The COMPLETE BOOK of
DREAMS

The COMPLETE BOOK *of*
DREAMS

JULIA & DEREK PARKER

DK PUBLISHING, INC.

www.dk.com

A DK PUBLISHING BOOK
www.dk.com

PROJECT EDITOR Tracey Williams
ART EDITOR Ursula Dawson
MANAGING EDITOR Krystyna Mayer
MANAGING ART EDITOR Derek Coombes
DTP DESIGNER Cressida Joyce
PRODUCTION CONTROLLER Maryann Rogers
U.S. EDITORS Erin Claremont and Kristin Ward

First paperback edition, 1998

First American Edition, 1995
4 6 8 10 9 7 5 3

Published in the United States by
Dorling Kindersley Publishing, Inc.,
95 Madison Avenue
New York, New York 10016

Library of Congress Cataloging-in-Publication Data

Parker, Derek.
Parkers complete book of dreams/by Derek and Julia Parker. --
1st American ed.
p. cm.
Includes index.
ISBN 0-7894-3295-1
1. Dreams. 2. Dream interpretation. I. Parker, Julia.
II. Title.
BF 1091.P25 1995
154.6'3--dc20   94-27918
                                                    CIP

Color reproduced by Colourscan, Singapore
Printed and bound in Singapore by
Star Standard Industries (Pte.) Ltd.

CONTENTS

—◆— INTRODUCTION —◆—

DREAMS AND DREAMING fascinate all of us. This is partly because we all dream — and most of us remember at least a few of our dreams — and partly because dreams are so mysterious, yet so vivid and memorable, that they must mean something. In fact, most (and perhaps all) dreams do mean something, although there are various opinions about exactly what they signify.

THE PRIVATE THEATER

There is no reason to work on and use your dreams, unless you feel inclined to do so or unless you believe that they can help you. It may be that dreams do their work whether we strive to understand them or not. On the other hand, there is no doubt that dreams can be a conscious source of inspiration, and a fountain of relief and reassurance when we are in difficulty.

Dreams often seem meaningless to anyone but the dreamer, but it is important to remember that in the theater of dreams the dreamer is the only member of the audience. So, the contents of a dream may be — and usually are — deeply meaningful to the dreamer.

SOURCES OF INSPIRATION

There is no doubt that dreams draw profoundly on our imaginations, and much work remains to be done on the connection between dreams and the area of the brain that produces creative art. Sometimes, we emerge from our sleep with rational and useful thoughts, and there are many examples of works of art that have arisen apparently spontaneously in dreams, and have simply been set down by the creator. The poem "Kubla Khan," for example, was dreamt by its creator, the poet Samuel Taylor Coleridge.

Having taken a dose of opium (to which he was addicted) Coleridge fell asleep in the farmhouse he was renting on Exmoor, between Porlock and Linton, just as he was reading a passage about Kubla Khan in a travel book by the 17th-century writer Samuel Purchas. Telling the story, Coleridge says:

"The Author continued for about three hours in a profound sleep, at least of the external senses ... On awakening he appeared to himself to have a distinct recollection of the whole [poem, of two or three hundred lines], and taking his pen, ink and paper instantly and eagerly wrote down the lines that are here preserved. At this moment he was unfortunately called out by a person on business from Porlock, and detained by him above an hour, and on his return to his room, found, to his no small surprise and mortification, that though he still retained some vague and dim recollection of the general purpose of the vision, yet with the exception of some eight or ten scattered lines and images, all the rest had passed away like the images on the surface of a stream ..."

The novelist Graham Greene used dreams to practical effect in the construction and writing of his books, the composer Stravinsky dreamed an octet, the psychologist Otto Loewi attributed his winning of the Nobel Prize to a dream, singer and songwriter Paul

THE FACE OF DREAMS

In his Progress, *the contemporary artist Lucien Mathelin imagines a face made out of familiar things; a dream of such a face might suggest a dreamer preoccupied with ephemera.*

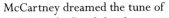

McCartney dreamed the tune of "Yesterday," and the chemist F.A. Kekulé dreamed about the ring structure of the benzene molecule (as a snake with its tail in its mouth).

The latter case is an example of how dreams work in ciphers. Kekulé did not dream the actual solution to the problem on which he was working – he was given a symbol that, when he considered it, clearly represented the answer. We are not given easy answers by our dreams, nor do they always come up with brilliant examples of our creative genius. The novelist Anthony Burgess once woke from sleep convinced that he had dreamed the solution to the question of life, but he actually found that he had written on the wall, with his wife's lipstick, the words:

"Let his carbon gnoses be up right
And wak all folowers to his light."

However, when we examine them, the apparently nonsensical plots and characters of our dreams often become rational and sensible, commenting profoundly on our waking situation, our problems and difficulties.

Dreams have something of the quality of much 20th-century art: the paintings of Dali, Picasso, and other surrealist and abstract painters; the poetry of Ezra Pound and T.S. Eliot among others; and the novels of such writers as Gabriel Garcia Marquez, all use symbolism in the way in which dreams use it.

DREAMS EXPLAINED

This book does not claim to be able to interpret readers' dreams for them, but hopes to show how they can begin to interpret their own dreams. Chapter One looks at how dreams and dream interpretation have been considered throughout history, it summarizes the mechanics of sleep, and attempts to answer the larger question of why we dream. Chapter Two turns to practical matters: how to remember and record your dreams, assess them, and begin to interpret them.

DREAMS IN WONDERLAND
Lewis Carroll's Alice *books are quintessentially dream-like: Alice suddenly grows to giant size (above); the Walrus, the Carpenter, and a number of oysters converse (right).*

The final chapter of the book should be helpful to those who want to be their own dream analysts. Chapter Three offers possible interpretations for some of the most common dream themes, such as animals, music, color, childhood, food, money, and landscape. This chapter also contains information about nightmares, erotic dreams, and apparently predictive dreams. The final section of the book comprises the Dream Thesaurus, which includes further information to help you interpret your dreams. If you are puzzled by a dream, think of the symbol that seems most prominent and look it up in the Dream Thesaurus. There will be a reference to one or more of the themes mentioned in Chapter Three. Further instructions on how to use the Dream Thesaurus are given on pages 40 and 184.

In addition, some of the theme pages include short dream analyses, which illustrate aspects of the relevant themes. Longer and more complex dream sequences are described on separate pages, and each description is accompanied by the explanation that has emerged after discussion with the dreamers.

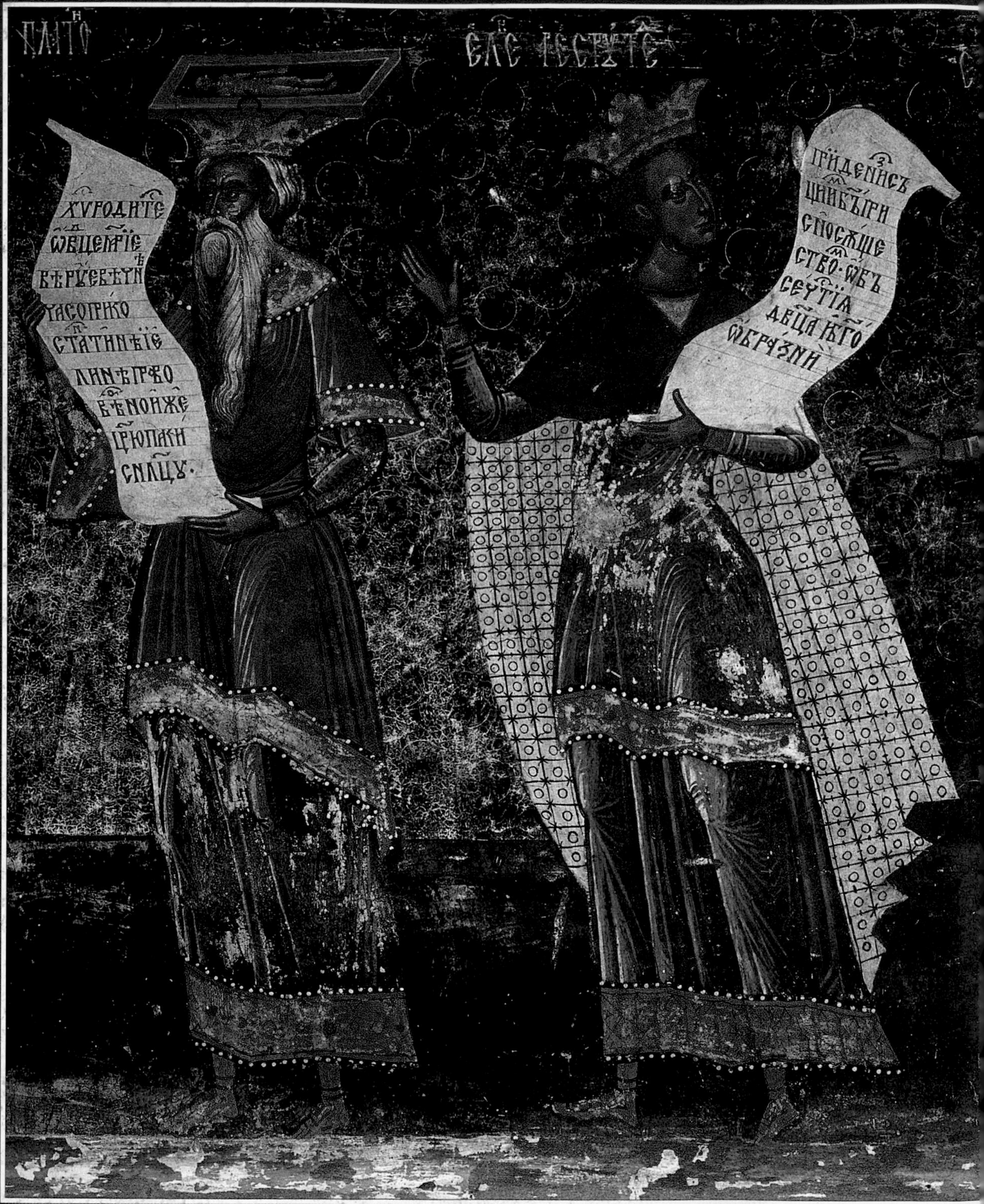

YOU AND YOUR DREAMS

IN AN AGE WHEN, increasingly, the consolations of religion are not as clearly available as they once were, it becomes more and more important to draw conclusions about our own identity from other sources. We may ask ourselves: "Why are we here, and what are our lives for?" While our dreams will not give us conclusive answers to such questions, they may help to clarify what we feel about ourselves and how we should live our lives.

Our consciousness is expressed as fully and revealingly in dreams as it is in waking reality—just as our unconscious works as strongly in our waking lives as it does in our dreams. The conscious and unconscious are so closely interrelated as to be almost meaningless without each other; and it is when that relationship becomes disjointed and disconnected, that we begin to suffer at best feelings of uncertainty, and at worst psychological disturbances.

Learning to interpret your own dreams will enable you to recognize the messages your unconscious is sending you about yourself.

16TH-CENTURY FRESCO FROM SUCEVITA MONASTERY, SHOWING PHILOSOPHERS OF THE ANCIENT WORLD

—◆— DREAM HISTORY —◆—

AS FAR AS WE KNOW, all animals dream, and humans probably started
to dream even before they were sufficiently intelligent to think
about the process. It has been suggested that some of the earliest
prehistoric cave paintings are records of dreams.

ANCIENT DREAMERS

Dreams were originally believed to be messages from
the gods, or supernatural communications of some
kind. During the 12th dynasty (c.1991–1786 BC), the
Egyptians were certainly attempting to interpret their
dreams, for they published a book setting out some of
the conclusions they had reached about dream symbols.
It was in ancient Egypt that the process of "dream
incubation" began: a person who was emotionally
disturbed, or wanted to ask the gods for help would
be put to sleep in a temple, and the priest (or Master
of the Secret Things) would interpret the dreams.

The Greeks were seriously considering dreams at
least as early as the 8th century BC, for in Homer's
Iliad, Agamemnon receives instructions from the
messenger of Zeus in a dream. With the aid of priestly
interpreters similar to those of the Babylonians and
Egyptians (from whom they inherited many occult
techniques), the Greeks also believed dreams to be
divine messages. They also used dreams in medicine,
sending sick people to particular temples in those
places where the "gods of the body" had their shrines.

Ailing Greeks would visit these temples, and after the
performance of various religious rites, would sleep, and
hope to have a dream that promised their return to
health. They would frequently stay at the temples for
weeks, or even months, until they had the "right" dream.
The temple of Aesculapius at Epidaurus was perhaps the
most famous of these places of dream pilgrimage.

The earliest dream interpreters in Greece hover in
the uncertain world between legend and reality. Pliny
the Elder (c.AD 23–79) suggested that the earliest
interpreter was Amphictyon, son of Deucalion (who
in Greek mythology was the son of Prometheus).
However, the historian Herodotus (c.484–424 BC)
claimed that the people of Telmessus, in Caria
(southwest Asia Minor) specialized in dream
interpretation; indeed, King Croesus (the last king of
Lydia) consulted them about an important dream.

EARLY GREEK THINKING

The first step into modern dream interpretation was
taken in the 5th century BC: the Greek philosopher
Heraclitus (c.544–483) suggested that a person's
dream world was peculiar to them, and
was not necessarily a result of outside
influences – even those of the gods.
Most Greek philosophers concerned
themselves at some time with dreams and
what they might mean: Plato (c.428–
348 BC) realized how radically dreams
could affect a personality or a life. In the
Phaedo Plato describes how Socrates
studied music and the arts because he
was instructed to do so in a dream.

A century after the death of Heraclitus,
Aristotle (384–322 BC) finally put an end
to the idea of dreams as messages from
the gods, and tried to study the dream

DREAM PILGRIMAGE
*This picture shows the Greek ruins of the
sanctuary of Aesculapius at Epidaurus – here
the sick were sent, in their dreams, the gods'
prescriptions for their cures.*

THE GREEK PHILOSOPHERS (LEFT)
*A 14th-century Italian manuscript shows Socrates,
Aristotle, Plato, and Seneca.*

HIPPOCRATES AND GALEN (BELOW)
*In this picture, Hippocrates is teaching his aphorisms
to students, with a commentary by Galen.*

process in a rational way. He points out (in his *De divinatione per somnum*) that "most so-called prophetic dreams are to be classed as mere coincidences, especially all such as are extravagant," and later asserts that "the most skilful interpreter of dreams is he who has the faculty of absorbing resemblances. I mean that dream presentations are analogous to the forms reflected in water." In his *Parva naturalia*, Aristotle suggested that dreams were in fact fragments of recollections of events of the day.

He also advanced the theory that dreams were a reflection of the bodily state, and a doctor could therefore use a patient's dream as a means of diagnosing an illness. This idea was supported by Hippocrates (*c.*460–357 BC), the founder of modern medicine, and is prevalent today. Galen of Pergamum (AD 129–99), a Greco-Roman physician, followed the same line. For example, he recorded that a man dreamed that his left thigh was turned into marble, and soon after lost the use of his left leg as the result of a palsy. A wrestler he was treating dreamed that he was standing up to the crown of

his head in blood; Galen inferred that he "was in need of a liberal bloodletting, and by this means the pleurisy under which he labored was cured."

ROMAN THEORIES

Although earlier documents exist (notably the Egyptian dream book known as the Chester Beatty papyrus), the *Oneirocriticon* or *The Interpretation of Dreams* by the Roman Artemidorus (*c.*AD 150) is the first comprehensive book on the interpretation of dreams. In this enormous, five-volume work, Artemidorus argued that dreams were unique to the dreamer: the person's occupation, social status, and health would all affect the symbols in a dream. His interpretations were often extremely shrewd, for example:

> "A man dreamt that a friend and associate of his, with whose daughter he was having an affair, sent him a horse."

LESSONS IN METAPHOR
Aristotle taught that to understand dreams one must understand metaphor, in which one image describes another.

PHARAOH'S DREAM

A 19th-century painting by Jean Adrien Guignet shows Joseph interpreting Pharaoh's dream, saying, "The dream of Pharaoh is one ... God hath shewd Pharoah what he is about to do."

JACOB'S LADDER

Jacob dreamt of "a ladder set up on the earth, and the top of it reached to heaven: and behold the angels of God ascending and descending on it."

The groom brought the horse up two flights of stairs and led him into the bedchamber where the man himself was lying. Not long afterwards, the man lost all access to his mistress. For the horse signified the woman. The place however signified that the present arrangement would not continue, since it was impossible for a horse to be on the third floor." (1873 ed., p.487)

A second *Oneirocriticon*, written by Astrampsychus (*c.*AD 350) bears some resemblance to the dream books that the Victorians produced. Astrampsychus's volume contained statements such as "To wear a purple robe threatens a long disease" and "To hold or eat eggs symbolises vexation." However, some of the axioms in the book may be accurate, for example: "Sitting naked signifies loss of property."

BIBLICAL VISIONS

The Christians revived the belief that dreams were supernatural events. The Old Testament of the Bible is full of dreams: the most famous is probably Jacob's dream of a ladder or staircase from Earth to Heaven. Nebuchadnezzar, King of Babylon (who died in 562 BC), had an interesting dream reported in the *Book of Daniel* (Chapter IV). In the dream he saw a tall, strong tree standing at the center of the Earth, with beautiful foliage beneath which wild beasts took shelter, and in which birds nested. But then a messenger from Heaven ordered the tree to be felled, and the King to be chained to its stump to live like a beast feeding on grass. The King summoned a dream interpreter, Daniel, who told him that the tree represented his power and glory, and that his abasement in the dream was to teach him that he should acknowledge a heavenly power as high above himself as he was above the beasts of the field. The dream was, however, seen as actually prophetic.

St. John Chrysostom (347–407) preached that God revealed himself through dreams. He also made the remarkably modern statement that we are not responsible for our dreams, and should not therefore be ashamed of any images that appear in them. Both St. Augustine (354–430) and St. Jerome (*c.*342–420) claimed that the directions of their lives were affected by their dreams.

Most religions had considerable respect for dreams. Mohammed (*c.*570–632) "received" much of the text of the Koran in a dream, and interpreted his disciples' dreams for them.

Later, the pendulum swung the other way: the Inquisition held the view that dreams were more often than not the work of the Devil, since the Church was the interpreter of God's word, and so revelations made to individuals in dreams could only be diabolic. Martin Luther (1483–1546), who was the founder of Protestantism, shared this view: sin, he said, was "the confederate and father of foul dreams."

ST. AUGUSTINE

MIDDLE EASTERN IDEAS

Early work on dream interpretation was not confined to the Egyptians, Greeks, Romans, and Christians. In Persia, "Sifat-i-Sirozah" (an unidentified writer) devised a scheme relying on time: a dream could only be interpreted according to the particular day it occurred. The Zoroastrians (followers of the national religion of the Uranian people from the time of the Achaemenids to the close of the Sassanian period) were particularly devoted to this theory, which set out rules for each day of the month, for example: "The second day is that of Bahman … Events dreamed of will occur in four days, but the hopes which may be cherished will be disappointed."

The most notable early Arabic dream interpreter was Gabdorrhachaman (*c.*720), whose theories first appeared in the West in 1664, published in French as *L'Onirocrite Mussulman*. He considered that dreams were prophetic, and could only be interpreted by those who possessed "a clean spirit, chaste morals, and the Word of Truth." Gabdorrhachaman's aphorisms seem to have been based on his own instinct rather than on any particular understanding of symbolism: "He who dreams that his tongue has shortened immoderately will utter much folly and ribaldry."

DREAMS OF THE DEVIL
Sano di Pietro's painting of the dream of St. Jerome depicts the aggressively sarcastic Doctor of the Church, who asserted that overtly sexual dreams must be sent by the Devil.

MOHAMMED'S ASCENT
This painting shows Mohammed's ascent to Heaven from the Temple Mount in Jerusalem. In a dream he had on the way there, he encountered Moses, Abraham, and Jesus.

own suggested to him that dreams might arise so quickly that they were almost simultaneous with the stimulus that produced them. Maury was ill in bed, with his mother sitting beside him. He dreamed that it was during the Reign of Terror of the French Revolution, and he was condemned and led to the guillotine. As the blade of the guillotine fell, he woke up to find that the top of the bed had fallen down and had struck the top of his spine just as the guillotine would actually have struck him.

However, this line of thought proved to be relatively unimportant, and it was the development of the theory of the unconscious that marked the beginning of the modern attitude toward dream interpretation. Johann Fichte (1762–1814) and his disciple Friedrich Schelling (1775–1854) had already begun to suspect that dreams revealed our unconscious fears and desires, but it was with the publication in 1900 of Sigmund Freud's *The Interpretation of Dreams*, that modern work on dream interpretation really began.

JOHANN GOTTLIEB
FICHTE

MODERN THINKING

FRIEDRICH WILHELM
JOSEPH VON SCHELLING

Freud (1865–1939) set out the theory that, although they may be prompted by external stimuli, wish-fulfillment was the basis of most dreams. According to him, our dreams reflected our deepest desires, rooted in our infancy, and always held a serious meaning. He stressed the erotic content of dreams: for example, long, pointed objects represented the penis, and hollow objects or containers represented the vagina.

Carl Gustav Jung (1875–1961) collaborated with Freud for some years, but disagreed with him on this very point: hidden sexual problems were not, Jung argued, at the root of most dreams. Freud believed that dreams were the result of concealed desires, and continued, on the whole, to conceal them; Jung, on the other hand, felt that dreams revealed our deepest wishes and longings, enabling us to realize our unconscious ambitions, and helping us to fulfill them.

EUROPEAN ATTITUDES

Robert Cross Smith (1795–1832), from Bristol, set up as an astrologer under the name "Raphael" and became enormously successful (his *Prophetic Almanac* sold over 100,000 copies a year). Two years before his death, he published *The Royal Book of Dreams*, in which he devised a procedure for interpreting dreams by the use of "ciphers." These would reveal such maxims as "Thy dream presages a saturnine enemy," or "A full, merry, and right joyful dream; it tells of banquets and feasting."

Modern dream interpretation may have begun with Alfred Maury, a French doctor who is reputed to have studied over 3,000 dreams. He believed that dreams arose from external stimuli. A particular dream of his

Jung suggested that dreams are, in fact, important messages from ourselves to ourselves, and messages that we ignore to our loss.

Most modern psychologists tend to lean toward Jung rather than Freud, and certainly it is his view that makes books like this possible. Freud would have denied that someone could be taught to interpret their own dreams; whereas Jung believed that, although it was a difficult task, it could and should be done, for dreams were "meant" to be understood.

OTHER THEORIES

Theories about dreams have continued to be developed since Freud and Jung published their respective views. Some psychologists, like Medard Boss in *The Analysis of Dreams* (1958), have suggested that it is pointless to have any theory about dreams — that they are simply another facet of life, as meaningless as waking existence. Similarly, some psychologists believe that dreams merely "wipe the tape"; they dispose of memories that would otherwise clutter our minds with numerous remembered experiences and emotions. The Gestalt technique sees dreams as aids to the organization and structuring of information, so the dreamer should consider every element of the dream, which will relate to some "unfinished business" of the mind.

Montague Ullman and Nan Zimmerman concluded:

"If I were to sum up the various approaches by means of analogies, I might use the steam kettle for the Freudian-related approaches, a rotating mirror for the Jungian approach, and someone filling in holes for the Gestalt approach. In the case of the steam kettle, something under pressure succeeds in getting out but in a different form. In the case of the mirror, the rotation of the mirror reflects an unknown side of the self. The Gestaltist is busy preparing solid ground by filling holes left over from the past." (1983, p.62)

Only a tiny minority would now argue that dreams are not important means of helping people to live fulfilled lives. The Greek philosopher Zeno (*c*.490–after 445 BC) held that the study of our dreams was essential to self-knowledge. That is still the case.

CINEMATIC TECHNIQUES

Cinema directors use dream-like images to heighten tension — as in this scene from Alfred Hitchcock's Spellbound.

—◆—The Mechanics of Sleep—◆—

THE IDEA OF SLEEP is so commonplace that, unless we are deprived of it or are troubled by recurring nightmares, we do not often think about it. Yet it is one of the most puzzling happenings in human life. The idea of losing consciousness, of ceasing to be ourselves, and of relinquishing all control over our thoughts and movements, is dreadful to us, and yet it happens every night when we sleep.

IDEAS AND EXPERIMENTS

For centuries, people thought of sleep as a period when humans rested their bodies and their minds. Other ideas were less obvious; for example Aristotle's notion that during sleep the vapors that rose from the stomach after food were dissipated. However, that kind of theory was pursued for hundreds of years. Even in the early part of the last century, it was believed that during the day blood rose to the brain and caused congestion there. During sleep, the blood drained back into the rest of the body (and therefore it was best to sleep without a pillow, so that the blood could flow more easily from the brain). Early in this century, scientists suggested that certain chemicals, such as lactic acid, carbon dioxide, and cholesterol, collected in the brain during waking hours and were then depleted during sleep. The question remains, when these theories have been rejected: what is the purpose of sleep? Most of us need, or think we need, eight hours sleep each night, but this may not be true. The former British Prime Minister Margaret Thatcher was reputed to function with only about four hours of sleep a night, and dream laboratories have records of people for whom this is also the case. However, no examples have been found of any individual who can go without sleep altogether. People who say they "never sleep" have invariably been found to take, at the very least, occasional "naps" lasting for five or ten minutes.

Attempts to discover how little sleep the human body needs began many years ago. In 1896, there were experiments at the Iowa Psychological Laboratory during which a subject was kept awake for three days, and at the end of the experience felt "quite as well as ever, and did not feel sleepy the following evening."

In January 1964, Randy Gardner, a 17-year-old high-school student from San Diego, remained awake for 11 complete days observed by doctors from a nearby United States Navy sleep laboratory. Although during that time he sometimes felt nauseated, had difficulty reciting tongue-twisters, and suffered lapses of memory, after sleeping for 14 hours when the experiment was over, he suffered no emotional or physical ill-effects. In addition, over the next two nights he slept for just six-and-a-half hours longer than usual.

THE DREAM OF ST. URSULA
This image shows one of the Venetian artist Carpaccio's paintings in the series The Legend of St. Ursula.

No cases have ever been recorded in which physical illness has resulted from lack of sleep, although the brain probably does need sleep, since measurements of brain activity have shown some chemical changes during sleep deprivation.

REM RESEARCH

The modern understanding of the nature of sleep began just over 40 years ago. In 1952, a researcher noticed that at certain times during a period of sleep the eyes of the subjects could be seen stirring beneath their closed lids — as though they were watching moving figures. These motions were called "rapid eye movements," and the phases of sleep were called REM periods. Three years later, scientists Eugene Aserinsky and Nathan Kleitman published a classic paper on the subject. It was found that during REM sleep the flow of blood to the brain increased, as did the brain's temperature, particular brain wave patterns showed up on an electroencephalograph (EEG), and both the penis in men and the clitoris in women became erect. Irregularities in breathing and heartbeat were noted during REM sleep, and a reduction in electrical activity in certain muscles.

THE SLEEPING BRAIN
The brain during sleep: the yellow areas are active, and the purple, inactive.

It was also discovered that if a person was awakened during REM sleep, he or she could usually remember vivid dreams; while only about six percent of people awakened during NREM (non-rapid eye movement) sleep claimed to have been dreaming. It seemed to be the case that only during NREM sleep were humans really "unconscious," and apparently indulging in complete rest. Although about half of the people awakened during this period believed they had been dreaming, they thought that their dreams were more like daydreams — seeming less surreal than "real" dreams.

These discoveries were so interesting that they led to an intense period of the study of sleep patterns, and most of our knowledge about the nature of sleep emerged from studies made over the next 20 years.

THE ALMIGHTY BRAIN
In this painting, the contemporary artist Andrzej Dudzinski suggests the complex levels of brain activity during sleep.

ELECTRICAL ACTIVITY
Wires attached to the head of a sleeper in a laboratory record the changes in electrical activity in the brain.

SLEEP CYCLES

When we fall asleep we enter a cycle of sleep — a pattern that is usually repeated several times during the night. Scientists identify four stages of sleep: the first stage is simply a transition from wakefulness to real sleep; while stage two may be described as "normal" sleep. During stage three there is another transition, or sinking into a deeper sleep — that of stage four.

During sleep, what is happening in the brain can be measured by the use of an EEG. Electrodes placed on

A SLEEP CYCLE

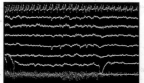

AWAKE
A print-out from an EEG reading of electrical activity in a subject when awake.

STAGE ONE SLEEP
During this stage, the brain is working less effectively than when the subject is awake.

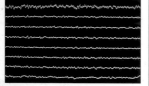

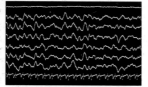

STAGE TWO SLEEP
The waves become slower, and are interrupted by brief bursts known as "spindles."

STAGE THREE SLEEP
This stage stops strong electrical impulses. It would be difficult to wake the sleeper.

the scalp pick up brain waves of about one-millionth of a volt in strength, which are amplified and traced on paper or recorded on tape, where changes in frequency (the number of waves taking place within one second) can be seen. Four types of EEG have been particularly studied: Beta waves (fast waves that show when the brain is animated or anxious); Alpha waves (which show during periods of meditation, when the brain is wakeful but relaxed); Theta waves (occurring during drowsiness or light sleep); and Delta waves (slow waves that are seen during times of deep sleep).

When we first go to sleep, we sink very quickly into stage four, NREM sleep, then after about an hour enter a period of around ten minutes of REM sleep, when dreams occur, before "climbing" back through three layers of NREM sleep. The whole cycle lasts around 80 or 90 minutes. During perhaps four cycles repeated throughout a single night's sleep, the phase of REM sleep will lengthen slightly, and just before we wake in the morning may last as long as an hour, so that during an eight-hour period of sleep we spend around six hours in NREM sleep, and the remaining two in REM "dream time." Just under half of us wake only from NREM sleep, and these include those people who claim that they "never dream" (*see page 16*). It has been suggested by some psychologists that these people unconsciously wake themselves at a time when they are not dreaming, because they want to repress what their dreams are telling them.

SLEEP FOR PHYSICAL REST

It seems likely that during NREM sleep, the body and mind are resting, and that this is the kind of sleep we need in order to rest and "recreate" ourselves, and for various bodily functions to take place, including growth. This kind of sleep is also highly rhythmical; it is geared to the pattern of our days, together with an enormous number of physiological functions that also go by the clock. When we fly quickly from one part of the world to another, and have to cope with an eight- or ten-hour time change, our "body clocks" take some time to adjust, and in the meantime our blood sugar, body temperature, white corpuscle count, adrenal gland activity, and many other functions all become temporarily out of gear, causing jet lag.

DREAMS OF THE FUTURE
Arnold Schwarzenegger starred in the science fiction film Total Recall, *in which dreams are implanted in the mind.*

In some people, travel across time zones can produce psychiatric symptoms, probably because their NREM sleep pattern has been disturbed.

THE NEED FOR SLEEP

REM sleep seems less physically than psychologically important. While people deprived of NREM sleep appear literally tired, and are clumsy and sluggish, those deprived of REM sleep become overly sensitive, are unable to concentrate, and have bad memory recall. REM sleep also helps us to cope with stress. Moreover, it has been found that while those deprived of NREM sleep suffer only temporary inconvenience, deprivation of REM sleep and therefore of the periods during which we have most of our dreams, results in people becoming disturbed. Sleeping tablets, for instance, can reduce the amount of REM sleep we get; then when the tablets are withdrawn we can fall into a temporary pattern of unusually high amount of REM sleep, the effects of which can lead to delirium when we wake.

Most healthy adults sleep for between five to nine hours a night. It is certainly possible to teach yourself to do with less sleep – to reduce your sleeping time by an hour or two a night – without doing yourself any damage (you can also teach yourself to sleep longer than you do at present).

People often underestimate the time they spend asleep. They may believe that it has taken them an hour or two to get to sleep, when they have really only lain awake for 15 or 20 minutes. Similarly, waking in the night they may believe they have spent much more time awake than has actually been the case.

SLEEP AND AGE

As we grow older our sleep pattern changes. Most of us, sometime between the ages of sixty and seventy, begin to find it more difficult to sleep for eight hours every night – and also difficult to stay awake for the whole of the day. The two things are connected: when we begin to take naps during the day, nature deducts this time from our night's sleep. Also, many older people begin to doze at around ten o'clock in the evening; they may then go to bed and fall asleep almost immediately – only to wake earlier than usual. One way to combat this is to take a half-hour nap when you begin to feel tired, and then stay up until around midnight, after which you will probably sleep soundly until eight or nine o'clock in the morning.

It appears that the reason for sleeping does not lie wholly in the fact that sleep allows the mind and body to recover from the daytime activities. Perhaps we also need sleep because we need to dream, and that need may extend further in nature than we think. Newborn babies spend about half of their sleeping time in the REM state; and REM sleep has been observed in most mammals, and in birds and reptiles.

—◆— WHY DREAMS HAPPEN —◆—

ALL HUMANS, AND MANY ANIMALS, dream. When people who claim that they "never dream" are awakened from REM sleep, most of them remember a dream. A relatively small proportion still claim not to have been dreaming. Most people who assert that they are non-dreamers suffer not from a lack of dreams, but from the inability to recall them (*see pages 16 to 19*).

The two most important dream theories are those of the Austrian psychiatrist Sigmund Freud (1856–1939) and his Swiss associate, Carl Gustav Jung (1875–1961), who parted from his mentor after a disagreement. Anyone wanting to work with their dreams must start by considering the theories of

CARL GUSTAV JUNG

SIGMUND FREUD

these two men. They are summarized here, but books are available that will explain their theories more comprehensively.

THE VOICE OF THE UNCONSCIOUS

Freud asserted that dreams were the result of our repression of certain desires, but that those desires were usually so foreign to our waking natures that our dreams could refer to them only through symbolism. He believed that if these desires were openly expressed they would appall us – and in fact, we would not accept that they could belong to us. Freud suggested that dreams had a manifest content (what happened in the dream) and a latent content (what the dream was trying to tell us). Most of the desires expressed in our dreams, he believed, were sexual; he lived in an age when the expression of sexuality was extremely restricted, and it was natural to suppose that the repression of such a powerful force must lead to psychological disturbance. Such dreams, he believed, fulfilled their purpose even if the dreamer was unaware of their meaning – for the emotion represented in them had been expressed, if only obliquely. It may be that dreams which we do not remember do their job in much the same way as those we recall: many things can be effective without being fully understood. However, as Jung put it:

> *There is no doubt that we can enhance [their] effect considerably by understanding [them], and this is often necessary because the voice of the unconscious so easily goes unheard.*" (1916, p.137)

"What nature leaves imperfect is perfected by the art," says the alchemical dictum. This is not as absurd as it may seem. Most of us, during our waking hours, fail to follow arguments through

FUSELI'S NIGHTMARES
Henry Fuseli (1741–1825) explored the murky layers of horror and fear in paintings like this, which seem to stem directly from dreams.

to their logical conclusions – particularly if they are leading toward catastrophe. We prefer to forget the whole matter, often with disastrous results, especially in the realm of our emotional lives.

FREUDIAN THEORY

Freud's attempts to explain the curious nature of dreams included the theory that dreams often blended two or more symbols, so that a man in a dream could represent both the dreamer's father and his employer, or a machine could represent his job and his hobby.

He also believed that the mind was divided into two "sections": the conscious and the unconscious (he later renamed the unconscious the "Id"). He suggested that the unconscious "contains everything that is inherited, that is present at birth, that is laid down in the constitution – above all, therefore, the instincts." Freud claimed that it was in the unconscious where the wishes and desires expressed in our dreams were hidden.

A SHAKESPEARIAN DREAM
Fuseli's darkly erotic paintings explored the world of the subconscious long before it was explored by psychiatry. Here he illustrates Bottom's dream from Shakespeare's A Midsummer Night's Dream.

Jung put it differently: "… the dream is a natural occurrence, and … nature shows no inclination to offer her fruits gratis or according to human expectations."

Freud thought that all "healthy" people were to some extent repressed, and that they used a lot of mental energy in sustaining those repressions. He suggested: "… a healthy person … is virtually a neurotic, but dreams appear to be the only symptoms which he is capable of forming."

When working with our dreams, we must deal with two elements: the dream as we remember it, and what it symbolizes – that is, the code and its translation. The main way in which Freud encouraged

that there was such a thing as the "collective unconscious" — a part of the mind that contains a store of information common to all humans. This was his explanation for the fact that people from widely different cultures, from opposite ends of the Earth, can have dreams in which specific symbols occur and appear to have the same meaning.

Jung recognized our waking selves, with our conscious poses and behavior patterns, as the persona. He believed that those of us who are too concerned with outward appearance and with what others think of us, have a dream character that represents our hidden selves. Plato, in his *Republic*, wrote "in all of us, even in good men, there is a lawless wild beast nature which peers out in sleep." Jung called this character "the Shadow."

One of the main ways in which Jung and his disciples approached the interpretation of a dream, was to ask the dreamer to expand it (to talk about it at length and explore it), but without criticizing it, or thinking of it as silly or objectionable. This is a way of outwitting our private censor. The simplest way is to talk to someone, rather than to write the dream down, although practice makes it possible to use the written method when we are alone. Also, talking frankly about our dreams can often be difficult.

his patients to start work on their dreams was by "free association" — by thinking about the symbols in the dream and saying, or writing down, the first thing that occurred to them. The basic idea was to prevent the patients from trying to work out the dream by the sort of process we use when we are considering something that has happened to us in our waking lives. For instance, if you see a man crossing the road, you may wonder where he is going, whether he will be hit by an approaching car, or whether the woman he is approaching is his wife. But if you think of such a scene in a dream, and write down your first thoughts, you may arrive at "old age" (the man), "death" (the busy road), and "love" (the woman). These images will be personal to you, and may not occur to any other dreamer in the world.

JUNGIAN ANALYSIS

Jung, who at first worked closely with Freud, shared many of his ideas. However, while Jung certainly recognized the unconscious, or Id, he also suggested

THE IMPORTANCE OF DREAMS

When interpreting your dreams, do not make the mistake of thinking that every dream must have the same importance. Although some psychiatrists will suggest that there is no such thing as a meaningless dream, there is a great difference between this point of view and the claim that all dreams contain equally important messages. Many dreams refer to relatively insignificant events or thoughts of the past day, and are easily forgotten. Others remain in our memories for many years, and these are likely to be important. To quote Jung again:

"Significant dreams ... are often remembered for a lifetime, and not infrequently prove to be the richest jewel in the treasure-house of psychic experience. How many people have I encountered who at the first meeting

could not refrain from saying: 'I once had a dream!' It was
the first dream they could ever remember, and one that
occurred between the age of three and five." (1974, p.16)
Such dreams, Jung believed, would probably contain
references to symbols that could be found in the
collective unconscious, and were likely to appear in the
dreams of people all over the world, whether primitive
or highly sophisticated.

This does not mean that members of different
societies do not differ in the way they interpret their
dreams; they are more or less important
to different peoples. A Jesuit missionary
in the 17th century complained that the
Iroquois Indians made no distinction at
all between dream and reality, and if a
dream gave what seemed to be an
instruction, they followed it minutely:
"This people would think itself guilty
of a great crime if it failed in its
observance of a single dream."

TRIBAL BELIEFS

Members of some other communities
also closely associate dreams with reality.
In Borneo, a man who dreams that his
wife has committed adultery is likely to
act as though that has actually happened;
while if a Kamchatkan man dreams that a
woman has made love to him, that
woman is believed to owe it to him to
make the dream come true. It has been
reported that a Paraguayan Indian once
dreamed that a missionary had shot at
him, and on waking set out to kill the
missionary. The Inuit of Hudson Bay and
the Patani Malays believe that during
sleep the soul leaves the body, and so to
wake anyone who is sleeping is to put
them in danger of losing their soul.

Local social circumstances and
conditions certainly govern some dream
patterns. A man of the Yir Yoront tribe
of Australian aboriginals, for instance,

will only have a sexual dream about a woman who the
tribe will allow him to marry. If he begins to have a
dream about an inappropriate mate, something is
supposed to happen in the dream to interrupt his
pleasure. Other types of dream, however, are more
universal. For example, it has been found to be the
case that men and women have basically different
dreams: men dream about other men more often than
they dream about women; while women dream with
equal frequency about both males and females.

FANTASY AND INVENTION
Spanish artist Goya (1746–1828) shows a
man surrounded by the horrific creatures
of nightmare in his painting entitled
Bewitched Man.

INTERPRETING YOUR DREAMS

DREAMS ARE RARELY what they seem, and the events in dreams may not have anything to do with the "reality" of the world outside our minds. One of the difficulties about interpreting dreams is that you can be yourself, or anything else – even any number of things – in a dream. This could give rise to several different interpretations. Which interpretation applies will depend on your waking situation, and certainly on the emotions you felt in the dream. Your mood will also be very important; you should relate it to a similar mood you may have suffered recently in your waking life. The result of the dream, when you consider it, may be to warn or encourage you, or at the very least to make you think more thoroughly than you might otherwise have done about the waking situation to which it refers.

The difficulty, when we first begin thinking about our dreams and what they have to say to us, is that most of us rarely "see" the message. This chapter will help you to recognize and understand the symbols offered to you in your dreams, as well as to learn to interpret them in the context of your waking life.

PIETER BRUEGHEL THE ELDER (C.1525–1569),
THE TRIUMPH OF DEATH

◆— REMEMBERING YOUR DREAMS —◆

DREAMS ARE EXTRAORDINARILY ELUSIVE, and some people never remember any of their dreams, or claim that they do not dream at all (*see page 16*). Of the rest, most have had the experience of waking from an interesting and strange dream only to find that it begins to fade the moment we wake. Then the harder we try to recall it, the faster it recedes from our memory.

PROBLEMS OF RECOLLECTION

Even if we are unable to recall a dream soon after we wake, occasionally during the following day an action or word will jolt our memory, and part of the dream will suddenly reappear. It may then be possible to reconstruct more of the dream, but this is not good enough if we want to work seriously on our dreams. So as a first step to interpreting or decoding our dreams, we must find a way of "holding on" to them at least long enough to record them. Actually putting words onto paper, or a cassette tape, is the only reliable way of ensuring that we remember our dreams.

We may ask why the contents of dreams should be more difficult to remember than the details of, say, a subject we may be studying for an examination, or even the random events of an ordinary day. No convincing answer has ever been given, although it may have something to do with the reason why we often find our dreams so difficult to interpret. Our conscious mind seems to be reluctant to allow us full understanding of our dreams.

One psychologist has talked about our "catastrophic expectations" in relation to dreams — we unconsciously believe that our dreams can have nothing good to say to us, so why should we make an effort to remember them? On a more practical level, the reason probably lies in the very nature of dreams. The events in dreams are usually (to our waking minds at least) entirely irrational, so the memory finds it difficult to grasp them. It is also true that if we remembered all of our dreams, we would be burdened with the vivid recollection of five or six long scenarios every night of dramatic scenes that — on the surface at least — seem like nonsense. So it may be just as well that we do not remember all of our dreams; and it seems to be the case that — even when we have become practiced in recalling them — we only remember the dreams that have something interesting to say.

MNEMONIC METHODS

You can work at recalling your dreams just as you can work at interpreting them, and usually with success. Simply talking to someone about your dreams will often prompt you to remember those you have the following night. If you find that you rarely recall your dreams, you could try saying to yourself just before sleep: "I shall have a dream tonight, and I will remember it when I wake." Then, when and if you do so, you should say: "I remember one of my dreams." You will then almost certainly be well on the way to better dream recall.

SURREALIST STILL LIFE
Surrealist artists freed their work from their normal association of pictorial ideas and surrendered, as in dreams, to the irrational dictates of their subconscious visions.

us. So when you wake, do not immediately reach for a piece of paper and a pencil. Instead, lie still and try to remain to some extent inside the atmosphere of the dream. You should not try to think about your dreams in detail, and above all do not will yourself to remember them, since they will slip away from you. Just let the dream remain in your mind until you feel confident enough to begin to record it. Then reach out for the flashlight and the pencil and notebook, or tape recorder, and make a note of a few key words from the image or symbol that is most vivid in your mind. You will find that by just jotting down a few phrases, you will be able to grasp the dream. The dream should then be with you for several hours, and you can record it properly later in the day.

Even when we have grown accustomed to the process of dream recall, and can remember most of the details of a dream, we may sometimes wake from what seems to be an important dream, and we cannot recall it. However, even if a dream seems to have vanished, it is often possible to salvage something. Even a fleeting image, or a single word written in a notebook, may begin to germinate in our mind. It may be prompted by an incident later in the day and images may gather around it, until the dream gradually reassembles itself.

The psychologist Dr. Frederick S. Perls devised a method to help dreamers who find it particularly difficult to interpret their dreams. You can use this method to recall your dreams: you simply "ask" your dreams why you cannot remember them *(see page 33)*.

You should find that as soon as you start recording and working on your dreams, you will have no difficulty in recalling them. In fact, some people give up trying to work with their dreams, because they find themselves so deluged with dream memories. However, no time spent working on your dreams will be wasted, since you should find yourself suffering less from stress.

GRADUAL RECALL

For most of us, the major problem is not remembering that we had a dream — or several dreams — but what actually happened in those dreams. We should not become overly anxious, since the more desperately we try to grasp the elements of a dream, the more it escapes

DREAM IMAGES IN FILM
In Jean Cocteau's film La Belle et La Bête, *live arms hold a row of candelabra.*

RECORDING YOUR DREAMS

HOWEVER WELL YOU REMEMBER your dream – or think you remember it – you should always either write it down or make a sketch of it. This is not only good practice – since you will establish a pattern that will be useful – but it also means that you will have a record to work with, which should help you to see any patterns that occur in your dreams.

MAKING NOTES

There is no substitute for writing down your dreams. You could use a tape recorder to make notes, or you could draw your dreams; but actually putting it down in words is the only way of recapturing as much of a dream as possible, and of being able to work on it without becoming confused.

The first step comes before you start your diary, with the rough notebook or pad of paper that you keep at your bedside. This should be accompanied by a flashlight, so that if you wake in the dark you do not have to switch on a light. (Remember that too much movement can encourage the dream to vanish before you can write even a quick note about it.) Do not attempt to write down the dream in full; a few words should ensure that you recall the main contours of the dream, which you can write up properly that day (*see page 30*). You should never allow yourself to think that

a dream is too unimportant to note down. The most simple, seemingly insignificant, or even "meaningless" dream may turn out to be extremely important when you consider its possible symbols during the course of the day.

WRITING UP THE DREAM

Writing up the dream in full should ideally follow your first notes as quickly as possible, although once you have set down your rough notes, it is surprising how vividly the dream will come back to you when you begin to think about it.

The dream diary itself should be fairly large, and when open should have a double-page area large enough to allow you to write the narrative or story of the dream on the left-hand page, and the interpretation on the right (*see page 30*). In the process of interpreting your dream, you may need a lot of space in which to make notes and perhaps draw diagrams to help you. First, always date the page. The date may have some significance in the dream, and will be of interest as you begin to build up a file of dreams. Next, you should make a note of the prevailing atmosphere of the dream, and of your own emotions about it. Did it seem to be a "happy" or an "unhappy" dream? Did you feel placid, excited, friendly, afraid, amorous, or angry throughout the dream? If you felt different when you woke up, you should note that, too: after having an apparently cheerful dream, on waking you may be plunged into a sad feeling of nostalgia or regret. It is then important to note any predominant color in your dream.

A DREAM SKETCH
Andrzej Dudzinski's record of one of his dreams shows how a sketch, made on waking, can help us to retain such images.

THE LAND OF OZ
In the film The Wizard of Oz, *Dorothy's acquaintances, the Tin Man, the Scarecrow, and the Wicked Witch of the West, appear in her dream.*

If you have made rough notes on more than one dream during a single night, make sure you record them in the order in which they occurred, and label them in that order. Sometimes we can clearly see that a dream has been prompted by something that happened quite recently. If this is obviously the case, make a note of it (but always with a question mark). Your dream will rarely be "about" this trigger event, but the event or image may give you a clue in interpretation. It may also be useful to make a note of the last thing you remember thinking about before going to sleep: this can sometimes show you a "way into" a dream.

Now, most important, write down your dream as fully as you can. Do not worry that you may not be writing elegantly, or even grammatically; it is most important to write down everything you can remember about the events in the dream, in the order in which they occurred.

Finally, you should jot down a few words "about" the dream – whatever occurs to you. A name, a situation, or an event may come to mind. Some psychologists also suggest that without thinking hard about it, you should give your dream a title, which will help you focus on the most important image.

BEGINNING ANALYSIS

Once you have your dream diary in front of you, with the record of the dream on the left-hand page, you are ready to start the real work of interpretation. Everyone will devise their own way of going about this, but to begin with, it will certainly be worth jotting down a few first thoughts on what the dream may be about. Do not make the mistake of doing this too anxiously, or even thoughtfully: remember, the dream has come from your unconscious, and that is

where the clue to its meaning must also lie. If you are sufficiently relaxed about the whole situation, you may find that the moment you set your pencil to paper, you will write a word that will lead you to the dream's meaning. However, this rarely happens, especially when you are starting your dream work. More often than not, your mind, and the paper, will remain blank.

If the dream as a whole seems to have no bearing on anything in your life, begin to think about every separate image in it, and try to relate these images to some meaningful emotion or event. Remember, however, that things may not be what they seem. You may be represented by anything in the dream, so try to recall what the objects were "doing." If a telephone was ringing, could you be that telephone, with a message for someone? Or was the telephone someone else, with a message for you? If the ringing telephone was standing on a table, which for a reason you cannot understand seemed important, could the message be from or for someone whose name rhymes with "table"?

USING THE BOOK

At this point, you should follow the suggestions on pages 40–41. Look up the major symbols in the Dream Thesaurus (*see pages 184–206*), and read the main entry to which you are referred. If nothing there seems to make sense, follow the minor lines of thought also suggested in the Dream Thesaurus. You should be aware that none of these may apply either, since dreams are as individual as their dreamers.

◆— THE DREAM DIARY —◆

THE FOLLOWING EXTRACTS are examples of how a dream diary might work. The dreamers were asked to try to use the entries in this book to help to interpret their dreams. In each case, the interpretation is fully "written up", but you may only need to make a rough note of your conclusions. You will also probably like to devise the layout of your dream diary for yourself.

JENNIFER'S DREAM DIARY

DATE 21 January 1995.

ATMOSPHERE Rather excited at first, but then becoming slightly calmer.

COLOUR Conscious of the colours of the peacock's tail, otherwise none.

POSSIBLE TRIGGER Perhaps discussion with a colleague about career prospects?

NARRATIVE I was playing tennis against an unidentified champion. We were on a very brightly lit indoor tennis court. I never got the chance to serve, but I somehow managed eventually to win the match. As I went up to collect my medal from a member of the royal family, and stepped forwards and bowed to her, instead of handing me the medal the princess slapped my face. A movement on the court caught my eye, and when I looked down I saw it was a peacock. The princess appeared at my side, bent down, and cut off all the colourful tail feathers. She then handed them to me and said "Burn these".

NOTES A game often alludes to one's lifestyle and attitude to problems. Any sport involves both skill and dedication, and a medal is a recognition of achievement. A member of the royal family is probably an authority figure, perhaps involving memories of parents and the inhibitions of childhood. A peacock is proud, sometimes strident, and may represent self-assertion.

INTERPRETATION The first thought that occurred to me was that the dream referred to my promotional prospects as work, but this was not the case. The peacock symbol seemed to suggest that perhaps this was a dream about my image or the way I project myself. Working backwards from this, I decided that the game was in fact the general game of life, in which we use our skills to present ourselves. The fact that I always won the game without ever having to serve suggests that in some way I am having a fairly easy life, or that I am not utilizing the skills I possess. The authority figure in the dream slapped my face: could this be a suggestion that I am disapproved of by authority or by society? She then went on to cut off the (my?) peacock feathers (cutting me down to size?) and burn them. I remembered that on the previous day I had had an argument with someone who stepped in front of me in a queue, and afterwards felt that I had been too strident. Perhaps the dream was telling me to be less harsh in my judgements. As for the tennis match: am I winning too easily? Am I hoping to become a champion without the effort of really applying myself?

AUTHORS' NOTES

Jennifer seems to have made an accurate interpretation, although support from other dreams may or may not confirm it. Note that she got the trigger for the dream wrong at first; often the true origin of the dream appears when you have thought about it (although a first thought may reveal a profitable line of analysis). The fact that she realized she had been too harsh in rebuking someone for a petty offence probably did prompt the dream.

The member of the royal family may have represented her mother, who was a dominant figure in her life. She is very much a "self-made" woman, whose personality is defensive, and she disapproves of her daughter's "showy" image. But she seems to have been right: the dream was principally suggesting that she was winning too easily, and that she will never be a true "champion" unless she modifies her approach and instead of displaying her talents, uses them in attack rather than defence.

TERRY'S DREAM DIARY

DATE January 14, 1995.

ATMOSPHERE Generally upbeat.

COLOR Bright landscape, very green grass, darker green trees, and the contrasting bright colors of the shirt and tie.

POSSIBLE TRIGGER Unable to pinpoint the trigger.

NARRATIVE I was at first on a boat, on a rather sluggish sea with a slightly nauseating swell. But then it turned into a house, which was familiar without actually being a house I recognized. I was in a hallway, then went into a brightly lit, white room with large windows looking out onto a country landscape. I saw a goat tied outside on the lawn, looking rather woebegone. I gestured to it to get off the lawn, but saw that it was tied to a stake. I stripped off all my clothes and put on new, clean pants, then slacks and a bright shirt and tie. I wanted to go for a walk but I thought the windows were locked; however, I found I could walk through them – the glass vanished, or there had never been any. I saw the goat running off, now looking very spirited and lively. I walked across the lawn and opened a gate that led into a field of corn.

NOTES Sea: water often means emotion. House: dreamer's body or personality. Window: eyes. Landscape: freedom. Goat: sexuality. Clothes: self-image. Underwear: sexuality.

INTERPRETATION Am I afloat on a sea of emotion, but getting nowhere, and feeling sick (of life in general)? The boat changed into a house, which is supposed to represent the body or the personality. But it also indicated a shift from instability to stability. Perhaps I have been thinking too emotionally about something. If windows can represent eyes, and I saw a pleasant landscape through them; perhaps I have been "dreaming of green fields" – being overly optimistic. Or do I desire more freedom than I've recently had, since a symbol of some kind of landscape can apparently suggest freedom in dreams.

A goat can represent male sexuality, but I wanted it to go away. Surely I do not want to rid my life of sex? However, the goat looked fed-up, and was tied to a stake, so I wonder what that means. (It was at this point that Terry says he "saw" the true meaning of the dream.) The trigger was obviously my feelings about my girlfriend, who I have become very bored with; she is unadventurous not only sexually but in every other way. My sexual boredom seemes to be represented in the dream by the tethered goat. I stripped and put on clean underwear and bright clothes. This could indicate that I want to change my present sexual life for a more active new one. When I finally got out of the house (there was no real obstacle to my leaving), the goat ran off looking for action. The gate is another symbol of wanting to broaden my horizons. Corn is often a symbol of fecundity in dreams.

AUTHORS' NOTES

Terry's interpretation shows how often the meaning of a dream can come in the course of examining it, when everything seems to fall into place and the meaning seems obvious. It can also be the case, as it seems to be here, that a dream may have two parts that are not clearly relevant to each other. The first part of the dream needs further examination; Terry may have hit on the key to it when he asked whether it refers to instability, and his perhaps being "sick of life." More work should be done on this.

Terry seems to have made an accurate analysis, although he may have missed some aspects of the dream. He emphasized that he put on clean, new underwear, and this may suggest that he wanted to "clean up his act" in some way, sexually. There was no image in the dream of his girlfriend, and the suggestion might therefore be that his idea of sex, while not "dirty," has perhaps been as something flippant and disposable. The dream suggested a need to make a new start, and there certainly seemed an implication that his sex life needs a little cheering up. However, the image of the cornfield may carry a suggestion that he feels ready for fatherhood.

— ANALYZING YOUR DREAMS —

EVERY DREAM IS A MESSAGE from yourself to yourself, expressed in a
code that only you can learn to understand and interpret. In his essay
"On the Nature of Dreams," Jung wrote: "Even if one has great
experience in these matters, one is again and again obliged, before
each dream, to admit one's ignorance and, renouncing all
preconceived ideas, to prepare for something entirely unexpected."

About Freud, Jung said, "He recognized that no
interpretation can be undertaken without the dreamer.
The words composing a dream-narrative have not just
one meaning, but many meanings." For example,
dreams often make use of puns and slang terms, and
these will differ depending on language and culture.

WHO'S WHO?

While there is a good chance that you will always be
you in your dream, it is equally important to
remember that you can also be any other person,
animal, or inanimate object. Therefore, it is at this

point where the overall interpretation of a dream
becomes far more complex. In order to discover how
this could work, you may have to think of yourself as
the chair leg, the family dog, or one of your relatives,
for example. The symbol of the object, animal, or
person in the dream is commenting on your feelings
about it. For example, your dream chair leg may be
trying to support the other legs, which were broken.
In waking life, are you the sole supporter of your
family? Do you have to support three other people?
The family cat may be shedding in your dream, and all
her fur comes out as you brush her. Are you having to
work too hard and too long and thereby losing your
good looks? A relative may have said something
particularly hurtful to you in your dream; have you,
in waking life, behaved like this to another person?

It is important to understand that you have to work
your way around every symbol in your dream in this
particular manner if you are to interpret it fully.

MOOD

It is sometimes the case that we cannot recall any
actual symbols in a dream, we simply remember a
vague mood. In such cases you should ask yourself
about that mood. Did you feel depressed or happy?
Were you frightened and apprehensive, or assertive
and enthusiastic? About what? If you do not know the
answer, allow your mind to flow over the feelings. If
you cannot proceed, you should simply relate that
mood to your waking life, since it may be commenting
on at least one problem or aspect that you have to
concentrate on at present. Perhaps the mood related to
something that occurred recently — a retrospective
influence, in which case you can either put your
thoughts to one side, or you can ask yourself why the
mood is still hanging over you.

BECKONING MONSTERS
Goya, in his painting The Sleep of Reason Produces
Monsters, *shows how waking tensions can summon fiends to
our dreams — here in the form of predatory birds and cats.*

SUMMONING DREAM IMAGES
Richard Dadd's Come unto these Yellow Sands *owes less to Shakespeare's* The Tempest *than to the dream-like inspiration of his own mind.*

ATMOSPHERE

Recalling the physical atmosphere in a dream is usually helpful in its interpretation, because the atmosphere is probably making a statement about the present state of our emotions and our feelings about current problems. If you were cold or hot, or wet, do you have some powerful and passionate feelings, or are you reacting emotionally coldly? If either is true, your dream may be suggesting that you should "cool" your attitude, or that you should express your emotions more forcibly. If you were becoming sunburned in your dream, there may be a warning about taking risks. But did the atmosphere also color your mood in your dream, making you energetic or lethargic? All such points should be considered, since they may be showing you how you are reacting to the atmosphere in your life.

COLOR

Many people are unduly concerned that they do not dream in color. It seems to be the case that people who are acutely aware of color in their waking lives will have colorful dreams, while those who are less aware of color will have less colorful dreams (*see page 75*). Whether you dream in color or monochrome, if some object's color is particularly striking in a dream, you should not only assess that color as a separate and relevant symbol, but also assess it in relation to the object. This would be an especially important symbol if you do not usually dream in color.

ANIMALS

Animals (*see page 42*) often represent our basic instincts, urges, and needs. In dreams they often take the forms of people known to us, or emerge as representing abstract emotions such as jealousy or fear. We can become any animal that appears to us in dreams, so when this happens you should

---

THE HARPY
This mythical creature seduced men by her song, then killed them.

---

consider what that specific animal represents to you. There may be a pun in your interpretation – for instance, if a pig appears in your dream, have you behaved chauvinistically or greedily in waking life?

ASKING FOR HELP

It may be a good idea to ask your dreams for more help; you can actually ask your dreams to explain themselves. If this sounds strange and even ridiculous, remember that you are the source of your dreams, and there is no reason why you should not remind yourself that your messages are too opaque or ambiguous.

Having failed to understand a dream that seems important, just before going to sleep the following night, recall the dream, tell yourself that it was too enigmatic, and ask for a clearer one. It is usually the case that you will send yourself a dream that, while it may not seem anything like the first one, will have the same theme and the same message, or offer a clue that will help you to interpret it.

Another classical means of asking a dream what it means was devised by Dr. Frederick Perls, the distinguished Gestalt psychotherapist. Take two chairs, and place them opposite each other. You then sit in one, and imagine that your dream is sitting in the other. Ask the dream why you cannot understand it, then move to the other chair, and as the dream, answer yourself. Move between the chairs as you first ask and then answer questions.

The process can go on for some time, but eventually you (as the dream) will deliver a phrase that immediately rings a bell. When that happens, the intent of the dream should be clearly revealed.

—◆— INTERPRETATION PROBLEMS —◆—

LEARNING TO INTERPRET your dreams is like solving a difficult crossword puzzle. Some people have the kind of mind that enables them to grasp the nature of the problem quickly and easily, while others feel they will never be able to do it. It is important to approach dream interpretation in a relaxed frame of mind, since tension will aggravate any problem you may have.

LEARN TO RELAX

If you become worried easily (by any problem) and find that when trying to work with and analyze one of your dreams you quickly begin to become exasperated by its difficulty, it may be a good idea to practice your favorite relaxation technique. You should always try to settle down to the work of interpretation alone, in a private corner of your home, away from the bustle of your waking life. If you wake during the night from a fascinating dream, after making a brief note of it, do not immediately try to work out "what it means."

SURRENDER TO YOUR DREAMS

It is important to surrender to your dreams, so you should not try to resist what they seem to be saying. A worrying dream will only repeat itself in other forms, and more importantly, in defying its message you will be denying your inner nature.

Dreams describe your innermost self. All too often your conscious mind denies it (perhaps prompted by your upbringing, education, or social situation). As Jung put it, a dream "shows inner truth and reality … as it really is: not as I conjecture it to be, and not as [the dreamer] would like it to be, but as it is."

So do not shrink away from the apparent meaning of a dream the moment it seems to go against the grain of your nature. Follow the line of thought to the end, and only when you are sure you have the meaning of the dream pinned down, give serious thought to its message – which may not be the same as its meaning. For example, a dream may show you as a serial killer: this does not mean that you have killed or could ever kill a large number of people; but it may mean that you are staggering under some undesirable personality trait or characteristic that needs to be exterminated.

You may find when you start interpreting your dreams that it is easier than you expected at first, but becomes more difficult as you progress. Your dreams may seem to become more "difficult," which simply means that they are being more successful in disguising their meaning. This is quite a common problem, and it may stem from the very reason why dreams disguise their meanings in the first place: because they know that you are pursuing them, they make an extra effort to elude you. However, this is actually a sign of your success. A "difficult" dream is more likely to be important, than one that is clear on first examination.

YOUR INNER LIFE

A dream may be obscure to you not just because it seems to have no bearing on your life, but because it may be commenting on your inner life – a life of which you are barely conscious during your waking hours.

A dream may not simply be the result of some waking guilt or love, ambition or failure, problem or pleasure. Dreams refer to your wildest fantasies, to your most remote animal instincts, to beliefs you are not aware that you hold, and fears that you would not confess even to yourself. Dreams could also refer to areas of your mind of which you may be unaware. Our minds are like icebergs: for every wish or fear of which we are conscious, ten times as many lie deep below the surface, in our unconscious – and our dreams could refer to any of them. This is another reason never to reject the apparent "meaning" of a dream.

WHAT IS THE ANSWER?

There is a famous story of the American writer Gertrude Stein, who when she was dying turned to her companion, Alice B. Toklas, and asked: "What is the answer?" Receiving no reply, she smiled, and said "Then what is the question?"

We may ask ourselves the same question with regard to dreams, because it is easy to be discouraged about them. Distressed at being unable to make progress with our analysis, we may ask ourselves whether dreams are worth all the time we are devoting to them.

PHANTOMS AND FANTASY
Odilon Redon (1840–1916) often painted phantoms and figments from dreams, visions, and nightmares. He called this painting The Dream.

—◆— PROBLEM DREAMS —◆—

DREAMS CAN BE DISTURBING for a variety of reasons. Some can follow
us for years, worrying us by their persistence and our inability
to understand them. How do we deal with nightmares, and why
do they occur? What are we to make of dreams in which we
know ourselves to be dreaming? Or dreams that warn
us of approaching catastrophe?

RECURRING DREAMS

It is safe to assume that a recurring dream (and such
dreams can return regularly over a period of years,
often from childhood to middle- or old-age) will have
something important to say to us about the way we are
conducting our waking lives; so it will be worth trying
to discover what its message is.

The way to do this is to keep a careful and detailed
record of the dream (*see pages 28 to 31*). We may think
that the dream is exactly the same each time it occurs,
but in fact this is rarely the case. Often there are
differences – even if very small differences – between
them, and it is usually the case that the nature of these
variations holds a clue to the meaning of the dream.
Such a dream is usually the result of some emotional
weakness in our nature that can, over the years, cause
us to be hurt, or to hurt ourselves in some way. It is
when this happens that our dream often recurs, and
although the dream may remain the same in its
essential elements, in our waking lives it can apply
to different sets of circumstances that provoke us
to display the same weakness.

It is only when we begin to strengthen the area of
ourselves that the dream is criticizing that it will begin
to change more radically, and then finally (if we resolve
our original problem) vanish.

LUCID DREAMS

Lucid dreams – in which we not only know that we are
dreaming, but can also control our dreams – occur to a
minority of people. There are techniques you can use
to teach yourself to control your dreams, but opinions
about the wisdom of doing this differ widely. Lucid
dreams can be enjoyable experiences, since you can,
for example, choose to fly, to jump off a precipice, or
to travel from country to country.

VISIONS FROM LITERATURE
*Arthur Rackham (1867–1918), one of the great English
illustrative artists, took much of his inspiration from dream
fantasies, fairy stories, and poems such as Milton's* Comus.

There is also the view, however, that lucid dreams
work against the main purpose of dreaming, which is
to teach us something and help us come to terms with
our own personalities. If we interfere with our dreams
we deprive them of their own self-will; that is, we
repress the part of our unconscious that is trying to
reveal ourselves to ourselves.

Some dream clinics encourage lucid dreaming as a
means of dealing with recurring nightmares. Learning
to control your dream, you can enter it with all your
faculties, and ensure that your monsters are restrained
and the nightmare is "cured." This, however, is to
ignore the reason why you are having the nightmare in
the first place; and the pressure that provoked it,
denied expression in your dreams, will only emerge
somewhere else in your waking life – perhaps in a
more harmful way.

NIGHTMARE WORLDS
Gustav Klimt (1862–1918) painted beautiful men and women who often seemed to inhabit a somber world; the faces of these Mermaids *emerge from the bodies of sea-snakes.*

Some people argue that lucid dreaming can be a means of reaching a higher state of consciousness, in which our minds can unlock potential that we have failed to discover in our waking lives. There is much interesting work going on in this field of research, and given the remarkable latent creative power revealed in dreams, it is clear that they could contribute much to the development of our spiritual lives. Whether this type of development can best be achieved through lucid dreaming is, however, another matter.

PREDICTIVE DREAMS

Unless you are seriously interested in the very idea of the possibility of predicting future events, it is both unwise and unnecessary to allow the idea of predictive dreams (*see page 62*) to preoccupy you. In the vast majority of cases, predictive dreams are too vague and imprecise to be either useful or frightening.

NIGHTMARES

Nightmares are dealt with at length on pages 154 to 155. It is possible to dispose of nightmares – sometimes simply by coming to understand them and remedying whatever tension is causing them, and sometimes simply by the passage of time. Recurrent nightmares (*see opposite*) usually indicate a particularly serious problem in your waking life with which you need to come to terms.

There are groups of people all over the world who meet to discuss their problem dreams, and nightmares in particular. It is sometimes difficult to find these groups, but local health authorities often have information about them.

SEXUAL DREAMS

Some people (especially those who are not at home with their own sexuality, perhaps because of repression or inhibition) are worried when they wake from sexual dreams in which they have taken part in, and perhaps enjoyed, activities that would horrify or shame them in their waking lives.

Sexual dreams – like all dreams – can occur for many different reasons. Sometimes they are simply the result of sexual deprivation. Young boys and girls, in puberty and after, often experience sexual dreams that culminate in orgasm. Those who are responsible for sexual education, such as parents and teachers, should explain that this is a normal part of growing up, and is nothing of which to be ashamed.

Those adults whose sexual dreams are troubling must remember that they are not living in medieval times, when people believed that such dreams were sent by the Devil. However horrifying our dream actions (sexual or otherwise) may be, they originate in our own minds. If distressing dreams or nightmares recur, and seriously disturb you, professional psychiatric advice should be sought.

DREAM THEMES

IT CANNOT BE EMPHASIZED enough that your dreams are personal to you, and that it is impossible to interpret them in terms of any dream anyone else has ever had. When Jung was talking to his patients about their dreams, he would start by asking: "What do you think about it? When you think about that dream, what occurs to you in connection with it?"

His theory was that we are capable of interpreting our own dreams, and, indeed, when talking about our dreams, we often arrive at the right meaning without any prompting. Nevertheless, some help is useful and there are certain themes that appear in most people's dreams which often lead in roughly the same direction. This chapter contains a selection of these themes. You may find it difficult to decide just what the main theme is, since it will not necessarily be a prominent image in the dream.

Let your mind dwell on your dream, and carefully consider your feelings about it. The "feeling" you have about it, rather than a memory of an incident, may suggest the focus of the message your unconscious is sending you.

WILLIAM BLAKE (1757–1827),
NEBUCHADNEZZAR

HOW TO USE THIS SECTION

YOUR DREAMS ARE THE MOST private aspects of your life. No one can tell you, with absolute assurance, what your dreams mean, so it is best to learn to interpret your dreams for yourself. This is not an easy task, and a certain amount of work is involved. When considering your dream, you may want to turn straight to the appropriate Dream Theme (you will find this in the Dream Thesaurus in small capital letters). What you find there about the symbol that has presented itself to you may immediately strike a cord. However, if this is not the case, follow the instructions given on these pages and on page 184. Finally, always remember that your dreams are personal to you; it is possible for two people to have exactly the same dream and for it to have quite different meanings.

THE WORLD OF NATURE

FANTASY & FABLE

ARTS & SCIENCES

THE HUMAN BODY

BUILDINGS & INTERIORS

EVERYDAY THINGS

HUMAN EMOTIONS

HUMAN ACTIVITIES

HUMAN CONDITIONS

RITUALS & RELIGION

THE DREAM THESAURUS

THE DREAM THESAURUS

Each image is related to one or more of the main dream themes on pages 42 to 183. These themes are listed in small capitals below each entry in the Dream Thesaurus, and are followed by the relevant page number.

The words in italics below the themes are pointers to follow if the suggested theme or themes do not seem to apply to your particular dream.

The underlined entries are the main dream themes.

THE MAJOR SYMBOL

Consider the main image in your dream and look this up in the Dream Thesaurus.

DREAM THESAURUS PAGES

POINTERS

If none of the suggested themes seems to apply, go back to the Dream Thesaurus and look at the "pointer" words in italics.

EXCLUDED ENTRIES

It is impossible to include every entry in the Dream Thesaurus in the main dream theme pages. Although your dream image will relate to one or more of the themes, the actual word may not appear on the theme page to which you are referred.

SIMILAR IMAGES

If the principle image in your dream does not appear in the Dream Thesaurus, consult the nearest suggestion. For example, if you dream that you are dancing a tango, look for the entry "dancing."

REFERENCING

Look up the suggested theme or themes.

DREAM THEMES PAGES

DREAM THEMES

The capitalized words in the main text are the dream images mentioned in the Dream Thesaurus — each of these words is an entry in the Dream Thesaurus. The capitalized words are also pulled out and listed alongside the main text for easy reference. The numbers below many of the pulled-out entries in the Dream Themes section refer to other theme pages on which those particular dream images appear.

ANALYZING YOUR DREAMS

As well as referring to the theme section, follow the general instructions given in Chapter Two to successfully interpret your dreams.

THE WORLD OF NATURE

FANTASY & FABLE

ARTS & SCIENCES

THE HUMAN BODY

BUILDINGS & INTERIORS

EVERYDAY THINGS

HUMAN EMOTIONS

HUMAN ACTIVITIES

HUMAN CONDITIONS

RITUALS & RELIGION

THE DREAM THESAURUS

MAMMALS AND REPTILES

MOST PEOPLE DREAM more readily about domestic animals than about wild ones: dreams of household pets often center on our own characteristics, mirrored in those of cats, dogs, birds, and even fish. Freud suggested that dreams of wild animals represented our most sensual passions, and sometimes the "evil instincts" that lie deep in our unconscious.

HORSE
144, 170
DOG
43
CAT
43

Statistics show that the animals who most often appear in dreams are HORSES, DOGS, then CATS, and women seem to dream more often of horses than men do. Early records show that Artemidorus of Daldis (*c.*2nd century) lists horses among the common dreams of women. Some psychologists have suggested that the horse represents male sexuality.

DOG
43
CAT
43
RAT
MULE
ELEPHANT
LION

Dreams of animals are fairly difficult to interpret because of the many possible associations. The meaning of your dream of an animal is almost certain to refer to your feelings (either past or present) about that animal. Were you or are you frightened or comforted by it; have you ever been attacked by it? Then there are the traditional associations: DOGS are said to be faithful, CATS clever or wise, RATS cowardly and devious, MULES stubborn, ELEPHANTS to have remarkable memories, and LIONS to be brave. There are also many mythical allusions connected to some animals.

PET
131

Your dream may be of a caged lion in a zoo; of the Cowardly Lion in the film *The Wizard of Oz*; of the Nemean lion of legend; of the lion on a coat of arms; or of the Leo of the Zodiac (*see page 69*). So the reference may be to restriction, to cowardice, to the overcoming of some difficulties, to pride and status, or to any characteristics of the astrological Sun-sign Leo. Consider the context of your dream, your waking feelings about the creature in it, and as many details of the animal's behavior and appearance as you can remember. The animal (especially if it is a domestic PET) may represent an aspect of your personality or character that you instinctively feel you should employ in a particular situation. If in your dream you were hunting an animal with a view to killing it, it may represent a personal characteristic that you may feel you should eliminate. If an animal is chasing you in a dream, this may suggest that in waking life you are in flight from some area of your personality that is stubbornly demanding expression.

APE
MONKEY
CHIMPANZEE
BABOON
ASS
DONKEY
BEAR
BUFFALO

The following suggestions should only be treated as possible starting points for interpretation. The APE is intelligent, but tends to be tricky and mischievous (like the MONKEY, CHIMPANZEE, or BABOON); it is also highly imitative, so there may be a sense of emulation in your dream. Who is about to play a trick on you, or be sly, malicious, or cunning? Or is it you? The ASS and the DONKEY are seen as meek but sturdy, and sometimes foolish, creatures; could this be an allusion to your attitude toward work? The BEAR is a symbol of strength and danger, but is also regarded as a lovable creature. The BUFFALO

THE WORLD OF NATURE

FANTASY & FABLE

ARTS & SCIENCES

THE HUMAN BODY

BUILDINGS & INTERIORS

EVERYDAY THINGS

HUMAN EMOTIONS

HUMAN ACTIVITIES

HUMAN CONDITIONS

RITUALS & RELIGION

THE DREAM THESAURUS

BEAVER
ANT
44
BULL
CAMEL
CAT
42
COW
HERD
GOAT
RAM
JACKAL
KANGAROO
MOLE

represents power and resolution; in your dream were you one of a herd? The BEAVER, like the ANT, symbolizes hard work and perseverance, while the BULL represents masculinity, sexual energy, rashness, brute force, and anger. A rampant bull creating havoc may suggest that you are overly optimistic about your sexual prowess. The CAMEL is an obedient and forbearing animal, storing up food for fuel during lean times. The CAT has been associated with witchcraft; it can also be spiteful and self-defensive. In almost every religion the COW represents the maternal instinct. Could this be a comment on your waking attitude to motherhood? If you were one of a HERD of cows, beware of paying too much heed to others' opinions. The GOAT and the RAM both suggest rampant sexuality, while the JACKAL has the reputation of being tenacious but cowardly – feeding off others. A KANGAROO travels fast, but what is it hiding in its pouch? Is the dream merely an allusion to a particular Australian? A MOLE burrows, hidden beneath the ground; is this the way you are or should be

MOUSE
SHEEP
TIGER
PIG
BOAR
SOW
SNAKE

working? Are you as timid as a MOUSE; or as silly as a SHEEP, which always appears overly obedient, compliant, and part of the herd? Perhaps you are as assertive as a ram or as fierce as a TIGER? The PIG is invariably associated with greed. It is also seen as diligent and friendly (but the BOAR is more closely identified with antagonism, and the SOW with breeding). SNAKES are all too often automatically regarded as phallic symbols (*see Erotic Dreams, page 96*), but are you being a "snake in the grass" – sneaking up on someone? Or is it happening to you?

DOG
42
SQUIRREL
ZOO
ANTLERS
FUR

You should always consider the context of the dream: was the DOG fierce but tethered, and therefore under control; or was it confined to its home? Was the dream SQUIRREL storing up nuts for the winter? If so, what sort of winter do you fear may be approaching? An animal in a ZOO is not only confined, but is observed by others. In waking life, are you the subject of close attention or admiration? Physical differences between the animals may be important: the ANTLERS of the deer and the spikes of the hedgehog may be a reference to irritation or vexation; soft FUR is more approachable, but is possibly an indication of reclusiveness.

— ◆ WINGED CREATURES ◆ —

A BIRD IN FLIGHT often represents aspiration, spirituality, and freedom. Dreams of winged creatures may refer to a need for some form of release in waking life; it may sometimes be symbolic of the freedom to adhere to a certain belief or conviction.

ALBATROSS
BAT
BUDGERIGAR
PARROT
CHICKEN
COCKEREL

The ALBATROSS if killed, brings bad luck; on the other hand, it is a high-soaring bird with an enormous wing-span, so the reference may be to freedom. The BAT may either signify blindness (to what?) or an instinctive sense of direction. BUDGERIGARS and PARROTS are notable chiefly for imitation; who are you mimicking or mocking? The CHICKEN is seen as an anxious, over-domestic bird. Are you an over-possessive hen? The COCKEREL is alert and vigilant, giving the

CUCKOO
DOVE
EAGLE

early-morning call. This may suggest a need to communicate a message – and in no uncertain fashion; but you should also consider the common allusion to male sexuality. A dream of a CUCKOO may refer to a stranger trying to insinuate themselves into the family, or even a strange and unwelcome element in your emotional life. The DOVE is the bird of peace and love: does this represent your partner? The EAGLE often has a particular significance for Americans, but in general

THE WORLD OF NATURE

FANTASY & FABLE

ARTS & SCIENCES

THE HUMAN BODY

BUILDINGS & INTERIORS

EVERYDAY THINGS

HUMAN EMOTIONS

HUMAN ACTIVITIES

HUMAN CONDITIONS

RITUALS & RELIGION

THE DREAM THESAURUS

THE WORLD OF NATURE

FANTASY & FABLE

ARTS & SCIENCES

THE HUMAN BODY

BUILDINGS & INTERIORS

EVERYDAY THINGS

HUMAN EMOTIONS

HUMAN ACTIVITIES

HUMAN CONDITIONS

RITUALS & RELIGION

THE DREAM THESAURUS

HAWK
GEESE
NIGHTINGALE

it is a powerful symbol of victory. As with a dream of a **HAWK**, there may be an allusion to your powers of observation, or to a wish to take an overall view of problems, or of life in general. The hawk is chiefly a bird of prey: above whose head are you hovering intently? Although **GEESE** are portrayed as foolish birds, they are also good watchmen; **NIGHTINGALES** are generally admired, but it is their song that is most remarkable. Have you been "singing" – in other words, boasting or

OSTRICH
OWL
PEACOCK
SWAN
FLOCK

talking out of turn? Conversely, are someone's words seducing you? Have you been ignoring important facts like the **OSTRICH**? Or is your dream referring to the wisdom of an **OWL**? The pride of the **PEACOCK** is matched by its strident self-assertion. The grace of the **SWAN** is joined to the power with which its unseen feet propel it through the water. A dream of being part of a **FLOCK** of birds is likely to have much the same connotation as being part of a herd (*see page 43*).

—◆— SWIMMERS AND CRAWLERS —◆—

THERE IS A STRONG SYMBOLIC connection between Christianity and fish, and the fish's element is water (*see page 46*), so there may be a powerful emotional factor in a dream about fish. The fish has also often been a phallic symbol, and is the symbol for Pisces in the Zodiac. Often busy, insects are determined and active, so dreaming of insects may symbolize your own hard work or aspirations.

CRAB
64
AQUARIUM
OCTOPUS
EEL
TADPOLE

Dreams of particular fish will have a significance if the symbol touches your personal life. **CRABS** move sideways, so consider whether you are taking evasive action. Their claws gather sand, a symbol of acquisitiveness and possessiveness but also of clinging or hoarding, or of resentment. A dream that involves an **AQUARIUM** may refer to certain constricting emotional conditions; a goldfish bowl may simply allude to boredom. A dream **OCTOPUS** may suggest business, multiple activities, or deals; **EELS** may appear slippery and inveigling; and a **TADPOLE** in your dream may suggest a transformation of some kind in your waking life.

STING

You may have been stung by an insect in the dream, in which case did it represent an enemy or event in your life? The **STING** may be an emotional one: someone may

have hurt you, or gossip may have stung you. Is your conscience stinging you? If you were frightened or repelled in your dream, try to make an association with a "real" threat in waking life.

ANT
43
ANTHILL
CATERPILLAR
BUTTERFLY
FLEA
GNAT
MOSQUITO
MOTH
SCORPION

The **ANT** in particular is associated with industry, and the **ANTHILL** may refer to your workplace. The metamorphosis of **CATERPILLAR** into **BUTTERFLY** seems to suggest a longing to improve your image (especially but not exclusively in women). A **FLEA** is celebrated for ubiquity – for jumping rapidly from one body to another. Do you have the sort of mind that leaps from one subject to another? A **GNAT** or **MOSQUITO** may have much the same significance, although the latter is largely associated with irritation, and at worst the spread of disease. To whom in waking life may this symbol allude, and what precautions should you take? **MOTHS**, too, must be regarded with suspicion: they eat away at valuable clothing and cause much damage that is not immediately visible. The **SCORPION** has a sting in its tail: is this referring to you or to an enemy?

◆—FIRE—◆

A DREAM INVOLVING FIRE usually has a comment to make on our physical and emotional potency and the way in which we express it in waking life. If fire is associated with water (*see page 46*) in a dream, the allusion is almost certainly emotional: a dream of a fire being put out by water, for example, may suggest physical energy being restrained by the cooler processes of thought.

**HEARTH
BONFIRE
BEACON**

You should always try to consider the context of your dream. A fire burning in a domestic **HEARTH** is likely to allude to your personal life, while a **BONFIRE** on a hill will have a more public significance. A **BEACON** or bonfire suggests a public declaration: it will almost certainly be a symbol of communication, successful or otherwise. What kind of message do you need to communicate? On the other hand, is someone trying forcefully to impress you with a message that you are resisting? A dream in which there is a fire out of control, destructive, and quick spreading, may suggest that your waking emotions are out of control, and that you are not taking heed of constraint or disapproval. If in your dream you were succeeding in controlling the flames, it may be implying that you are actually in control of certain waking situations (even if you are doubtful of this).

CANDLE

What was the fire feeding on in your dream, and what might it represent in waking life? In your dream, did you have feelings of regret, delight, or resignation about the object on fire? A fire consuming a whole building (*see page 100*) or a room (*see page 103*) may suggest that you are being consumed by an uncontrollable passion. On the other hand, the tiny flame of a **CANDLE** is able to spread considerable light, just as in waking life a relatively small expenditure of energy can have remarkable results when properly applied. A dream of blowing out a candle may signify an end of some kind in your waking life; for example, the ending of an emotional relationship or of a particular period of your life. Men sometimes dream of extinguishing a fire by urinating on it, and this frequently implies disapproval of a message, or of someone else's point of view or morals. In a dream, this method of preventing the message from spreading appears to be forceful, tactless, and determined.

**FURNACE
FORGE**

A **FURNACE** is perhaps the most forceful and practical expression of the power of fire. All of the fire's energy is devoted to making something: in waking life, this may represent an ongoing project or the presentation of a new idea. A dream in which you were using a fire to **FORGE** something; for example, some kind of weapon (*see page 118*) or a tool (*see page 115*), may hold more than one meaning. Are you already a creative person in waking life, about to start a new project, or is the dream hinting that a portion of your energy should be more creatively employed in some way?

THE WORLD OF NATURE

FANTASY & FABLE

ARTS & SCIENCES

THE HUMAN BODY

BUILDINGS & INTERIORS

EVERYDAY THINGS

HUMAN EMOTIONS

HUMAN ACTIVITIES

HUMAN CONDITIONS

RITUALS & RELIGION

THE DREAM THESAURUS

THE WORLD OF NATURE

FANTASY & FABLE

ARTS & SCIENCES

THE HUMAN BODY

BUILDINGS & INTERIORS

EVERYDAY THINGS

HUMAN EMOTIONS

HUMAN ACTIVITIES

COOKING
BARBECUE
STOVE
73
BRAZIER

The other major use of fire in dreams is in the preparation of food. What were you **COOKING** and what might this item represent? It could symbolize an idea or a plan, or it may simply refer to the basic business of providing for a family. A dream of a **BARBECUE** rather than a **STOVE** suggests something less serious: it may be a reference to your social life. A **BRAZIER** is used for comfort, and to produce warmth under auspicious circumstances: in your dream, was this for you or for someone else? What waking situation should be alleviated by a little warmth and understanding?

POKING

Dreams in which one is tending a fire are frequent. There is sometimes an allusion to interference: for example, if you were **POKING** a fire in your dream, there may be a suggestion that in waking life you are intervening (perhaps uninvited) in a certain situation. Were you trying to make the fire burn more fiercely and destructively, or were you attempting to extinguish it? A dream in which you were fueling a fire may imply that an idea of yours needs more input, more research, and the presentation of more facts. But why were you feeding the fire? Consider your motives, and react accordingly.

—✦— WATER —✦—

DREAMS IN WHICH WATER plays a considerable part are often concerned with the dreamer's emotional life. The reason for this is obscure, but psychologists have suggested that it has connections with the amniotic fluid in which we float in the womb. It is not by accident that the water of a well has always represented wisdom.

FLOATING
WATERFALL

A dream that one is **FLOATING** safely and calmly in warm water is one of the most comforting, secure dreams imaginable: flotation tanks (popular as a means of relaxation) are the equivalent in waking life. However, dreams are not always as simple as that. Water appears in dreams in many contexts, and most of them are commenting on your emotional state. Some are clearly referring to your birth. Dreams of a **WATERFALL** or of a swiftly running stream have this connotation. A dream in which you are swept along in a warm stream of water through a tunnel,

POOL
LAGOON
150

emerging to fall into a **POOL** or a **LAGOON**, may contain an allusion to the process of birth (it is alleged that we all carry in our unconscious the memory of being born).

BATH
146
SEA
47

Dreams of being immersed in water, for example in a **BATH** or in the **SEA**, may allude (depending on your feelings about the experience) to your current waking emotional state. It may be a sign of emotional security, or (if the sea in the dream was rough and you were afraid of

DROWNING
SHOWER
146
JACUZZI
RAIN
49
UMBRELLA
SWIMMING-POOL

DROWNING) insecurity. A dream SHOWER or a bath in which you are thoroughly cleaning yourself, may allude to a need to cleanse your emotions of false or negative elements, while a JACUZZI may have a sexual connotation. A dream of being thoroughly drenched by RAIN may be suggesting that you are guided too easily by your emotions; however, you may have been sheltering beneath an UMBRELLA. In waking life, are you protecting yourself from emotions that you are afraid of? Being in a SWIMMING-POOL may remind you of the importance of leisure time and the need to relax.

SEA
46

The SEA is commonly a symbol of the mother: a dream of being overwhelmed by a wave, or sucked down into the depths, may imply that you are being smothered or dominated by your mother; while calmly riding the waves, or swimming or paddling in a warm sea, suggests an ideal relationship. Struggling against the tide, and making progress, may suggest that you are gaining strength against a repressive relationship.

STREAM
RIVER
BOAT

Dreams of being carried along in water – whether a swift-flowing STREAM or a RIVER – are generally references to passing time and to being carried along from birth to death. However, they may also refer to the stream of your emotional life, and the meaning of the dream will be indicated by other clues – mainly by how you felt (for example, frightened, confident, or happy). Dreaming that you are in a BOAT may allude to the circumstances in which your emotional life is lived: the boat may represent your

STEAMER
CANOE
DINGHY
BUOY
SHIPWRECK
162

family, home life, or current emotional relationship. Look for clues in the dream, such as the boat's name or the color of the sails. The context of the dream, and the type of boat involved, are important points to note. Was the boat sailing forward confidently, or was the vessel foundering? Was it a solid, safe STEAMER, or a fragile CANOE or DINGHY? If it was moored to a BUOY, how secure was it and what did it represent? The craft may refer to a person, your job, or your financial situation, for example. A SHIPWRECK has obvious connotations: what is happening to your emotional life?

FOUNTAIN
GEYSER
HOSEPIPE
PLUMBER
148

There are sometimes clear sexual symbols in dreams. A dream of a FOUNTAIN, a GEYSER, or a HOSE will usually embrace sexual emotion rather than simply ejaculation. If the jet was weak or failing, the dream may be suggesting that sexual desire is not matched by emotional involvement (or the other way around). The presence of a PLUMBER may be alluding to another person, or your own conscience. A steady flow of water is probably symbolic of your confidence in waking life.

THE WORLD OF NATURE

FANTASY & FABLE

ARTS & SCIENCES

THE HUMAN BODY

BUILDINGS & INTERIORS

EVERYDAY THINGS

HUMAN EMOTIONS

—◆— EARTH —◆—

AS THE MOST BASIC of the elements, earth reminds us of our mortality.
Fire can enliven us, water can comfort us, and air can inspire us,
but we are in the end "brought back down to earth." In dreams,
earth can not only reflect humanity's remote beginnings, but also
the depths of our unconscious.

**MUD
SAND
DIGGING**
114, 144
BURROWING

Most people who dream of earth find the experience unpleasant. Dreams of being buried by earth, **MUD** or **SAND**, or of **DIGGING** or **BURROWING** into the earth, are often extremely disturbing. It is important to consider the context of the dream. Was someone actually burying you? If so, the reference may be to a rival at work, or a partner or authority figure who is (perhaps unconsciously) subjugating your personality to theirs. Or it may be that you are simply being buried by work or by anxieties.

CHAMBER

If a dream takes you to an underground **CHAMBER**, what you find there is most important (each dreamer will find something unique to them). The dream may be alluding to the depths of your unconscious, and the symbolism will be extremely important (although for that very reason often difficult to interpret).

EARTHQUAKE
48, 121, 158, 161
**SAND
GARDENING**

Dreams about earth may signify security; or, if you were burying yourself, a sense of insecurity may be at the bottom of the dream. The same may be true if the earth itself was shaking or opening beneath you in an **EARTHQUAKE**, or if you were walking on shifting **SAND**. If you were **GARDENING**, however, creativity is probably indicated: the dream may be referring to your psychological growth, or increasing emotional or financial security.

—◆— AIR —◆—

A DREAM IS RARELY "about" air; the element is usually only part of a
dream. We soar on air when we dream of flying (*see page 147*), or we
struggle through it when there is a high wind.

OXYGEN
94
SUFFOCATION

OXYGEN is the element we depend on for our basic survival, and any dream of being deprived of it, or of **SUFFOCATION**, is likely to symbolize some sort of deprivation – usually psychological or intellectual. A dream in which you are outdoors (*see page 58*) – and conscious of the clarity and coolness of the air, may signify that you need to give freedom to your thoughts. On the other hand, the dream may be acknowledging a recent waking feeling of release from a problem or confining situation. As in all dreams in which air plays a part, other constituents of the dream will probably be equally significant to your interpretation, and should not be ignored.

WIND
49
SMOKE

If in your dreams you are flying and you are aware of the air swirling around you, or if on the ground you are buffeted by a strong **WIND**; if **SMOKE** is carried on the air, obscuring your view; or if detritus is whirling around, you should consider the implications. In waking life, are you being forced into a situation in which you must consider ideas that you previously refused to contemplate? Are you worried about hostile "attacks" by certain people, or by the interference of numerous niggling problems in your waking life? How did you deal with the situation in your dream, and what does this say to you about your waking difficulty or predicament?

—◆— WEATHER —◆—

DREAMS IN WHICH THE WEATHER is a strong feature may be presenting us with a personal "weather forecast," telling us that there are storms or a sunny, calm spell ahead. However, this type of dream more often reflects the mood in our waking lives than actually forecasts what lies ahead.

BREEZE

It is quite often the case that the mood of the day is carried on into sleep, and this may be reflected in the general atmosphere of our dreams. However, dreams do not necessarily imitate the moods of our waking life; when we are at our most moody and pessimistic, a dream can be surprisingly cheerful, or if we feel low and sluggish, an invigorating **BREEZE** in a dream can suggest that we pull ourselves together and show some spirit.

STORM
121, 158
HURRICANE
SHELTER
SUN
WIND
48

A dream may contain comments on the climate of a personal relationship. A tiff with a loved one may turn into a dream **STORM** or even a **HURRICANE**, but there may be clues to avoiding the worst of the weather. For example, were you sheltered or looking for **SHELTER**? Did the **SUN** eventually shine through the clouds? **WIND** may represent change or a need for change – we speak of "blowing away the cobwebs."

RAIN
47

RAIN, associated with water (*see page 46*), usually has an emotional significance if it appears in dreams. How were you dealing with the situation in the dream, and what other clues might there be to your waking behavior?

HAIL
SNOW
160, 172
DRIZZLE
CLOUD
MIST

HAIL has similar associations to rain, but is much colder; **SNOW** is even more extreme and usually lies on the ground not only more thickly than hail but for longer. Your dream may be warning you of a spell of chilly emotional weather. A mere **DRIZZLE** may signify that the situation is less serious. Lowering **CLOUDS** may appear threatening, but was the sun breaking through? If you were "up in the clouds" you may have been flying (*see page 147*). **MIST** is a similar symbol: if the landscape (*see page 58*) is obscured, there may be a problem – or even a person – in your waking life that you are not seeing clearly. Can you see a way ahead? How much effort were you making, in your dream, to find the way forward?

THUNDER
158

In ancient times, **THUNDER** was considered to be the voice of the gods, and in dreams it often seems to have peculiar gravity. What is the voice saying? It will usually be a voice of disapproval, but it may not be obvious what is being disapproved of, although there should be clues in the dream.

THE WORLD OF NATURE

FANTASY & FABLE

ARTS & SCIENCES

THE HUMAN BODY

BUILDINGS & INTERIORS

EVERYDAY THINGS

HUMAN EMOTIONS

HUMAN ACTIVITIES

HUMAN CONDITIONS

RITUALS & RELIGION

THE DREAM THESAURUS

An object or person appearing in a dream of thunder may represent someone against whom you hold a grudge or who you are planning to oppose. It may also epitomize a characteristic in your mind of which your conscience disapproves. Remember that although the dream may be a warning that others will, or do, disapprove of some action or attitude of yours, it is also possible that the thunder is the voice of your own conscience, or an authority figure such as a parent, teacher, or superior at work. Did you understand what the thunder was saying? It is a strong image, and the advice offered is equally forceful.

LIGHTNING
158

If **LIGHTNING** flashed in your dream, what was it illuminating? The symbol may represent your sudden understanding of a problem or situation, or the suggestion that a quick decision or action is needed (or appropriate). If you have suddenly "seen the light," then the dream may be reassuring you that the light is a true one. However, remember that this kind of dream can be prompted by an outside source: for example, a car's headlights illuminating your bedroom window. Who or what was most affected by the type of weather in your dream? Were you personally exposed to the weather, or were you concerned for someone else? In the latter case, it may be that you fear the consequences of your actions on another person. If a building (*see page 100*) is at risk, you should attempt to translate the dream from the point of view of what was damaged or under threat rather than first considering the weather itself.

DREAM ANALYSIS

"I was a child again, and riding my bicycle along the village street, but its wheels began to sink into sticky, muddy earth, so that I could barely move. Finally, however, the earth began to dry, and I found that I was able to cycle along quite easily once more."

This dream was from an elderly lady who was fighting a serious illness. The earth symbolized not only the illness but also her concern that she might die. As a child she had never been allowed a bicycle, so possessing one represented freedom. The bicycle was a symbol not only of something she badly wanted (her health) but also something that would help her make her way to recovery.

—◆— TREES —◆—

THE ROOTS OF OUR DREAMS lie deep in our unconscious, and since humans have always coexisted with nature (although many of us now spend most of our lives in cities), it is not surprising that trees and other plants often appear as dream symbols.

**BRANCHES
LEAVES
BIRDS**

The actual shape of a tree is significant: it can live for centuries, its branches spreading, dividing, and multiplying – like those of the human family tree. The **BRANCHES** of a dream tree may represent our family life, while **LEAVES** and **BIRDS** in the branches may reflect our thoughts. The noise made by the wind rushing though the branches was considered by ancient people to be the voice of nature; therefore, in a dream, representing basic truth-telling. You should look for clues in the dream as to what your unconscious may have been trying to tell you.

ROOTS

The **ROOTS** of trees usually spread even more widely than their branches, and because of the association with the Earth (*see page 48*), they may symbolize our past – the experience that informs our present thoughts and actions. A dream that the roots are in the sky is an ancient symbol of wisdom, the bringing into the light of basic, hidden, perhaps unconscious ideas and theories. Roots

OAK
ASH
BAY
BEECH
BIRCH
171
ELM
WILLOW

been associated with natural wisdom, philosophy, optimism, and prophesy. If you happened to associate an oak with your home, and therefore your family, your dream may be telling you to remember your background and rely upon it. It may be advising you to build upon the love and reassurance you had in your youth, and perhaps pay more attention to the advice of your parents. The ASH symbolizes optimism, creativity, and generosity: to dream of an ash was traditionally regarded as extremely fortunate. In mythology, the BAY tree was thought to guard against witchcraft, and still carries an allusion to the warding off of something unpleasant. The BEECH tree was said to represent selfishness, narrow-mindedness, sorrow, and even cruelty. The BIRCH, perhaps because of its tall, straight trunk, was considered a symbol of honesty, virtue, and honorable love. The ELM is a cold symbol, associated with old age (what was the state of health of the tree in your dream?); it also represents caution, responsibility, and endurance. The WILLOW tree was often associated with pregnancy, childbirth, and motherhood. It was also believed to symbolize emotional disturbances. It may seem unlikely that ancient traditional associations can work in the 20th century, but they often carry weight in dreams.

TRUNK
109
RINGS
SAP

are joined to branches by the tree TRUNK, which may represent family tradition. However, it may also symbolize our individuality: there are many roots and branches, but only one trunk. This may refer to the head of the family. If you cut a tree trunk across, by counting the RINGS marked in it you can tell its age. In a dream, these rings may represent our past experiences, and the wisdom we have gathered as we have moved through life. A tree's SAP is usually symbolic of blood.

OAK

Specific trees may be significant to the dreamer: so try to identify the emotion you feel for a special tree (it may evoke a childhood memory). It is not only the symbol in a dream that is important, but also the emotion that we relate to the symbol. For example, in the West, the oak is a symbol of great strength and durability. OAK trees were often considered sacred and have

DREAM ANALYSIS

"I saw a group of men cutting down a large tree in a park; a crowd of birds hovered in the air above it, and I realized that the destruction of the tree would mean their deaths. Some of the men were shooting at the birds. I protested to the leader of the men, but he said, 'It doesn't matter — they're bright birds, and they'll survive.' Then I saw that one big bird was flying off with several others on its back."

The dreamer had been engaged in long-term planning in the firm he worked for, but his superiors had rejected all his best ideas and seemed intent on ignoring him altogether (the tree probably represented the dreamer). The words of the workman's leader (the dreamer's boss) suggest that the dreamer is not as ineffectual as he might think, but that he should amalgamate some of his ideas, thereby making a stronger impression.

THE WORLD OF NATURE

FANTASY & FABLE

ARTS & SCIENCES

THE HUMAN BODY

BUILDINGS & INTERIORS

EVERYDAY THINGS

HUMAN EMOTIONS

HUMAN ACTIVITIES

HUMAN CONDITIONS

RITUALS & RELIGION

THE DREAM THESAURUS

—◆— OTHER PLANTS —◆—

PLANTS HAVE OFTEN been seen as the clearest indication on Earth of the spiritual power of the universe and, as Jung put it, have been "regarded with awe and contemplated with philosophical wonderment." This does not mean that all dreams involving plants carry messages of great importance; they can be as playful as any other dreams, and may deal as often in puns or in sly allusions.

THE WORLD
OF NATURE

FANTASY &
FABLE

ARTS &
SCIENCES

THE HUMAN
BODY

BUILDINGS &
INTERIORS

EVERYDAY
THINGS

HUMAN
EMOTIONS

HUMAN
ACTIVITIES

GRASS
HAY
GARDEN
54, 173

It is important to think of any possible personal references: if you were cutting the GRASS in your dream, what aspect of your waking life needs to be "trimmed" or "cut back"? The dream may be saying something about the leisure time in your waking life, since grass is often associated with relaxed afternoons in the sun, or picnics. If you were gathering the grass to make HAY, on the other hand, the dream may be prompting you to make the most of a current situation in your waking life, and to seize the moment to your advantage. Dreams in which you were working in your GARDEN may have a parallel with some form of waking work, but perhaps involving your family rather than your career. You should consider your waking life, and search for the comparison. If you do not have a garden in waking life, such a dream may be one of wish-fulfillment (*see page 150*).

BASIL
BROOM
109
DOCK LEAVES
NETTLES
FERN
GARLIC
HONEYSUCKLE
GROUND ELDER
DEADLY NIGHTSHADE
THISTLES
BRAMBLES

Plants, especially herbs, have many ancient references and traditional associations: for example, a dream of BASIL may allude to sweetness, kindness, and deep affection. BROOM usually grows in wild places and on common ground, and is frequently a symbol of freedom, determination, and the conviction that one will succeed. The branches of this bush were often used to make a sweeping brush or "broom"; hence its meaning in a dream of sweeping away unwanted people or things. DOCK LEAVES are used to soothe the irritation caused by stinging NETTLES; so the dream may be making a comment on the way in which you should approach something painful in your waking life. FERN was used as a divining plant, so there may be a reference to your hopes (or fears) for the future. For centuries, GARLIC has been regarded as a powerful guard against witchcraft: against what in your waking life do you need protection? The root of the garlic is also a strong medicine: dreaming of this may mean that you need to take care of your health. Climbing plants, and HONEYSUCKLE in particular, may symbolize various types of ambition; but to dream of GROUND ELDER suggests an even stronger ambition. Although nowadays DEADLY NIGHTSHADE is not seriously considered as a murder weapon, its association with violent, untimely death is still strong: against whom do you harbor such forceful, antagonistic feelings? THISTLES (unless you are Scottish) and BRAMBLES are prickly symbols, and also hint at antagonism toward you or on your own part. They may suggest that you need to find a way over difficulties that are in your path.

FLOWERS

DREAMS OF FLOWERS can often be reassuring. In waking life, there are few people who do not associate flowers with pleasure and relaxation. Apart from simply enjoying them, we use flowers as gestures of love, reassurance, comfort, and sympathy. It is generally in one or another of these contexts that flowers of all kinds frequently appear in our dreams.

BOUQUET GARLAND

If you dream of sending someone flowers, or presenting (or receiving) a **BOUQUET**, you should try to identify the other person in the dream. It may be someone you respect, love, or have compassion for; someone who you wished loved or respected you; or someone who has more regard for you than you may consciously believe. A dream of giving flowers to an anonymous person, or of receiving them from someone you cannot identify, may suggest that your self-respect is in need of encouragement. A **GARLAND** of flowers has a similar — though perhaps more formal — association.

WREATH

A dream of sending someone a **WREATH** of flowers could certainly be associated with unconscious feelings of guilt and hostility, but not with the same strength as dreams of attacking, or being attacked by, the person with whom the dream is associated. It is more likely to be a gesture of sympathy evoked by a conscious or unconscious understanding that the recipient has lost or lacks some quality. Have they lost your friendship? Dreaming of receiving a wreath may have the same significance: who sent the wreath? Could it be someone with whom you have recently lost sympathy or quarreled?

THE WORLD
OF NATURE

FANTASY &
FABLE

ARTS &
SCIENCES

THE HUMAN
BODY

THE WORLD
OF NATURE

FANTASY &
FABLE

ARTS &
SCIENCES

THE HUMAN
BODY

BUILDINGS &
INTERIORS

EVERYDAY
THINGS

HUMAN
EMOTIONS

HUMAN
ACTIVITIES

HUMAN
CONDITIONS

RITUALS &
RELIGION

THE DREAM
THESAURUS

GARDEN
52, 172
**DEAD
FLOWERS
DESTRUCTION
WORM
GRUB**

The appearance of the flowers in your dream may be significant: if they were formally arranged (perhaps you were arranging them) there may be a suggestion that your social life is too carefully organized, or perhaps needs putting in order. Flowers running riot in a **GARDEN**, or strewn around your home, would seem to suggest that your life is full of pleasure. But what else was happening in the dream? Were you tidying the flowers, or were you scattering more around? A dream in which flowers predominate in a garden may suggest (unless you are a passionate flower-grower) that your life needs more color, and that you should be less preoccupied merely with the practical business of making a living. A dream of **DEAD FLOWERS** is often depressing, and may convey a message of regret or danger. The **DESTRUCTION** of flowers (attacked perhaps by a **WORM** or **GRUB**) contains a similarly ominous tone.

**WATERING
FEEDING
BLOSSOMING**

If you were **WATERING** or **FEEDING** flowers, there may be a hint that you need to work on a relationship. Flowers in bud, or **BLOSSOMING**, in dreams may symbolize the flowering of an idea or a new relationship; or that you are entering a new phase in your life. Freud considered flowers to be a female symbol, because

of their cup-shaped blossoms and because a bee enters them in order to fertilize them. In male dreams, a flower can represent women or a particular woman. The flower could also symbolize an idea that has been fertilized in your mind.

**WILD-
FLOWERS
FLOWER
BEDS
CUT
FLOWERS**

WILDFLOWERS emphasize natural qualities, relaxed beauty, and scorn for the highly organized artificiality of **FLOWER BEDS**. The latter, with the blooms carefully placed, may seem impressive rather than endearing, suggesting the cautious organization of talent rather than its full flowering. **CUT FLOWERS** are displayed rather than allowed to give pleasure in their natural setting: they may be symbols of artificiality.

**ROSE
THORNY
BUTTERCUP
ORCHID
CAMELLIA
LILY**

Certain types of flower have individual associations for particular dreamers; if the emphasis in your dream seems to be on one particular type, try to recognize any possible connections. Some flowers also have traditional significance. The **ROSE**, for example, has been a symbol not only of love but also of courage: were the roses in your dream **THORNY**? The **BUTTERCUP** is traditionally associated with childhood; the **ORCHID** with beauty, admiration, and wealth; the **CAMELLIA** with delicacy; and the **LILY** with being elegant, cool, and remote.

—◆— FRUIT —◆—

FRUIT HAS TRADITIONALLY symbolized immortality, and the pleasures
of love. It is easy to see why fruit epitomizes the idea of immortality:
its seed symbolizes the beginning of all things, leading to ripe fruit
that produces more seed, and so the cycle begins again.

APPLE
107
PEAR
55
**PINEAPPLE
PEACH**
55
FIG
106

In Western countries, the **APPLE** is linked strongly to the ideas first of temptation, and then of sin and deceit (through the biblical story of Adam and Eve), and Greek mythology associated the apple with sexual attraction. The people of China regard the **PEAR** as a symbol of longevity, and in the West, the **PINEAPPLE** has been an emblem of fertility. The **PEACH** is important in many cultures:

in China and Japan it is seen as a symbol of immortality (the blossom is related to feminine charm) and in the West it is seen as an emblem of salvation. The **FIG** is a universal symbol of fecundity (probably because of its innumerable seeds) and sometimes of bisexuality (the leaf is seen as a phallic symbol and the fruit itself representing the vulva). These interpretations may apply in our dreams despite our not consciously being aware of them.

A dream of fruit can often have sexual connotations, perhaps because the food is sweet and luscious, and especially if we were eating it with great enjoyment. Erotic connotations are often evident in

PEARS
54
MELONS
PEACHES
54
BANANA

literature, where the ancient poets compare women's breasts to **PEARS** or **MELONS**, and boys' or girls' bottoms to **PEACHES**. The **BANANA** has more recently been seen as symbolic of an erect penis, and a banana appearing in your dream may have been attacking a puritanical idea, reminding you of an area of life you are denying, or suggesting that you are too easily shocked.

—◆— VEGETABLES —◆—

FROM ANCIENT TIMES, vegetables and vegetation itself have not only been seen as symbolic of the life force, nourishment, abundance, fertility, and resurrection but also of a dull, vegetative waking life. In dreams, vegetables can often symbolize the most basic human emotions.

The possibility of sexual innuendo cannot be dismissed, and is often linked to the shape of the vegetable concerned. The idea has too often been used in plays, films, photographs, and literature to be ignored. However, that idea is not inevitable. There may be an allusion to your diet; you may not be eating enough fiber, cereals, and green vegetables. A dream in which you are overcooking vegetables could suggest that you are concentrating too long or too hard on a problem, or "overcooking" a relationship, in the sense of allowing it to become too emotionally claustrophobic.

The symbolic significance of individual vegetables has never been as strong as the associations of particular fruits, and you will have to think carefully about all the possible allusions before concluding what a dream of beans, potatoes, or cabbages means to you. In the latter case, for example, in

some parts of Europe there may be an allusion to conception or childbirth, because children have been told that babies are "found in a cabbage patch."

BEANS
PEAS
ROOT
VEGETABLES

The way in which **BEANS** or **PEAS** climb up toward the sky may be significant, or the fact that **ROOT VEGETABLES** grow under the earth (*see page 48*). In waking life, this may allude either to aspiration or ambition, or to plodding thoroughness. Cooked or prepared vegetables may carry a different reference than raw ones in dreams: are they ideas that are developing or simply offering themselves to you, ready for growth and nurture?

THE WORLD OF NATURE

FANTASY & FABLE

ARTS & SCIENCES

THE HUMAN BODY

BUILDINGS & INTERIORS

EVERYDAY THINGS

HUMAN EMOTIONS

HUMAN ACTIVITIES

HUMAN CONDITIONS

RITUALS & RELIGION

THE DREAM THESAURUS

THE BLACK BULL DREAM

" I was walking along a smooth path, which was edged with small, colorful flowers. At first this was a delightful experience, but gradually the path changed: the ground beneath my feet became muddier, and I was trampling on the flowers. Even those by the side of the path were withering and dying. It became more and more difficult to walk, because the ground was so muddy and slippery; but in the distance was a beautiful column of light, which encouraged me to continue. I trudged on, and my feet became heavier as the mud collected on my shoes. Gradually, the column of light began to dim, and as it faded it began to change shape: it turned into a big, black bull that galloped toward me. Although the bull was very large, I was not afraid of him, and when he reached me he began to nuzzle me. I found that I was carrying a basket of fruit, and began to feed the bull with it. At first he ate the fruit eagerly, but then it seemed to turn sour, and he spat it at me. Then he galloped off.

I started to run after him and I knew that I was getting younger and younger. Even though this meant I could run faster, I could not catch the bull, and he gradually began to draw away from me. Suddenly a wall appeared in front of me, hiding the bull from sight. I was going too fast to stop, and ran into the wall. Although it seemed to be made of bricks, it turned out to be a pile of cushions. "

FLOWER-
STREWN PATH

PATH
TURNS TO
MUD

PILLAR OF
LIGHT
TRANSFORMS
INTO BULL

INTERPRETATION

Beth, a successful and prosperous businesswoman, had a lover. At first the relationship was exciting and beautiful – as represented by the flowers and the smooth path. However, as time passed she recognized that her lover was becoming secretive, uncaring, and rude. To keep him, Beth gave him expensive gifts, and money. This was symbolized in the dream by the bull eating the fruit she gave to him. Her lover would be nice to her when he wanted money, but he would be unpleasant and cruel at other times. This is represented by the changing pillar of light becoming the bull: the pillar was a phallic symbol; while the bull represented her lover's macho, dominating self. One day she came home from her office unexpectedly, to find him in bed with a younger woman. The final part of the dream is colored by wish fulfillment, since she became younger in the dream.

Her unconscious was telling her that she wanted to be the younger woman, but as she ran after the bull (she was trying to keep her lover in real life) the dream wall sprang up. This represented her common sense, which was saying that she should end the relationship. Beth decided that the fact that the wall was padded represented her own security and comfortable lifestyle, which would help to "cushion" any blows. The dream was both summing up Beth's present situation and reassuring her. She ended the unrewarding affair immediately after analyzing her dream.

BULL EATS
OFFERING OF
FRUIT

BULL THEN
REJECTS FRUIT

BETH
PURSUES
BUT FAILS
TO CATCH
BULL

WALL
APPEARS

WALL
TURNS INTO
PILE OF
CUSHIONS

—◆— LANDSCAPE —◆—

WHATEVER THE ACTION in your dream, the landscape in which it takes place will be extremely important to your interpretation. Were you stumbling through a forest, struggling through desert, climbing a mountain, or strolling through pleasant countryside? However important the other symbols in the dream, they will only be intelligible in the context in which they are set.

CLIFF
172
HIGHWAY
59
CITY
COAST

There is no reason to suppose that anything in a dream is placed there at random. On the contrary, we unconsciously choose the settings of our dreams, so if we are climbing a CLIFF, walking along a HIGHWAY, driving through a CITY, or sailing around a COAST, there is almost certainly a reason why. The cliff may represent a problem you are intent on surmounting; the highway may signify a clear road ahead; the city may symbolize a complex dilemma through which you must find your way; and the coast may represent welcome firm ground on which you can set foot as you solve an emotional difficulty.

When considering a dream, it is not always easy to reach a firm decision about the most important element in it. However, being conscious of the dream landscape around you will have a bearing on the interpretation. For example, if you are being chased by a monster, the setting of the dream may be as important as the creature in pursuit. This will certainly be the case if the environment is "used" in the dream — for example to help you hide, escape, or trick the pursuer — since it will offer hints about dealing with the waking situation represented by your dream ordeal.

HILL
144
MOUNTAIN
144, 172
SLOPE

A HILL, a MOUNTAIN, or even a gentle SLOPE may be considered as an image of a problem in your waking life, and it is important to examine how you were dealing with it: were you climbing confidently, with difficulty, or in fear? The dream will not tell you how those problems are going to be solved, but how in your innermost mind you believe

CHASM
GORGE
DITCH
HURDLE

yourself capable of dealing with them — or failing to deal with them. The appearance of particular difficulties may also have considerable significance. If a CHASM or GORGE suddenly opens beneath your feet, look in your waking life for an unsuspected difficulty; lesser dream impediments such as DITCHES or HURDLES, which you must leap or surmount, have similar references. The presence and behavior of companions on a dream climb or walk may reveal something about colleagues or friends and their reactions in the context of your problems.

DESERT
FIELD
STREET
59
RAIN FOREST
**DESERT
ISLAND**

Your waking feelings about the landscape of your dream will be important: a DESERT may be horrifying to one person, but may symbolize romance, escape, and desirable seclusion to another. Open FIELDS may be as boring to metropolitan-minded people as city STREETS are to a country-dweller. In dreams, a landscape will have different associations for almost every individual dreamer. A RAIN FOREST may represent a rich source of inspiration and growth to one person, while to another, with fears of snakes or wild animals, it will suggest apprehension and fear, possibly in an emotional context. A DESERT ISLAND will have a romantic association for some people, but to others it may mean isolation (this could be interpreted either as an intense desire to be alone or as a cry for an end to solitude) in waking life.

ABROAD
121, 135

A dream that you are ABROAD in a foreign landscape may suggest some confusing, uncharted situation through which you must find your way. Or do you simply need a holiday? Dreaming that you are in

ARCTIC
ANTARCTIC
BEACH
127, 150

the **ARCTIC** or **ANTARCTIC** – cold, isolated, and covered in ice and snow – is likely to be a comment on some aspect of your emotional life. If your dream of a **BEACH** was not one of wish-fulfillment (*see page 150*), consider your emotions at the time: were you running along the sands with a feeling of freedom, or plodding through heavy sand dunes?

ALLEY
AVENUE
STREET
58
TRACK

A dream of an **ALLEY** may represent a predicament in which you have little or no choice, while an **AVENUE** (a broad, pleasant route) may signify support for a path you have chosen to take. A straightforward **STREET** may have the same significance, but a rough **TRACK** may well have the opposite meaning. However, it does not necessarily indicate an unhappy route, especially if it was an interesting and exciting path and you were following it with some confidence.

BOUNDARY
FRONTIER
FENCE
GATE

A dream featuring a **BOUNDARY** or **FRONTIER** may suggest either challenge, criticism, and restriction, or the ability to sail through problems. Were you challenged in your dream? If so, look for a weakness in a waking situation where your progress may be checked. Dream **FENCES** that confine you to a particular landscape imply some form of restriction in your waking life. Were you looking for, and did you find, a **GATE**? Or were you, in fact, content to be limited in your movements? The allusion may be to a need for security in your waking life.

CAMP
EXPEDITION

The informality of a **CAMP** in a dream, as opposed to a town or city, may insinuate uncertainty, transience, and a temporary resting place. Could this relate to a personal or professional relationship? Dreaming of an **EXPEDITION** through an unknown landscape may refer to a need

EXPLORER

for support in an unfamiliar or trying situation, or perhaps to the fact that you should explore a project or idea more thoroughly than you were expecting. Your dream failure or success as an **EXPLORER** will obviously be important.

HIGHWAY
58

HIGHWAYS of every kind are most likely to represent a waking journey: this may be a symbolic journey in your career, or in your private, financial, or social life. Your actions on the dream journey will be important. Whether you were racing or caught in a traffic jam, anxiously steering along a dangerous, winding country lane, or strolling the wrong way up a one-way street, will all be significant to the interpretation of the dream.

MINEFIELD

A dream of a **MINEFIELD** may be referring to a waking life full of difficulties and potential dangers. The dream may either be reflecting your worries or (more likely) be suggesting how you should deal with them – by calling in an expert and treading with care. What were your feelings in the dream? Were you apprehensive and afraid, or were you feeling confident? Were you about to step on a mine when you suddenly awoke?

PARK
PICNIC

Although a dream **PARK** or **PICNIC** seems likely to be a reference to relaxation and pleasure, your feelings about the dream and your emotions in the dream are important. It may be interpreted as wish-fulfillment (*see page 150*): are you denying yourself time for such leisure activities in your waking life? It is also important to look for other symbols in the dream: particularly what you were actually doing, and who was with you.

If the perspective of the landscape in your dream was awry, then you are probably not "seeing things straight" in waking life. In your dream, look carefully for a symbol that is suggesting that some aspect of your waking life is in some way out of proportion.

THE WORLD
OF NATURE

FANTASY &
FABLE

ARTS &
SCIENCES

THE HUMAN
BODY

BUILDINGS &
INTERIORS

EVERYDAY
THINGS

HUMAN
EMOTIONS

HUMAN
ACTIVITIES

HUMAN
CONDITIONS

RITUALS &
RELIGION

THE DREAM
THESAURUS

—◆— THE SUPERNATURAL —◆—

EVEN THE MOST PROSAIC and materialistic of us have dreams that include supernatural creatures or incidents. These dreams can be unsettling unless we accept them as metaphors for events or emotions in our waking lives. However, there is no evidence that they are actually connected with the supernatural, although psychics may sometimes claim otherwise.

THE WORLD OF NATURE

FANTASY & FABLE

ARTS & SCIENCES

THE HUMAN BODY

BUILDINGS & INTERIORS

EVERYDAY THINGS

HUMAN EMOTIONS

HUMAN ACTIVITIES

CROSS
181
CRUCIFIX
181

People with a deep religious conviction will have a different response to dreams in which religion (*see page 180*) or religious symbols play a part, than nonbelievers. There is a long tradition in almost every religion of dreams as messages from a supernatural power. Many people may still be inclined to accept dreams in which religious symbols, or the leaders of faiths, appear as direct instructions from that power. For those who have been brought up in a particular faith, it is likely that the dream is instructing or prompting them to act in conformity with the moral stance of that faith. However, for these people – and certainly for the more recently converted – such dreams are always worth examination, since they may relate more to wish-fulfillment (*see page 150*) or emotional conviction than to the tenets of religion. These dreams are probably strong hints to regard some waking problem in the light of your religious belief. A dream of a religious symbol, such as a **CROSS** or **CRUCIFIX**, may suggest that you should consider the spiritual element of your life or (depending on the context) that there is a part of your life that needs moral as well as practical attention.

CHRIST
181
BUDDHA
ALLAH
ISVÀRA

The leader of a religion – for example, **CHRIST**, **BUDDHA**, **ALLAH**, or **ISVÀRA** – will usually appear only in relation to a vital episode or decision in your waking life. They are frequently seen in dreams or "visions" by people who are dying, although there is no suggestion that such a phenomenon is predictive of death. Indeed, as is the case with dreams of death (*see page 86*), such an appearance may signal a vital change in your life – most likely in your moral stance.

SPELL
MAGIC
WITCH
62
WIZARD

A dream in which someone casts a **SPELL** on you, or uses **MAGIC** either to help or hinder you, may refer to someone in your waking life who seeks to influence you, or people or events around you. It is rare that the person casting the spell is actually someone you recognize, but there will usually be a clue in the dream to enable you to identify him or her. That person is likely to be someone you neither understand nor trust in waking life, and the dream may reflect this lack of understanding. The dream may also comment on the validity of your reactions. The success or failure of the spell will be important: if it is successful, the **WITCH** or **WIZARD** may be offering valuable advice, to which you should pay attention. Future dreams may be needed to clarify the situation, so you should "ask" (*see page 33*) for a further meeting with the witch or wizard.

The 17th-century physician, Sir Thomas Browne, believed that "guardian spirits may sometimes order our dreams: and many strange hints, instigations or discourses which are so amazing unto us may arise from such foundations".

ANGEL
DEVIL
62

However, an **ANGEL** or **DEVIL** in your dream is most likely to be related not to any religious experience, but to the good or evil instincts in you. Its behavior in the dream may be that of prompter or tempter, no doubt relating to a recent or impending decision or action of yours in waking life. It is unlikely that it will tell or show you directly what it (your inner self) wants you to do, or wants to deter you from doing, but other symbols appearing in the dream should make its advice clear.

SPHINX
CENTAUR
64
MYTHICAL
CREATURE

Occasionally, a strange creature, such as a **SPHINX**, a **CENTAUR**, or a less well-known **MYTHICAL CREATURE**, may appear in your dreams. As with myths (*see page 64*), these can sometimes visit us even when in waking life we are not conscious of their meaning. The creature's appearance in your dream may be connected to its ancient significance: the sphinx as a

MINOTAUR

symbol of great wisdom; the centaur as an exhibitionist; or the **MINOTAUR** as a dangerous instinct hidden deep in your personality. The dream itself may be reflecting your present behavior, or your attitude toward life, and encouraging or discouraging you from it.

GHOST

Only young children are likely to see a **GHOST** – as a vague shadow – in their dreams. These may be the result of a fright in waking life (although even in children, the "ghost" may be recognized as the shadow of a real and disliked figure, such as a school teacher, a disagreeable neighbor, or another hostile adult). Adults who see ghosts in their dreams usually see the shadows of deceased friends, relatives, or enemies. Often, when the dreams are examined, the ghosts represent not the people concerned but the shadows of some of their qualities.

THE WORLD OF NATURE

FANTASY & FABLE

ARTS & SCIENCES

THE HUMAN BODY

BUILDINGS & INTERIORS

EVERYDAY THINGS

HUMAN EMOTIONS

HUMAN ACTIVITIES

HUMAN CONDITIONS

RITUALS & RELIGION

THE DREAM THESAURUS

If you have such a dream, you may recognize some of these qualities in yourself; qualities that you thought were dead but are threatening to return. Conversely, there may be a suggestion that the good qualities of your ghostly visitor have died in you, and deserve resurrection. Dreams of ghosts can often be reassuring rather than frightening.

**INCUBUS
SUCCUBUS
DEVIL**
61
WITCH
60

The words **INCUBUS** and **SUCCUBUS** were traditionally used (chiefly by the church) to describe a male or female spirit — usually unidentifiable — that visited women or men while they were asleep, to make love to them. Clerics, who have traditionally considered any interest in sex to be sinful, identified the incubus and succubus with **DEVILS** or **WITCHES**; they were considered to be dangerous and evil. However, it is now recognized that most people, at some point in their lives, have overtly sexual dreams. These dreams are particularly common in adolescents, who should be reassured that the experience is entirely normal.

A dream of magic or the supernatural that turns out to be a special effect produced by a **CONJURER** should be considered as a warning: things in waking life may not be what they seem. Who is trying to deceive you? Look for clues in the dream as to the identity of the conjurer. On the other hand, are you the conjurer performing magic tricks in the dream? If this is the case, is the dream reflecting some unease or anxiety about a current plan or negotiation in your waking life that rests on your skill rather than on solid facts?

CONJURER
178

PRECOGNITION AND PREDICTION

DREAMS THAT APPEAR to predict the future are often the most intriguing and interesting. While many such dreams can be explained, there are a few that genuinely seem to have predicted future events.

There is a tradition of psychics using dreams as a means of prophesy, that stretches back at least to the Babylonians (1700 BC). They interpreted their prophetic dreams in a particular way: if a dream of the fall of a temple was followed by a calamitous war, the next time a priest dreamed of the fall of a temple, it was thought to predict a war. This may not be a very scientific method, but it was followed for centuries. During some periods of its history, the Christian Church also regarded dreams as a way in which God showed his chosen people the future: St. Augustine claimed that his mother "saw" his conversion, in a dream, nine years before it took place. The Bible, with its many predictive dreams, was produced in support of this theory.

As late as the 16th century, bishops took careful note of their dreams, and in the same way, prophets predicted many events — from the rebirth of Christ to the end of the world.

Although there is modern evidence that some dreams appear to reveal future actions or events, most of these can be rationalized. In dreams, as well as in waking life, we spend some time anticipating what may happen as a result of certain actions or circumstances. For example, if you dream of an accident occurring to a particular person on a certain busy street corner, you have probably (consciously or unconsciously) realized that that person is in danger of having an accident in that particular place.

The best examples of this phenomenon are the many assertions from around the world that dreams predicted the assassination of President Kennedy. In some cases, the dreamers made notes of such dreams at the time, and there can be little question of their veracity. However, it must be remembered that President Kennedy was one of the world's best-known men, and that presidents are vulnerable to assassination. Also, in Great Britain alone, 55.5 million people dream up to ten dreams a night, giving them 555 million dreams a night. Add to that the population of the United States, and we have 3,105 million dreams a night. Given these statistics, it would have been strange if several people had not dreamed of Kennedy's assassination. In addition, there is no reliable record of anyone dreaming the precise nature of his death, the place, the time, or the name of the assassin. It seems to be the case that such dreams, as Jung put it, are "no more prophetic than a medical diagnosis or a weather forecast. They are merely an anticipatory combination of probabilities which may coincide with the actual behavior of things but need not necessarily agree in every detail."

Notwithstanding the above, some dreams do seem to be genuine precognitive phenomena, and almost every dream analyst will have come across them. If you are interested in this aspect of dreaming, if you have had predictive dreams, or if you want to look more seriously at the subject, it is important to keep a detailed dream diary. If you have a dream that seems to predict a serious event on a considerable scale (for example, an earthquake), make a detailed note and have it witnessed, seal it in a self-addressed envelope, and send it through the post office so it will be date-stamped. Do not open it.

ASTROLOGER
122

Dreams of personal disaster are common causes for concern. For example, someone who dreams of an airplane crash or who has had an **ASTROLOGER**, **PALMIST**, or **TAROT**-reader predict one in a

DREAM ANALYSIS

"I dreamt I went to school and there was no school there. Something black had come down all over it."

This ten-year-old girl went to school at Aberfan, and was killed when a slag-heap collapsed on top of her school. The story seems well authenticated, and no explanation has been found for the apparent precognition of the dream.

PALMIST TAROT

dream, may be worried if he or she is flying the next day. However, dreams of this kind usually arise out of fear; most people only fly occasionally, so they may experience some tension, and will be susceptible to such nightmares.

In 1966, in the Welsh coal-mining village of Aberfan, a slag-heap collapsed down a mountainside and buried a school, killing 128 children and 38 adults. There were a number of reports of dreams predicting this event, and a Dr. J.C. Barker examined some of them for the Society for Psychical Research's publication, *Journal* (vol.44, no.734). One dream, reported before the event, recorded children trying to get out of a room, and "hundreds of people all running to the same place; the looks on [their] faces were terrible. Some were crying and others holding handkerchiefs to their faces." Other dreamers described "screaming children buried in an avalanche of coal" and "a school, screaming children, and creeping black slimy stuff." Included in these accounts were two specific references to Aberfan (*see Dream Analysis, above*).

— ✦ MYTHOLOGY ✦ —

ONE OF THE STRANGEST aspects of dreams is the way they can bring
before us ancient mythological figures of which we are convinced we
know nothing. However, as Jung put it, "The great ones of the past
have not died, as we think; they have merely changed their names."
Our dreams may also relate to modern legends, such as Batman.

**THE WORLD
OF NATURE**

**FANTASY &
FABLE**

**ARTS &
SCIENCES**

**THE HUMAN
BODY**

**BUILDINGS &
INTERIORS**

**EVERYDAY
THINGS**

**HUMAN
EMOTIONS**

**HUMAN
ACTIVITIES**

**HUMAN
CONDITIONS**

**RITUALS &
RELIGION**

**THE DREAM
THESAURUS**

The Greek and Roman myths, and the
figures of the zodiac (*see page 69*), survive because they are universal. They
represent human characteristics that are
always with us – love, lust, greed, and
anger. These characteristics are
enshrined in myth and legend, in stories
that affect us today as they affected those
who heard them from storytellers
thousands of years ago. These myths lie
deep in our unconscious, just as the
remains of ancient civilizations lie buried
in the earth, waiting for archeologists to
uncover them. The personalities of myth
will only be instantly recognizable to
those who have studied them. They may,
however, be recognized by their
characteristics, and by studying their
personalities and legends we can learn
much about them and about ourselves.

CENTAUR
61
UNICORN
CRAB
44

Any figure that appears prominently in a
dream (particularly if it seems archetypal
but unidentifiable, or appears to act in a
dogmatic or authoritative manner) will
be worth measuring against the
mythological figure it most closely
resembles. Then measure yourself against
its characteristics and try to mark the
similarities or contrasts. Mythological
creatures such as the CENTAUR, the
UNICORN, and the CRAB of Cancer (*see
page 69*), also have their significance:
little is known about centaurs, but we
do know that they are brutish (half-man,
half-beast) and associated with sexual
frenzy; while the unicorn is a gentler
creature, wooing his virgin by placing
his head in her lap.

JUPITER
ZEUS

The Roman JUPITER figure is the Greek
ZEUS ("father of the gods") and may
resemble any authority figure of your

SATURN

dreams; for example your father,
employer, or teacher – anyone who
demands obedience and commands
respect. As Jung pointed out, here is "the
archetypal leader, the voice of collective
authority, the Lord, King or tyrant, but
also Protector, the figure … whose word
is law." Sometimes the Jupiter figure is
noble, respectable, and virtuous; while at
other times he exhibits himself as a
"whited sepulchre." Jupiter was known
for his philandering and his extremely
cavalier attitude to the moral code that
he attempted to impose on others. Such
a dream may be an injunction against
some action of yours in waking life, but
it may also be proposing that you are
above such petty considerations as good
behavior. It is important to remember
that Jupiter himself was occasionally
rebuked and ridiculed by his subjects: no
one is actually invulnerable. Jupiter in his
"thou shalt not" mood is possibly closer
to SATURN, whose name is used to
describe a mood of dark disapproval.

VENUS
151
APHRODITE

The Roman VENUS figure is APHRODITE,
the Greek goddess of love. The figure is
beautiful, but wayward: her temple in
Cyprus was a celebrated center of sexual
luxury, where intercourse was regarded
as a form of celebratory prayer. For men,
the appearance of an unknown but
extremely beautiful woman may simply
be a call for sensual satisfaction; a wish-
fulfillment dream (*see page 150*) directed
not at a particular woman but at women
in general. Her behavior in the dream
will be significant, reflecting your own
conscious or unconscious desires – what
you need from a mate. There may be a
strong hint about your attitude to, or
treatment of, women. Occasionally

this Venus figure may appear in a dream as a threatening sexual figure (*see Nightmare, page 154*) – usually to men who feel sexually insecure. Venus is intent on "getting her man," and is the opposite of the mother figure to whom many sexually insecure men more easily relate.

MERCURY
151
HERMES

THE WORLD OF NATURE

MERCURY was the Roman messenger god (**HERMES** in Greek mythology). Although every dream is in a sense a message (from you to you), a dream in which someone actually delivers a message to you is one that you cannot afford to ignore. Think first of the nature of the message, but then (and in particular) about the actual messenger. Mercury was also a trickster, impulsive and self-centered, and controlled and dominated by his appetites. He can remind us of our adolescent selves, those youthful appetites that we may never quite grow out of. Was the messenger in your dream to be trusted, or was there a suggestion of duplicity? There may be the implication that some "message" in waking life is not as reliable as you might like to think.

FANTASY & FABLE

MARS
151
HERO
136

MARS – the Roman god of war – may be represented in dreams by any figure that is attacking you or anyone else in the dream. You may even have assumed the guise of Mars. The god of war is the dynamic **HERO** in Greek mythology, who may be a soldier intent on winning in battle, a businessman in a boardroom dispute, or a social climber determined to reach the top. Hero's trademarks are courage, determination, aggression, and the assertion of his own will. His actions, in your dream, may be addressing any problems you have in the area of your ambitions or goals.

ARTS & SCIENCES

**SUPERMAN
MARILYN
MONROE
JAMES BOND
THE QUEEN**
115, 162

The modern mythological heroes and heroines may be based on fiction or on fact. **SUPERMAN, MARILYN MONROE, JAMES BOND**, or **THE QUEEN** may appear in our dreams as archetypal figures, and represent – like the ancient gods – certain actions or aspirations. They may be encouraging us to be braver, more ambitious, or more adventurous; we may

THE HUMAN BODY

not always find them appealing figures, and may not want to follow their example. It is important to remember, however, that you, as the dreamer, have summoned these characters. If a Mars-like figure appears in your dream, armed and ready for battle, it is almost certainly because the part of your unconscious that has commanded his presence in your dream wants to urge you into action. In the same way, if a Mercury-like figure appears in a dream, there may be a hint that either you or someone close to you is engaged in subterfuge.

BUILDINGS & INTERIORS

These figures, if we properly understand their appearance and intention in dreams, are all assisting in the process of our "individuation" – helping us to "find ourselves" (this may indeed be one of the main purposes of all dreams). They are, like all dream symbols, often difficult to "place." For example, a child may dream of symbols that, on the surface, relate to old age, but in the child's case they may be associated with the progress from childhood into adolescence, or from adolescence into adulthood. The heroes or heroines of mythology, even in modern disguise, can represent our "shadow" (*see page 97*), a personality representing the hidden, repressed, and unfavorable aspects of our personality, with which we are (as Jung put it) "in constant battle for deliverance." Usually, in mythology, the hero wins his battle against the foe, whether man or monster; when he loses, he goes into the darkness that represents a kind of death. This may also happen in a dream, but it is important to remember that dreams are creative; they lead us through the darkness into the light.

EVERYDAY THINGS

FAIRYTALE

FAIRYTALE myths often occur in modern times – particularly in women's dreams. Psychologists have noticed that the story of "Beauty and the Beast" has been acted out, in various forms, in the dreams of women confused by the difficulty of male/female relationships in a world where masculine and feminine attitudes have not yet been fully reconciled.

HUMAN EMOTIONS

HUMAN ACTIVITIES

HUMAN CONDITIONS

RITUALS & RELIGION

THE DREAM THESAURUS

THE MAZE DREAM

"*I was visiting a stately home with my family, and we decided to go into the maze. Almost immediately, I lost sight of my wife and sons, and found myself alone and feeling increasingly worried. The hedges of the maze were very high, and very thick. I could not see or hear anyone else, but I was gradually aware of an unpleasant breathing noise, which grew louder as I approached the center of the maze.*

Ahead of me, I saw a break in the hedge, which I knew was the entrance to the center of the maze. As I approached the gap, however, I knew that something nasty was waiting for me beyond it. I knew that I had to go in, but could not bear to see what awaited me, so I turned around and walked backwards through the gap. The breathing noise stopped, and there was complete silence. I wanted to run, but now saw six or seven different exits, and knew that if I took the wrong one I would be caught by whatever was behind me.

Then I saw a trail of computer tape lying on the ground, so I picked it up and followed it, knowing that it led out of the maze. I knew that the monster had given up its pursuit because it knew I was escaping. But the breathing had resumed and I knew I would have to return to kill the monster, or it would attack my family and me."

MONSTER IS BEYOND GAP

NORMAN FOLLOWS TRAIL OF COMPUTER TAPE

HEDGES ARE
HIGH AND
THICK

GAP
APPEARS IN
HEDGE

INTERPRETATION

Norman was a computer programmer
with no special interest in mythology,
but his dream related clearly to the
Greek myth of the Minotaur (a bull-
headed monster that was shut up in a
maze, and killed by the Greek hero
Theseus). Ariadne, whom Theseus
loved, had given him a ball of thread
to unwind as he entered the maze.

The dream appeared to relate to a
situation which had developed at
Norman's workplace. He was in line
for promotion to an executive post,
and he had a sole rival for the position.
This rival was cast, in the dream, as a
Minotaur because Norman's wife, who
was interested in astrology, had once
commented on his tenacity, saying
"What can you expect of a Taurean?"
(the symbol of Taurus is the bull). The
maze represented the intricate system
by which his suitability for the job
would be judged. He suspected that
his rival might be ahead of him in the
race for promotion (represented by
the center of the maze). His wife had
been attempting to reassure him that
all would be well as long as he followed
his instincts and used his experience
(the computer tape). The dream was
prompting him to accept her advice.

Norman had "lost sight" of his
family because he had been preoccupied
with work, and the family relationship
had suffered. The hedges of the maze
were higher and thicker than he had
expected, which referred to the fact
that he knew that the post would be
more taxing than he had first thought.
The breathing sound may have referred
to the doggedness of his rival, who had
always pretended to Norman that he
was not interested in promotion. The
fact that Norman failed to face him (he
walked backwards through the gap in
the hedge) referred to his diffidence,
and his dislike of confrontations.

—◆— THE MANDALA —◆—

THE MANDALA IS AMONG the powerful symbols that frequently appear in our dreams, and which, despite being unrecognized, usually have something of great significance to say to us. The mandala symbol consists of a circle enclosing a square, and there is usually a figure in the center of the square. This figure will often represent ourselves.

Jung originally gave this motif the Hindu name "mandala," or "magic circle," and believed that it frequently represented the human psyche. The symbol appears in many parts of the world as a pattern of existence: Romulus planned ancient Rome on the lines of a mandala, and many other ancient cities – including Jerusalem – also took that form. The Hindu temple is built as a mandala, representing the four corners of the Earth revolving around its center, or "the ego revolving around itself in time and space" – that is, a complete intregration of your outer and inner selves. In Hindu and Buddhist art the mandala represents the universe, and the inner world of the human psyche.

**KALEIDO-
SCOPE**
168

While the significance of the mandala could be discussed for many pages, this would not necessarily be helpful to the average dreamer. Unfortunately, when it is recognized it remains one of the most difficult dream symbols to interpret, simply because its meaning is so mysterious and seems to be associated with the depths of the dreamer's psyche. It can express the idea of our whole life, from birth to death. Rose windows in cathedrals often represent this journey. The mandala may appear in your dreams as a **KALEIDOSCOPE**, or in geometric patterns made with compasses. Any colors associated with the mandala symbol may be important – as colors often are in dreams.

**CIRCLE
DISC
GLOBE
WHEEL
HOOP**

It is worth considering that any symbol taking a circular form – a **CIRCLE** itself, a **DISC**, a **GLOBE**, a **WHEEL**, and even a child's **HOOP**, may be a mandala. Although the symbol is often difficult to recognize, because of its importance it will often declare itself simply by insisting on recognition: it will "tell" you that it is important by refusing to leave your thoughts. Occasionally, on waking from a dream you may not be able to erase a particular image from your mind, however inconsequential it may seem. Any such image is probably important, and if it is circular it may well be a mandala. Whether it is or not is not especially important to the dreamer, as long as it is recognized as an important symbol. It is likely that you will recognize it as such, since it will remain in your thoughts.

It can be useful to draw our dreams, and this is especially true where a mandala is central to a dream. Some psychologists suggest that rather than literally drawing the symbol as you saw it in the dream, you should take this as a starting point and allow your pencil or brush to improvise. You should use colors in your drawing if possible, and include words if they occurred to you in your dream. You will probably find that you will want to draw some parts of the picture very carefully, while others will almost draw themselves – rather as though you are dreaming them. The resulting picture will show, it is suggested, the pattern of your present life, with threats or pleasures, and ambitions or fears, represented in it. The areas of the drawing that emerged from your unconscious will be most important in advising you of your true feelings and the direction you should take.

THE WORLD
OF NATURE

FANTASY &
FABLE

ARTS &
SCIENCES

THE HUMAN
BODY

BUILDINGS &
INTERIORS

EVERYDAY
THINGS

HUMAN
EMOTIONS

HUMAN
ACTIVITIES

HUMAN
CONDITIONS

RITUALS &
RELIGION

THE DREAM
THESAURUS

THE ZODIAC

DREAMS FOCUSING ON the Zodiac, and its mythical creatures and symbols, will have much to say about the human condition. Most dreams that highlight Zodiac symbols are likely to refer either to the characteristics of the mythical animals of the Sun signs, which are reflected in human behavior, or to people we recognize as belonging to particular signs.

**ARIES
TAURUS
GEMINI
CANCER
LEO
VIRGO
LIBRA
SCORPIO**

94

If you dream of a particular Zodiac symbol, you should consider these characteristics, and try to apply them to yourself or others. Traditional ARIES (the Ram) traits include assertiveness and the need to win. Arians are forthright, decisive, selfish, and ruthless. Reliability, common sense, sensuality, and practicality are all characteristics of TAURUS (the Bull). Taureans can also be stubborn, possessive, and gluttonous. Alertness, vivacity, youthfulness, and versatility are all traits of the GEMINI (the Twins) character, as are duality, duplicity, and being argumentative. Those born under the sign of CANCER (the Crab) are typically caring, protective, affectionate, and understanding. They also have a tendency to be grasping, clinging, worriers. Leadership, organizing ability, enthusiasm, creativity, and generosity are positive traits of LEO (the Lion). However, Leos can also be autocratic, domineering, and stubborn. Although someone born under the sign of VIRGO (the Virgin) may be analytical, clinical, health-conscious, practical, talkative, and modest, they also worry, nag, gossip, and are overly critical. The sign of LIBRA (the Scales) epitomizes romance, sympathy, kindness, and relaxation. Librans may be resentful, indecisive, too laid back, and sometimes spiteful. Those born under the sign of SCORPIO (the Scorpion) have powerful emotional and physical energy, and a sense of purpose. Jealousy, hate, and vindictiveness are also characteristic of Scorpio.

**SAGITTARIUS
CAPRICORN
AQUARIUS
PISCES**

Those born under the sign of SAGITTARIUS (the Centaur/Archer), are generally intellectual, enthusiastic, energetic, and optimistic, with a love of sport, and a breadth of vision. However, they can also be restless, off-hand, and may take unnecessary risks. CAPRICORN (the Goat) is ambitious, aspiring, progressive, and political, with an offbeat sense of humor. Other characteristics of this sign include grumbling, worrying, pessimism, meanness, and being downtrodden and emotionally cold. People born under the sign of AQUARIUS (the Water Carrier) are characteristically original, friendly, helpful, glamorous, and progressive, and usually have some artistic or scientific flair. Unpredictable, stubborn, cool, and distant, they are often in love, and have a tendency to be too romantic. The sign of PISCES (the Fishes) is typically kind, sensitive, loving, dreamy, creative, and emotional, but is also characteristically disorganized, deceitful, unrealistic, gullible, and sentimental.

 THE WORLD OF NATURE

 FANTASY & FABLE

 ARTS & SCIENCES

 THE HUMAN BODY

 BUILDINGS & INTERIORS

 EVERYDAY THINGS

 HUMAN EMOTIONS

 HUMAN ACTIVITIES

 HUMAN CONDITIONS

 RITUALS & RELIGION

THE DREAM THESAURUS

MUSIC

ALTHOUGH DREAMS ARE mainly visual, people to whom music is one of the most important elements of life may well dream of it. The dream is likely to be significant, usually on an emotional level, since the sound of music has relatively little to do with practical matters (apart from, of course, the practical skill that is involved in playing an instrument).

ORCHESTRA
176
CHOIR

You are most likely to dream of music if it is an important and enjoyable part of your everyday waking life. Composers have been known to dream complete works: for example, Stravinsky dreamed a sextet, and the tune of "Yesterday" came to Paul McCartney in a dream. How you interpret your dream will depend not so much on the nature of the music you hear (unless it is a specific piece that you are emotionally attached to in waking life) but on various other circumstances: whether you were listening to others perform; or whether you were playing an instrument in an **ORCHESTRA** or singing in a **CHOIR**. This may reveal something about you in a social or work context: the ease or difficulty you have in working or socializing with other people and how well

you are coping with this type of situation at the present time. In your dream, were you harmonizing or were you discordant?

OVERTURE
FANFARE
RECITAL
CONDUCTOR

There are circumstances in which what you hear may be important: an **OVERTURE** suggests the start of something new, while a **FANFARE** implies success. A solo **RECITAL** suggests that you are "on your own" in some respect, or reliant on only perhaps one or two other people – depending on whether you were accompanied by a pianist, a small band of players, or a large orchestra. In the latter case, are you conscious of being supported by a large number of colleagues in waking life? A dream of being a **CONDUCTOR** may symbolize responsibility: in waking life, are you in charge of a department or a firm? Or are you simply "showing off"?

INSTRUMENT
CELLO
GUITAR

Dreams of specific **INSTRUMENTS** may contain different references. The **CELLO** and the **GUITAR** have often been taken as representatives of the female body; the guitar, quite specifically, in poetry and erotic paintings. A man dreaming of playing on one of these, or perhaps on any stringed instrument, should consider whether it is an erotic dream or a dream that can be related to his basic sensual instincts. There may be a clue elsewhere in the dream that will help to identify the woman concerned. The quality of your performance will be important.

TRUMPET
CYMBAL

Were you "blowing your own **TRUMPET**" in your dream? A dream in which you were crashing a **CYMBAL** may be implying that you are making too much of a fuss about something in waking life.

THE WORLD OF NATURE

FANTASY & FABLE

ARTS & SCIENCES

THE HUMAN BODY

BUILDINGS & INTERIORS

EVERYDAY THINGS

HUMAN EMOTIONS

HUMAN ACTIVITIES

HUMAN CONDITIONS

RITUALS & RELIGION

THE DREAM THESAURUS

THE WORLD
OF NATURE

FANTASY &
FABLE

ARTS &
SCIENCES

THE HUMAN
BODY

BUILDINGS &
INTERIORS

EVERYDAY
THINGS

HUMAN
EMOTIONS

HUMAN
ACTIVITIES

HUMAN
CONDITIONS

RITUALS &
RELIGION

THE DREAM
THESAURUS

VIOLIN — A dream of a **VIOLIN** will often refer to its difficulty as an instrument: to the beautiful sound it makes when it is played properly or to the diabolical noise it produces when it is played badly. How were you playing it in your dream? Or was someone else playing to you? The effect on the audience in your dream will be important, as will your own feelings. Try to relate the dream to a current task in waking life, perhaps one with which you hope to impress others.

KARAOKE — Now universally popular, **KARAOKE** allows people to perform with an appearance of professionalism but without any kind of professional preparation or technique – and frequently without talent. Dreaming that you are taking part in a karaoke competition, or simply indulging yourself before an admiring audience, may be suggesting that there is an area of your life in which you are overly confident of your accomplishment or success. If the people in your dream audience were heckling or jeering, this possibility is emphasized. Simple enjoyment of the situation is, of course, also a possibility; and in addition there may be a suggestion of some talent in waking life wasted or waiting to be cultivated.

DRUM — The **DRUM** often has a similar meaning in dreams to the trumpet or cymbal. However, it is more usually associated either with news of some sort or with an attempt to keep other people in step. So unless you have something you wish to announce to the world, or you want to seek the attention of others, your dream may refer to your desire to bring someone around to your point of view. If you are marching to the sound of your own drum, it may emphasize your individuality and your desire not to be "one of the crowd," but to keep in step with your own hopes and aspirations.

ORGAN — A dream of an **ORGAN** may contain a reference to the male organ (possibly deriving from organ pipes). A dream of playing or listening to an organ may therefore allude to courtship or even to the sex act. How well were you playing the instrument in your dream?

PIANO — The **PIANO** is one of the most difficult instruments to play, and a good pianist can be sure of admiration and respect. A dream in which you were performing and receiving praise and applause is usually extremely reassuring. However, if you were simply practicing scales or unsuccessfully attempting a difficult piece, there may be a suggestion that there is a troublesome task in your waking life. This task may require more attention or practice; or are you taking on more than you can accomplish with your present skills?

DREAM ANALYSIS

"I was playing an enormous cello that I could barely put my arms around. When I put the bow to the strings, the bow bent and refused to produce any sound. Finally I lost my temper and shook the cello. It then began to shrink until it became a violin, so I put it under my chin and played beautifully."

The dreamer was in a relationship with a very independent woman, whose sexual experience was considerably greater than his own. He was inhibited by this, and had been suffering from impotence. His dream was suggesting that he should take more control and realize that they could "make beautiful music together" as equal partners.

◆ SKILL ◆

IN GENERAL, DREAMS INVOLVING physical skill will reflect the need for skill in waking life but usually (unless your profession calls for dexterity, or you are, for instance, a do-it-yourself enthusiast) in some other sphere than the purely physical.

If you are a carpenter or a keen amateur BILLIARDS player or ARCHER, it is likely that your dreams are using your skill in that sphere as a symbol for the skill needed in some other area of your life. Much of the interpretation will depend on your success in the dream: were you pocketing the balls successfully, or hitting the TARGET with your ARROWS? It must also be remembered that arrows are often sexual symbols (derived from the arrows of Cupid), so hitting the target here may symbolize a relationship, or a planned seduction (maybe of, rather than by, you). If you were an ACROBAT in your dream, were you performing tricks with ease? Were you keeping your BALANCE?

In a dream involving skill of some kind, you may have been a sad failure or you may have found your task extremely difficult. There may be a warning in the dream that you are taking things too

easily, or that you need to concentrate on the task in hand. If you were an ACROBAT failing to catch the hand of a partner, or finding your hands slipping from the TRAPEZE, you may be failing to grasp a situation comprehensively. If your dream involved performing complicated AEROBATICS with a team of flyers, in waking life you may be working well (or indifferently) with colleagues (*see Flying, page 147*).

There is always a chance, of course, that the dream is simply reflecting waking or unconscious anxiety: for example, it would not be unusual for a ballet dancer to dream that he or she could not perform a difficult step correctly, or for a professional billiards player to dream that he or she was unable to pot the black. Most people occasionally have anxiety dreams relating to their work, and they are generally nothing more than that.

ENERGY

ALLUSIONS TO YOUR energy level can take many forms in dreams,
but the appearance of any symbol that seems to represent it
should be noted. It is particularly important if a dream seems
to include a power failure of some kind.

ELECTRICITY
GAS
FUSE
131
STOVE
46
GASOLINE

An **ELECTRICITY** or **GAS** failure, or a **FUSE** blowing, may suggest that your energy level is low. Your dream may be advising you to pay attention to your lifestyle, and perhaps adjust your diet, get more rest, and consider ways of building up your energy. On the other hand, a dream that a gas fire (*see page 45*) or **STOVE** is burning well would indicate bounteous energy. It is also important to remember that symbols of fire and heat are often sexual. However, a dream of a car running out of **GASOLINE** may be reflecting a fear of low sexual energy or – for a man – even impotence.

FUSE
131

The blowing of a **FUSE** in a dream may warn you that you are close to losing your patience with someone or something, or that your energy is not being contained and fully used. Your dream may be suggesting that you need to do more exercise. Dreaming of

EXERCISE
144
RUNNING
144
WALKING
144
WEIGHTS
144

EXERCISE may mean a number of things, depending partly on the sort of exercise you were doing in the dream. If you were **RUNNING**, or **WALKING** strenuously, what are you hurrying to attain in your waking life? If you were running on a machine, are you scurrying along and getting nowhere? What goal do you wish to achieve in waking life? If you were lifting heavy **WEIGHTS**, in waking life do you feel as if some burden is being imposed on you? Alternatively, are you taking on the burden yourself and perhaps feeling resentful about it?

CREATIVITY

DREAMING OF ACTUALLY creating something may be less significant if
you are a naturally creative person than if you are not. If you have
never done anything with your hands, dreaming that you are making
a pot or writing a novel may carry the implication that you should
think of doing so – or at least make use of your imaginative faculties.

SEED
PIP
MANURE
119

If you have never pursued a creative hobby, your dreams may hint that you should. A dream of a **SEED** or a **PIP** may be placing the germ of an idea that will grow into something important; if you are planting a seed in the expectation of its growing into a fine tree or shrub, then the suggestion is that the germ of a waking idea will be worth following up. A dream of spreading **MANURE** may similarly suggest that a particular notion

PAINTING
74, 76
DRAWING
74, 76
POT
108

needs feeding and nurturing. If you are a creative person, a dream in which you are **PAINTING** or **DRAWING**, or making a **POT** may be referring to another aspect of your waking life that is just as important to you as your creative work. Try to recall every detail of the work you were doing, and relate it to an experience in your waking life. A dream like this may often offer a solution to a problem you are facing at work.

THE WORLD
OF NATURE

FANTASY &
FABLE

ARTS &
SCIENCES

THE HUMAN
BODY

BUILDINGS &
INTERIORS

EVERYDAY
THINGS

HUMAN
EMOTIONS

HUMAN
ACTIVITIES

HUMAN
CONDITIONS

RITUALS &
RELIGION

THE DREAM
THESAURUS

—❖— RECORDING —❖—

DREAMS IN WHICH YOU are carefully recording (for example, by writing about, drawing, or photographing) some scene or detail will underline the importance of the actual subject of your record. This will not necessarily be the subject itself, but what it may represent in your waking life.

THE WORLD OF NATURE

FANTASY & FABLE

ARTS & SCIENCES

THE HUMAN BODY

BUILDINGS & INTERIORS

EVERYDAY THINGS

HUMAN EMOTIONS

HUMAN ACTIVITIES

HUMAN CONDITIONS

RITUALS & RELIGION

THE DREAM THESAURUS

WRITING — A dream in which you are carefully **WRITING** down a series of names and addresses, may be a reminder either to remember your friends or to take note of your enemies. It may be useful to note the opinions of such characters in the dream if you are consulting them on a particular subject, or if you suspect them of interfering in something in your waking life.

PAINTING
73, 76
DRAWING
73, 76
VIDEO — A dream of **PAINTING** or **DRAWING** a landscape, or recording it on **VIDEO**, may refer to the need to note the details of a deal you are setting up, an important piece of business, or simply the circumstances of your waking life at the moment. Your dream may be advising you to make an effort to capture this particular scene or situation visually, or in words (*see Landscape, page 58*).

DRAWING
73, 76
VIDEO
PHOTOGRAPH
76 — The interpretation of this type of dream will largely depend on the success of your attempts at recording the situation or event: if a **DRAWING** fails to materialize satisfactorily, a **VIDEO** remains stubbornly out of focus, or a **PHOTOGRAPH** refuses to develop properly, there is clearly something wrong with your own vision of an important facet of your waking life. Your dream may be warning you that you have certain aspects of your waking life out of proportion or that you are not seeing them clearly.

— DREAM ANALYSIS —

"I was looking out of a window at a busy street and trying to write down the names of everyone walking by. They were all people from my past, and as I wrote each name the person concerned waved to me. When I looked at the paper, I found that it was blank, and I was disappointed."

This was the dream of a man who had recently retired from an exciting job. It had been suggested that he might write his autobiography, but he was hesitating because he thought he might offend some of the people concerned. The smiles of the passersby should have reassured him that this would not be the case, while the blank paper and his disappointment suggested that he would regret it if he did not get down to work.

❖ COLORS ❖

NOT EVERYONE DREAMS in color: people who are particularly
color-conscious in waking life will usually have "Technicolor"
dreams, and those who are less aware of the colors of
their environment tend to dream in monochrome. When a
color emerges strongly in a dream it is important to
consider it as a separate symbol.

RED

RED is the color of heat, passion, fire, and anger. If the color red features in your dream, it may mean that you are feeling extremely angry about a problem or about someone's behavior. In addition, because there is a relationship between red and energy, you should consider whether you are burning your energy in the most rewarding way. The dream may be hinting that you should be more energetic in waking life.

YELLOW ORANGE

YELLOW and ORANGE are positive colors, representing sunshine. A theme of cheerfulness and optimism should be with you if these colors were prominent in your dream; such a dream may be encouraging you to pursue your objectives. A murky yellow, however, may be commenting on the (perhaps unhealthy) state of your liver.

BLUE

BLUE is the color that represents our moods. The interpretation will largely depend on whether the color featured in the dream was dark and mysterious or bright, dazzling sky-blue. If it was the former, are you feeling nostalgic or depressed, or that your life lacks romance? In the latter case, are you about to "take off into the blue" – on vacation, or embark on an important and exciting new project?

GREEN

If the color GREEN emerges in your dream, there may be a suggestion that you are particularly in tune with the environment, and with green issues generally. Other symbols in your dream should help you to understand your attitude toward these important issues. In terms of your attitude and relationship with other people, you should consider whether you are feeling jealous or envious of another person's actions or achievements in waking life. If this is the case, perhaps you should reassess your opinion and outlook. In another way, your dream may be hinting that you have recently responded naively to a waking situation or suggestion.

BLACK

When BLACK emerges in your dreams it is to be taken seriously. To encounter black objects or general blackness in your dream may reflect a feeling of depression in your waking life: about life in general, about a particular area of life, or about someone who is special to you. If black recurs, carefully study what form it takes, and your mood in the dream. Soon, hopefully, you will see a more positive color, in which case you and your problems will probably have turned a significant corner.

WHITE

If WHITE was prominent in your dream, it is likely that you are feeling hopeful and positive. You may be about to make a new start in life (having come through a period of change). You should take note of what your dream is telling you; it may be that you have rid yourself of previous problems or responsibilities and are ready to begin again.

PURPLE

PURPLE is the color of authority, majesty, and the law. Consider whether you have been acting "royally" recently – for good or ill. Other symbols in your dream may reveal whether you should become a little more humble, or whether your regal purple was encouraging you to develop greater self-confidence.

THE WORLD
OF NATURE

FANTASY &
FABLE

ARTS &
SCIENCES

THE HUMAN
BODY

BUILDINGS &
INTERIORS

EVERYDAY
THINGS

HUMAN
EMOTIONS

HUMAN
ACTIVITIES

HUMAN
CONDITIONS

RITUALS &
RELIGION

THE DREAM
THESAURUS

◆ PICTURES ◆

TO DREAM OF PICTURES (for example, looking at paintings, going to the movies, or actually creating pictures of any kind) can either be a rewarding or a terrifying dream experience. It is generally the case that the picture we are looking at or making in our dream is a picture of our current waking lives; and what we see or depict is often the view taken by our inner selves.

PHOTOGRAPH
74
PAINTING
73, 74
DRAWING
73, 74
NEGATIVE
DARKROOM

If you were looking at a **PHOTOGRAPH** or **PAINTING**, your dream may have been underlining your sense of direction in waking life. Was the picture clear or out of focus? This may signify whether you are certain or uncertain of your actions or attitudes. Perhaps you were taking the photograph in the dream: this may be a symbol that you are in control. If you were **DRAWING** or painting, how did you cope with the perspective of your scene? Your answer may indicate whether the elements of your life are "in perspective." If you were studying a **NEGATIVE** in a dream, you may be looking at some problem or aspect of your waking life in a very negative way. You may also need to become more subtle in your approach to life. If you were in a photographic **DARKROOM**, are you waiting to see what is going to develop?

TELEVISION
82

If you were watching **TELEVISION** in your dream, what you were watching, and your dream attitude toward it, is of prime importance – but so is how you were watching. Were you slumped in an armchair? Alternatively, were you cooking a meal, doing the housework, or getting ready to go out, and watching the program out of the corner of your eye? Your dream may contain warnings: that you are too lazy to pay real attention to life; or that you are missing out on certain elements of life because you are too busy. However, if you dreamed that you were interested in the program, you are probably living a balanced life.

MOVIES
137

Dreams of the **MOVIES** contain similar meanings to those of television. However, the movie house is a public place, and we make more of an effort going to the movies than simply switching on the television; so your dream message may be attempting to make a stronger impact on you. This may be especially true if the theater screen was wide and you were impressed by the grandeur of the landscape or the characters portrayed in the film.

PINUP

Looking at **PINUPS** is usually a wish-fulfillment dream (*see page 150*) for both men and women. You may desire the dream pinup, or you may aspire to look like the figure of the same sex. The dream may also have a bearing on your attitude to sex, hinting that you are something of an exhibitionist.

CALCULATION

A DREAM INVOLVING MATHEMATICS or measurement is more than likely to be related to some kind of "calculation" or evaluation in waking life. It may involve a cold-blooded look at the events of your waking life and an attempt to be rational and unemotional about a particular problem or situation.

**ACCOUNTANT
COUNTING
EQUATION
COMPUTER**

A dream of an **ACCOUNTANT** attempting to make sense of a set of account books, or **COUNTING** an interminable column of figures, may be related to a problem or situation in waking life that seems to demand a cool examination. You are probably the accountant in your dream, unless you can relate that character to someone with an interest in your waking life. This may be someone who wants to understand you, discipline you, or bring you back to reality. The dream may be prompting you to throw away your usual emotional response and reach for a calmer and more composed attitude toward whatever is troubling you. Whether your efforts were successful or not will also relate to the waking situation. If you are facing a mathematical problem that does not add up, or an **EQUATION** that does not work out, have you overlooked a simple slip or error that could devalue your whole attitude in waking life? **COMPUTERS** are usually correct – unless human error intervenes – so if there is a continual computer error in your dream, has that clear way ahead you see in your waking life really been properly planned? Perhaps it is the case that your immediate future has not been "programmed" as accurately as you believe.

**BAROMETER
THERMO-
METER
METER
RULER**

Dreaming of the kind of measurement that involves an actual calculation of length, temperature, or flow, is likely to relate directly to attempts to control and evaluate your emotions. One of the clearest indications of this would be a dream of a **BAROMETER** or **THERMOMETER**, since these are instruments that measure the changing weather and temperature. In your dream, was the thermometer going up? Were your emotions high, and

becoming uncontrollable? Were you running a temperature? Was the barometer rising or falling, indicating stormy weather or a period of calm? This kind of dream is not necessarily predictive – it is not telling you that you are going to "lose your cool," or that a difficult period is approaching. The dream may be warning you of the turn of events in your waking life if you are not careful. With practice, you should be able to use such indications to modify your behavior and keep your temper, to avoid a storm. A dream of a gas or water **METER** may drop similar hints. Are you talking too much, or are you allowing your emotions to flow too freely in waking life? On the other hand, are you afraid that the price you eventually have to pay for such freedom will simply be too high? If in your dream you were taking measurements with a **RULER** or any other measuring instrument, it may reflect a desire to put a particular situation (or simply your emotions) into perspective. There may be difficulties, but the aspiration is there and it should not be denied.

DREAM ANALYSIS

"I was measuring the floor of a room in my new house for a carpet, but every time I got halfway through the job the tape measure began to shrink until it became useless. Finally, I took my shoes off and paced the length of the room; as I got to the wall, I turned and my fiancée came and kissed me."

The dreamer was about to be married and had been unsettled about the practical side of his life. He was not sure whether he was in a sufficiently secure position to support a wife. The dream was encouraging him to reject cold analysis and allow his emotions to take over (the bare feet are an important sign here). If he did so, happiness would follow.

THE WORLD
OF NATURE

FANTASY &
FABLE

ARTS &
SCIENCES

THE HUMAN
BODY

BUILDINGS &
INTERIORS

EVERYDAY
THINGS

HUMAN
EMOTIONS

HUMAN
ACTIVITIES

HUMAN
CONDITIONS

RITUALS &
RELIGION

THE DREAM
THESAURUS

THE COPPELIA DREAM

" *A production of the ballet* Coppelia *was being performed on some pretty outdoor terraces, with various scenes of the ballet being danced on different levels. I had mounted the production and was about to go on to dance the Act 1 Mazurka on my own. I was thinking to myself before I went on that it ought to have been an ensemble dance and not a solo, and hoped that the audience would not be put off by this. Then my music cue came and I burst forth, confidently, and performed the dance exactly as I had choreographed it for the production. When I had finished my performance, the music continued for the next dance, but I could not see if the other dancers were actually in their correct positions. However, someone assured me that they were.*

Later, when the performance was over, we were having a party for my birthday; at first, no one in the cast turned up, but they eventually arrived, and it was all extremely jolly. I was still wearing my Coppelia costume with its flowered, beribboned headdress and red shoes, and I felt really good in it. In due course, other people at the party admired it and commented on how nice I looked. "

DANCERS
PERFORM ON
TERRACES

SALLY DANCES
MAZURKA

THE INTERPRETATION

In waking life, Sally had choreographed and performed in scenes from this particular ballet, although for years she had been part of a large team of office workers. Just before she had the dream, she had been promoted to office supervisor; she had to change her relationship with her former colleagues, and now found herself in a far more responsible and lonely position. This is clearly indicated in the dream by her discovering that she was dancing alone in what should have been an ensemble. She was concerned about what the audience would think, which reflected her feelings about accepting the promotion. The dream was affirming that she had made the right decision – she came on stage confidently. However, the fact that she was unable to see the other dancers showed her concern about her colleagues' attitude toward her. The "someone" in her dream who told her the dancers were in position was probably her inner authority figure reassuring her.

When Sally was promoted, her colleagues were not sure how they should relate to her. She was aware of this, and the dream summed up the situation – her fellow dancers did not, initially, go to the party. However, in the dream's conclusion, they all admired her and her costume. The fact that Sally felt good in her costume was also positive: it signified that she would feel "comfortable" in her new job. Red is an assertive, strong color, and the shoes in which she danced so confidently showed her determination to succeed and overcome any obstacles.

Just before her new appointment, Sally had celebrated her thirtieth birthday; she was also aware that this was a "milestone" year, since she would begin to carry a lot of responsibility. This is one of the main themes of the dream, since Sally was responsible for the ballet production. The other symbol that emerged was the fact that the ballet was being performed on terraces, which represented the status of employees within the company (and her own progress). Sally's dream recalled a previous incident in her life. In doing so, it mirrored feelings she had experienced at the time she had been in charge of a large group of people – when they had to "dance to her command."

SALLY'S COSTUME IS
ADMIRED

NUMBERS

IF A PARTICULAR NUMBER is prominent in a dream, it may be worth considering its significance and symbolic meaning in terms of the ancient traditions of numerology.

ONE
TWO
THREE
FOUR

The number ONE is the number of communication, versatility, and reason. It may also refer to the self. Examine your own views, and see that they are communicated to the people around you. The number TWO signifies diligence, care, and perfectionism. This may make you unpopular with other, less meticulous people, but the dream may be suggesting that you should take more care. The number THREE suggests not only diplomacy and sensitivity, but also indecision. A dream involving this number may be prompting you to make up your mind about something in waking life, and to make your point tactfully. The number three can also suggest instability in certain areas of your waking life. Determination, force, passion, obsessiveness, and possibly jealousy, are the emotions traditionally represented by the number FOUR. It is also an even number suggesting a good balance of

FIVE
SIX
SEVEN
EIGHT
NINE

emotion and feeling. The number FIVE is traditionally representative of study and learning. It is also regarded as an optimistic number, and the number of justice. Number SIX signifies emotion, but rather than the passion of number four, it is a more sensual emotion directed at stability. The number six was customarily represented in wedding dresses and wedding ceremonies, and suggested long-lasting relationships. Individuality, freedom, and honesty are all represented by the number SEVEN. So too is tactlessness in the expression of feelings that may not be shared by less adventurous people. EIGHT is a number that has traditionally been associated with hard work, ambition, patience, and practicality. NINE is the number of inventiveness, originality, optimism, and independence of mind. However, this particular number is sometimes turned to perversity and unpredictability.

TIME

WE ARE RARELY REMINDED of the passing of time in our dreams, and it is difficult to know exactly how time is expressed in them. We are not in "real time" when we dream, since incidents or adventures that seem lengthy may actually be dreamed in a few seconds.

CLOCK
WATCH
SUNDIAL

A CLOCK or WATCH in a dream may be reminding us that there is either plenty of time (for example, to solve a problem, make a date, or plan a business enterprise) or that time is running short. Look at the style of the timepiece. Is the watch your own? Is the clock a familiar one? Conversely, are the items in the dream strange to you, and therefore representative of an outside influence or pressure? There is a difference between a modern timepiece and a SUNDIAL; a dream of the latter may be symbolic of an

CALENDAR

unrealistic aspect of your life. The dream may be suggesting that you should look for something in your waking life that is not quite real, or is out of fashion. A dream CALENDAR may be referring to your past. Were the pages being torn away to represent the passing of the years? Such a dream may well be commenting that time is passing more quickly than you think. If a particular date is displayed in your dream, it will probably have some significance, even if you are unable to "place it" immediately.

THE WORLD OF NATURE

FANTASY & FABLE

ARTS & SCIENCES

THE HUMAN BODY

BUILDINGS & INTERIORS

EVERYDAY THINGS

HUMAN EMOTIONS

HUMAN ACTIVITIES

HUMAN CONDITIONS

RITUALS & RELIGION

THE DREAM THESAURUS

THEATER

THE THEATER MAY BE SAID to be an examination, an interpretation, and a projection of human life. Our dreams of the theater fall into a similar category. Such dreams often make strong comments on our conduct in waking life, especially in a social context; they frequently accuse us of artificial behavior and of pretending to be what we are not – of "acting," in fact.

PERFORMING
178
STAGE
APPLAUSE
CATCALL
AUDIENCE
175
DANCER
OPERA

Unless we are dedicated amateur or professional actors, in which case the theater is important to us in a different way, dreams of **PERFORMING** suggest that we are concerned with our personality and how we appear to others. On the **STAGE**, we are on show just as we are in everyday life: we hope for **APPLAUSE**, and sometimes receive **CATCALLS**. The **AUDIENCE** is likely to represent the people around us in our waking lives: friends, neighbors, and associates. Try to remember what you can about the dream audience, and you should find clues in the dream as to their identity. Crowds, however, can often represent problems. Are you facing them boldly, knowing how to respond and what to say? Or are you acting your response? As an actor you will probably be playing the part of yourself, so your inadequacies (forgetting your lines or being unconvincing in your part) may symbolize inadequacies (of which you may be unaware) in your waking life. Dreams of being a **DANCER** or an **OPERA** star may be examples of wish-fulfillment (*see page 150*) but may also be

referring to your losing or keeping your balance, or being on- or off-key, in some waking situation.

AUDITION — A dream of attending an **AUDITION** may be referring to some kind of test in your waking life. It may symbolize an examination or an interview, but may also be a test you have set for yourself. How you behaved and how others reacted in the dream will be pointers to the way you should deal with the situation in waking life.

MAKEUP
GREASEPAINT — Actors use **MAKEUP** or **GREASEPAINT** to help to convince their audience that they are not themselves but some other character. In waking life, are you engaged in deceit of some kind – perhaps with the best intentions?

DREAM ANALYSIS

"I was rehearsing a play and the scene was set in an office. I kept bumping into the desks and saying other people's lines, but when I became embarrassed and tried to leave the stage, I could not find the exit. The other actors became annoyed and started shouting at me to stay."

The dream referred to the dreamer's career. Unsure of his new position after promotion, he had been trying too hard; he had been attempting to do everyone else's job as well

as his own. He realized what was happening and considered resigning, but the dream suggested that he should stay and try to reach an understanding with his colleagues.

THE WORLD OF NATURE

FANTASY & FABLE

ARTS & SCIENCES

THE HUMAN BODY

BUILDINGS & INTERIORS

EVERYDAY THINGS

HUMAN EMOTIONS

HUMAN ACTIVITIES

HUMAN CONDITIONS

RITUALS & RELIGION

THE DREAM THESAURUS

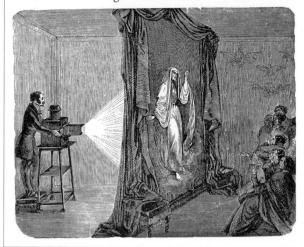

PROMPTER REHEARSAL In your dream, were you unsure of your words and actions, entrances and exits? Did you need help from a **PROMPTER**? Conversely, did you sail confidently through the **REHEARSAL** while other actors stuttered and stammered? Your dream may have been pointing out the fact that life is not a rehearsal; it may have been warning you that if you are not word-perfect (if you do not know how to behave in waking life), it is time you learned. The dream play you were rehearsing should provide a clue as to the area of life you should be thinking about. A dream in which you were rehearsing one particular scene may be suggesting that you are unsure of one aspect of your life, and need to pay attention to it.

TELEVISION 76 **FILM** Some dreams are clearly related to scenes from a **TELEVISION** play or **FILM** that you may have watched before going to bed. If you have such a dream, ask yourself why out of all the images you saw on television last night, your unconscious chose that particular one.

❖ SURREALIST DREAMS ❖

MOST DREAMS HAVE AN ELEMENT of the surreal – they delve into worlds that our waking minds seem incapable of either imagining or understanding. Surrealist dreams, however, are meaningful; they speak in metaphors, and are usually difficult to interpret.

It may be that the strange surreal dream worlds in which we often find ourselves are very important to us, representing a part of our personalities that needs expression and release. When the surrealist painters emerged in the 1920s, they showed pictures of impossible worlds in which watches melt, trains emerge from fireplaces, and a man looking into a mirror sees not his face but the back of his head. These painters were showing us, in visual form, images from dreamland – where such events and visions are "normal."

How do we attempt to understand such dreams, which often seem to have nothing to do with reality? The first step may be to regard them as quite literal. If you dream that a watch is melting, it may mean that time itself is melting away, and that you are perhaps not making the best of it. If, in a dream mirror, you see the back of your head, perhaps you should be examining aspects of yourself or your waking life that are not immediately obvious to you and that you may need to see or understand clearly.

❖ DREAM ANALYSIS ❖

"I was carrying a grandfather clock around the garden. The flowers around me all turned into watches, and the clock turned into a giant sunflower with a clock face. Then I was in my kitchen where a pan was boiling over, and as I ran to turn off the gas, flowers sprouted from the saucepan, then died."

The dream has a time theme running through it. The dreamer was in the process of applying for a job, and the dream reflected anxiety that time was running out – the situation was "coming to a boil." It was time to stop the discussions, "turn off the gas," and take action. The flowers seemed to relate to the job, which was in a bakery (in English "flower" is a pun on "flour").

Although the suggestions of a surreal dream may be straightforward, what are we to make of entire dream sequences that appear to have no meaning? They are certainly among the most difficult dreams to interpret ourselves, and often in analysis they only reveal their meanings after a considerable amount of work. Asking yourself for help with these dreams is a recognized technique that often works. Faced with trying to interpret such a dream, just before you relax into sleep on the following night speak firmly to your dream self: "I didn't understand that dream last night; please send me a clue." Very often, while not experiencing the same dream, you may find that you have a parallel dream. (This is a path you can follow with any "difficult" dream.) Another way of attempting to find the meaning – or at the very least uncover the main

symbols – of a surreal dream is to sit down with a pencil, clear your mind, think of the dream, and begin to "doodle." The symbols that flow from your pen will often relate to the dream (without your actually trying to draw any element in the dream yourself). This may provide a point from which you can begin to interpret your dream.

You can, of course, simply reject a difficult dream. However, it is often the very dream that you are unable to fathom that follows you around for days, weeks, and even months, and nags at you for understanding. In this case, it is likely that the dream has something important to say to you. It is the firm opinion of many psychologists that there is no such thing as a meaningless dream, so lengthy work on a dream that is annoying you may be worthwhile. You should not worry unduly, although it may be best to seek professional advice if the dream was so powerful that it begins to preoccupy you.

THE WORLD OF NATURE

FANTASY & FABLE

ARTS & SCIENCES

THE HUMAN BODY

BUILDINGS & INTERIORS

EVERYDAY THINGS

HUMAN EMOTIONS

—◆—CLOTHING—◆—

DREAMS ABOUT CLOTHING are extremely common and are usually telling us something about our self-image or our status. Dreams about clothing often focus on whether we are wearing the right apparel for the right occasion. We may have difficulty in dressing or appear in public either in the nude (*see page 96*) or without an important article of dress.

If you are uncertain about your clothing in a dream, the comment seems likely to be on your view of the position you hold, or should hold, in society. Have you found your right place, and are you comfortable about it? Dreaming of being untidily or improperly dressed when others around you are impeccably clothed seems to suggest that you have a feeling of inferiority or insecurity, or are not "fitting in" with the people around you. If you appear wearing formal clothes when everyone else is dressed casually, the dream may be suggesting that you have "ideas above your station" or are uncertain about your social identity; the dream may be a warning against snobbery. On the other hand, to be carelessly dressed in a formal setting – to the extent that perhaps others in the dream are offended – may also be suggesting that your behavior or attitude may be damaging your waking reputation or prospects. This may be true even though it may reflect a view that you should be accepted as you are.

APRON
OVERALLS

Dreams about clothing often contain visual puns. Dressed in an APRON or OVERALLS, are you covering something up or undertaking a practical – perhaps "dirty" – task? Someone dreaming of

CAMOUFLAGE
VEIL
COAT
BUCKLE
BELT
BUTTON
ZIPPER

wearing a CAMOUFLAGE jacket may be hiding something (perhaps their true feelings), while a dream of wearing a VEIL may carry the same message (although this also has religious or spiritual overtones). A carefully buttoned-up COAT or an item of clothing displaying BUCKLES suggests restraint, while casual clothing may refer to a lack of inhibition. A tight BELT may be warning you to restrain yourself or to watch your behavior. A dream of releasing BUTTONS or a ZIPPER may refer to a need for relaxation, or a desire to develop an easier relationship with the people around you, or with one particular person, whose identity may be suggested by other dream clues.

HAT
HOOD

Freud once remarked that "the hat is always a sexual symbol," but nowadays it is more likely to be an emblem of rather old-fashioned authority; although a man who dreams of taking off his HAT to someone is still consciously showing respect. For women, a hat is often a sign of status or pride. A dream of wearing a HOOD may suggest secrecy and concealment.

TIE
BIKINI
LINGERIE
UNDERWEAR

A TIE is sometimes a sexual symbol for men. Was it too tightly knotted or too "showy"? It is certainly true that almost any article of clothing may be a symbol of sexuality: particularly items that draw attention to what they are covering, such as BIKINIS, LINGERIE, and UNDERWEAR in general. Was the item of clothing in the dream worn or

SHOE
GARTER

dirty? If so, what does this say about your sex life or your attitude to your sexuality? You may have been proudly flaunting attractive underwear, satisfied with your attractiveness to others; although the dream may be telling you that you are too sure of yourself. Dreams of this kind of clothing can simply be types of enjoyably erotic (usually male) fantasies, probably of wish-fulfillment (*see page 150*). The **SHOE** and the **GARTER** have also traditionally been the focus of male desire, and may appear in dreams.

DRESSING
UNDRESSING
UNBUTTONING
UNZIPPING
PAJAMAS
NIGHTGOWN

The context of the dream is important. Were you embarrassed or proud? Were you **DRESSING** or **UNDRESSING**? If you were dressing, were the clothes you were putting on your own? If they belonged to someone else, were you expressing your admiration of or desire for that person? A dream in which you are **UNBUTTONING** or **UNZIPPING** your clothing may have no sexual implication, but rather suggest a desire to be freer, more open with others, and more relaxed than you are at present. Similarly, a dream in which you are ironing or preparing **PAJAMAS** or a **NIGHTGOWN** does not necessarily have a sexual connotation; it may simply mean that you need more sleep.

BOOTS
CLOGS
GLOVES

Were you wearing heavy **BOOTS** or **CLOGS** in the dream? If so, whose feelings are you treading on with your big feet? If your dream focused on **GLOVES**, you may need to handle a particular person or situation with special care. Alternatively, the suggestion may be that you need to protect yourself in some way. Freud associated gloves (into which a man inserts his hands) with sexuality or with contraception. Traditionally, a glove was a symbol of purity in a woman, while removing a glove displayed a desire to be open and honest.

SHIRT
STITCHING

A man's dream of a **SHIRT** may be associated with the concept of gambling – "betting one's shirt" on a horse. To dream of **STITCHING** clothes may be a hint that repairs are needed in some areas of your personal life.

FABRIC
LEATHER
SILK
CHIFFON

The texture of the clothes in a dream can be important. Dreaming that you are dressed in uncomfortable clothing (perhaps clothes made of irritating **FABRIC**) may be suggesting that a familiar part of your waking life is equally uncomfortable and irritating: for example, a person, a place, or a job. **LEATHER**, **SILK**, and **CHIFFON** are all regarded as sensual fabrics, so they may have sexual connotations in a dream.

COSTUME

If in your dream you are wearing clothes very different from your usual wardrobe, the implication may be that you are discontented with an area of your life – most likely your image. You should listen to what your dream is trying to tell you: is it time to settle down and be less startling or outrageous? Is it time to be your age, or to relax and try a new style? The color and texture of the clothes in your dream may suggest which area of your life needs remolding. You may dream that you are donning a historical **COSTUME**; either as part of your normal dress or for a costume party or a play. In the former case, you may be telling yourself that your attitude or image is old-fashioned and needs updating. The dream may also be hinting that you are playing a part and disguising your real self. However, you may feel more comfortable in costume than in ordinary clothes, in which case you clearly have an identity problem to solve.

THE WORLD OF NATURE

FANTASY & FABLE

ARTS & SCIENCES

THE HUMAN BODY

BUILDINGS & INTERIORS

EVERYDAY THINGS

HUMAN EMOTIONS

HUMAN ACTIVITIES

THE WORLD
OF NATURE

FANTASY &
FABLE

ARTS &
SCIENCES

THE HUMAN
BODY

BUILDINGS &
INTERIORS

EVERYDAY
THINGS

HUMAN
EMOTIONS

HUMAN
ACTIVITIES

HUMAN
CONDITIONS

RITUALS &
RELIGION

THE DREAM
THESAURUS

—✦— BIRTH —✦—

DREAMS OF BIRTH or of giving birth have a variety of meanings. They often convey joy and hope, with overtones of basic wish-fulfillment, but there are many other possible interpretations that have little connection with the process of reproduction.

GIVING BIRTH

If you are a woman and you dream of GIVING BIRTH, first ask yourself whether you actually have a desire to become pregnant. If that is the case, your dream is in the classic category of wish-fulfillment (*see page 150*). If you are with a partner and trying for a baby, your dream may be telling you — in advance — that you are pregnant. Dreams appear to be capable of diagnosis in advance of any doctor's tests. However, your dream infant is more likely to represent something else in waking life: it may be something you have created, or a new and much-cherished possession that you have worked hard to acquire, or even a carefully worked-out plan for the future.

LABOR

Were you actually suffering in the process of giving birth? Was the LABOR difficult? This may reflect any problems you have overcome — or are still fighting to overcome — in your waking life. If this is the case, the dream may have been reassuring you that the right result will eventually appear — assuming you greeted the dream baby with pleasure and satisfaction. If not, or if you awoke before seeing the results of your birth pangs, the dream may be telling you that your waking plans are incomplete and you are not ready to conclude them.

CORD

Had the CORD been cut in your dream? Were there problems in cutting it? Were you reluctant to have the cord cut? This symbol may refer to a grown-up family that is beginning to leave home. Or it may be that another element in your life seems to be slipping away.

ABORTION STILLBIRTH

A dream of an ABORTION or a STILLBIRTH may linger in your waking thoughts. The dream's message may be that you are following a fruitless path in life, or that certain pursuits are "dead" for you and should be abandoned. On the whole, however, dreams of birth are encouraging.

—✦— DEATH —✦—

DREAMS OF DEATH and dying are very common. They can be extremely frightening, but whether one was dying oneself or suffering the loss of a loved one, the dreams themselves rarely signify death. Traumatic and sad events in dreams may herald change.

FUNERAL CEMETERY GRAVE COFFIN

A dream of attending a FUNERAL does not mean that someone is about to die. If you were walking through a CEMETERY to the prepared GRAVE, your unconscious may be preparing you for some kind of change. If you were watching the COFFIN being lowered it is likely that whatever is about to change in your life is almost upon you. If you were about to be buried, try to relate this to how you are feeling; death is the ultimate change, and a change or changes in your waking life will have prompted the dream. Death suggests rebirth, and such dreams often occur at important periods of our lives: for example, during marriage or divorce.

GRAVESTONE TOMBSTONE

In your dream you may have been reading an inscription on a GRAVESTONE or TOMBSTONE, naming someone you know.

THE WORLD
OF NATURE

FANTASY &
FABLE

ARTS &
SCIENCES

THE HUMAN
BODY

BUILDINGS &
INTERIORS

EVERYDAY
THINGS

HUMAN
EMOTIONS

HUMAN
ACTIVITIES

MORTUARY

and a funeral party toward the grave, your dream may be reflecting on an approaching period of change in your waking life. If in your dream you had to visit a **MORTUARY**, perhaps you are unwilling to let go of what is past. Or has your past caught up with you? The mortuary may hold feelings of regret or guilt; there may be a problem that requires the attention of your conscience.

BEREAVEMENT
124
WIDOW
WIDOWER

A dream in which you have suffered a **BEREAVEMENT**, or have become a **WIDOW** or **WIDOWER**, may reflect feelings of loneliness in your waking life. Even if you are in a relationship, your dream may be suggesting that there is a lack of understanding between you and your partner. Has there been a breakdown in communication between you and your children? Are you feeling lonely or cut off in some way at work? Are you receiving enough support from people who are important to you? If you live alone, try to socialize more and extend your circle of friends.

EXECUTION
DEATH
WARRANT
EUTHANASIA

A dream that you have received an **EXECUTION** sentence or **DEATH WARRANT** offers dramatic symbols that indicate your need to change an element of your life. The interpretation would be similar if you were experiencing or requesting **EUTHANASIA**, but in such a case you are pleading with yourself to make the

If so, think about the characteristics of that person, because in such cases our dreams are telling us that we should eradicate or change ("kill") those qualities in ourselves. If in the dream you were sad when you read the inscription, it may well be that you should reconsider your attitude to the person concerned, or what they represent. For example, ask yourself whether you need to become more charitable, kind, or considerate – if those are the qualities you know abound in the person concerned.

VAULT

If a **VAULT** featured in your dream you may have to put a slightly different slant on your interpretation. In old cemeteries, it is possible to peer into family vaults and see the crumbling coffins: your dream may be suggesting that you can see that changes should be made, but are content to "look in" rather than make a clean break with the past.

UNDERTAKER

An **UNDERTAKER** in a dream may represent an authority figure in your waking life – someone who takes charge, and who "undertakes" a necessary and painful job for individuals who cannot do it themselves. You may be the undertaker, carrying a burden of responsibility. Are you assuming too much responsibility in life? If the undertaker was leading you

THE WORLD OF NATURE

FANTASY & FABLE

ARTS & SCIENCES

THE HUMAN BODY

BUILDINGS & INTERIORS

EVERYDAY THINGS

HUMAN EMOTIONS

HUMAN ACTIVITIES

HUMAN CONDITIONS

RITUALS & RELIGION

THE DREAM THESAURUS

KILLING MASSACRE

necessary change of attitude. Expressing violence in a dream by **KILLING** someone or performing a **MASSACRE** may indicate that you are extremely angry in your waking life. Are you perhaps angry with yourself, with another person, or even with society in general?

SKULL SKELETON

A **SKULL** or **SKELETON** appearing as a dream symbol is usually far less frightening than it may have appeared on waking. In fact, a skeleton symbol suggests that you are getting down to the "bare bones" of an important task, project, or problem. On the other hand, if you have any aches or pains in your joints, there may be a warning that something

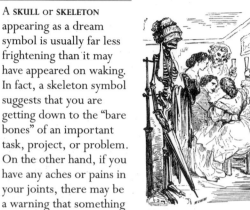

purely physical could be wrong. If the teeth in the skull were prominent, your unconscious could be suggesting that you get a dental checkup.

HEAVEN HELL
171

A dream of **HEAVEN** is clearly to be enjoyed – perhaps you are "in heaven" in your waking life, or your dream may have been purely escapist. If your waking life is particularly dreary at present, your dream of heaven may have been wish-fulfillment (*see page 150*). A dream of **HELL** may be reflecting on your present life and encouraging you to change it. However, you may have been cavorting in the underworld of Hades, and enjoying all sorts of weird and wonderful pleasures. On the other hand, a religious background may be rebuking you for some sin, or warning you that your present behavior could lead you into a worse kind of hell in the future.

—◆— CHILDHOOD —◆—

ALTHOUGH DREAMS OF CHILDHOOD may appear to be simply nostalgic, they often have a strong bearing on our current waking lives. A dream of the past may be manifesting an unconscious desire to escape from the responsibilities and problems of our waking life.

Dreams of childhood can also comment on self-importance, reminding us that however old we are, we still have the same basic needs and desires as a child. However rich our experience, we are not immune from making mistakes or miscalculating, or from being silly, cruel, or bad-tempered. In fact, our dream may be reminding us to take nothing – especially our own intelligence – for granted in our waking life.

TANTRUM

A dream about a child – perhaps a strange child – may well be a dream about yourself. Try to recall the child's behavior – whether it was friendly or unfriendly, smiling or throwing a temper **TANTRUM** – and consider whether the dream contains a message about your own current life and behavior. A child exhibiting selfishness or lack of

consideration may well be an image of your own shortcomings. Has your recent behavior or attitude in waking life been "childish"?

CRADLE
150
BABY-SITTER

A dream in which you were rocking a **CRADLE** could be making a reference to power; think of the saying "the hand that rocks the cradle rules the world." To dream of a **BABY-SITTER** may be a warning, or it may be a comment on your own security.

COMIC BOOK TEACHER
89, 174
BLACKBOARD

Sometimes in dreams of childhood we receive rather childish messages. We may be reading a **COMIC BOOK** or writing something uncomplimentary about a **TEACHER** on a **BLACKBOARD**. Such symbols in our dreams may be telling us how we feel about an authority figure or advising us to see the funny side of life.

⟡ YOUTH ⟡

WHILE A DREAM OF CHILDHOOD may often be nostalgic, dreams of being a youth again are often the product of wish-fulfillment (*see page 150*). Nevertheless, such dreams may also be inviting us to reassess our attitude toward young people, to attempt to regain our youth in some way, or perhaps to take a less elderly view of life.

As we grow older few of us can resist on occasions looking back wistfully at our teenage years. We may not necessarily want to go through the torments of adolescence again, but we may like to be able to marry our mature knowledge and experience to the physical strength and enthusiasm of youth.

ADOLESCENT A dream of youth may well be suggesting that we need to free ourselves from responsibilities that tend to burden us and recover some freedom of expression. Are you unnecessarily concerned about some complex issues that, if you examined them with an unbiased eye, might prove much simpler than you think? In fact, are you under self-imposed stress? Was the young man or woman in your dream acting in a particularly **ADOLESCENT** way? If so, your dream may be warning you that your present actions are less than adult: you may be showing prejudice, acting prematurely, or being spiteful or jealous in a way that you would regard as stupid and unproductive in a younger person.

live rather than live to work. It may be advising you to look for ways in which to enhance and enlarge a positive attitude toward your daily life.

SCHOOL
171, 174

If you were going to **SCHOOL** again in your dream, interpretation will largely depend on your attitude toward your school life. The implication may be that you need new intellectual challenges; you need to broaden your intellectual life, perhaps by studying a new subject or taking up a new pastime. However, many people hated their schooldays, and in such a case a dream that you have returned to them suggests that in some way the long shadow of your misery still lies over you. The dream may contain the suggestion that you still need to release yourself from the idea that you should work to

TEACHER
88, 174
CHILDREN
173

A dream of a particular – perhaps disliked – **TEACHER** may be commenting on an authority figure (for example, a superior at work) who is having a repressive and negative effect on you in your waking life. A dream that you were back at school and simply playing with a crowd of **CHILDREN**, probably suggests either that you are coping well with everyday problems, not taking life too seriously, and perhaps having a great deal of fun or, conversely, that you need to relax more. It should be quite clear which of the options applies.

THE WORLD OF NATURE

FANTASY & FABLE

ARTS & SCIENCES

THE HUMAN BODY

BUILDINGS & INTERIORS

EVERYDAY THINGS

HUMAN EMOTIONS

HUMAN ACTIVITIES

HUMAN CONDITIONS

RITUALS & RELIGION

THE DREAM THESAURUS

◈ THE FAMILY ◈

DREAMS FEATURING MEMBERS of our family can be reassuring. They may give us confidence and support, or they may concentrate on present or long-term problems from which there seems little prospect of escape. For those who have no family, such dreams are all too often wish-fulfillment (*see page 150*).

HUSBAND
146
WIFE
146
PARTNER
167

It is often the case that we are aware that our **HUSBAND**, **WIFE**, or **PARTNER** is present in our dreams, but they infrequently appear as themselves. The reason may be that they are a significant part of our waking lives, so the need for their obvious presence as themselves, in dreams, is small. However, the scene changes when we are distanced from our partner, and if we are separated not simply by physical miles but because of a breakdown in the relationship, their appearance in a dream may carry an important message. A negative dream of a partner when all seems well in the relationship may be a warning that there is an underlying problem. Examine the context of your partner's misbehavior in the dream. Your unconscious may have noticed a flaw in your partnership that you are consciously unaware of —

or are simply refusing to recognize. Remember, however, the possibility that the dream may relate to another negative area of your life: your partner may represent someone else close to you.

FATHER
MOTHER

Dreams in which one's **FATHER** or **MOTHER** appear represent not only the ultimate in authority figures, but also the characteristics we may have inherited from our parents. If you found some of your parents' characteristics distasteful or unpleasant and are fully aware of this, the chances are that you have come to terms with emotions that can certainly be hurtful. Parents who may have been difficult in waking life, may appear kindly and tolerant in your dreams, but a compassionate dream mother may be you; countering the consequences of her attitude toward you when you were a child. If your father was authoritarian, his appearance in your dreams may reflect a lack of self-confidence. Your dreams may be able to help you: you should search for positive symbols, and encourage them to reappear in future dreams (*see page 33*).

The World of Nature

THE WORLD
OF NATURE

FANTASY &
FABLE

ARTS &
SCIENCES

THE HUMAN
BODY

BUILDINGS &
INTERIORS

EVERYDAY
THINGS

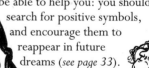

SON
DAUGHTER

Dreams in which your SON or DAUGHTER appear should, of course, be examined in relation to the other symbols in the dream. However, parents usually have a powerful intuition where their children are concerned, and it may well be that this is emerging in your dream. Try to think of it from a practical point of view: if your dream child was reproaching you for being worried or concerned, or for nagging, you should take notice.

BROTHER
SISTER

Your dream BROTHER or SISTER may represent the characteristics you admire or dislike about your own siblings and

the dream may be telling you something about your attitude toward those particular characteristics in yourself.

GRAND-
PARENT

The bond between grandparents and their grandchildren is very often strong and extremely positive. To dream of a GRANDPARENT who has died will more than likely be reassuring, telling you that you have inherited some of their wisdom. If your grandparents were strict, can you see the wisdom of their past reactions? If not, and you still feel hurt by this in waking life, you should ask your dreams for more help (*see page 33*).

—◆— THE BODY —◆—

A DREAM THAT ANY PART of the body is injured or painful will always be worth following up, since it is possible for illness to be self-diagnosed in this way before a doctor would see any signs. However, dreams also use the parts of the body as symbols in other areas of life.

It has long been realized that our dreams can signal ailments before we consciously recognize that anything is wrong with us, and certainly before there are any physical signs that may be seen by a doctor. Do not fear that every nightmare signals a serious illness, but if you have a dream that something is medically wrong with you (especially if the dream recurs) it will be worth consulting your doctor.

BLOOD
95
HEMORRHAGE
MENSTRU-
ATION
MENOPAUSE

BLOOD is an extremely important symbol, sometimes of the principle of life itself, and sometimes of the soul, of physical strength, and of rejuvenation. It may be a difficult symbol to interpret, but dreaming of loss of blood must surely in some way refer to loss of physical or moral strength. Dreaming of drinking blood may be not only a potent symbol of enmity but also of absorbing the power of your foe. A dream of a HEMORRHAGE may refer to being "drained" of strength, of a need for more nourishment, or perhaps simply for a holiday. For women, it may signify the onset of menstruation. A woman's dream of MENSTRUATION or MENOPAUSE

is likely to be a dream of change. It may be a sign of fear of the end of active life, but it may also signify the promise of a new life, free of "burdens" (for example, children). It may even reflect a fear of the end of sexual life.

SPINE
BACK
BACKBONE
HAND

Dreams of the SPINE, BACK, or BACKBONE are all symbols of the will — the capacity to be firm and determined. Are you failing to "stand up" to someone? The HAND is an enormously important part of the body. A dream of a disabled or injured hand may be a reference to some inability to perform a task (which may not be physical). The hand can also symbolize the whole pattern of one's life or psyche.

FEET
LAMENESS

A dream about FEET is sometimes an allusion to general progress. Have you been "going too far" in some way, are you simply weary of a task you are unable to see the end of? Dreaming of LAMENESS may signify an inability to proceed.

FACE

A dream of a FACE is likely to be about the image we present to the world — our idea of how we are seen by others, or how we

THE WORLD OF NATURE

FANTASY & FABLE

ARTS & SCIENCES

THE HUMAN BODY

BUILDINGS & INTERIORS

EVERYDAY THINGS

HUMAN EMOTIONS

HUMAN ACTIVITIES

HUMAN CONDITIONS

RITUALS & RELIGION

THE DREAM THESAURUS

EAR
EYE
NOSE
BLIND
130

wish to be seen. A swollen face may therefore refer to an overblown idea of our own importance; a blemished one to a defect in our character that we fear is obvious to others. Your dream of an EAR may be telling you to listen to the advice, criticism, or praise of others, while a dream of an EYE (particularly if it recurs) may simply mean that you need an eye test. On the other hand, a dream of being BLIND is more likely to refer to what you are unable to see, or refuse to see, than to any disease. A dream of a NOSE may well be an allusion to curiosity; to being "nosy." Dreams of pleasant or unpleasant smells may allude to the discovery of something pleasant or unpleasant about oneself or others – usually an intimate secret.

LIPS
MOUTH
BEARD
165

LIPS are often a symbol of the female genitalia and may play a part in erotic dreams. These dreams may simply be enjoyable and have no covert meaning. A dream of a MOUTH may have a similar connotation, although the allusion may be to taking in nourishment (or love). It is also worth remembering that although a BEARD is often a symbol of virility, it can also refer to the anima, or female part of a man's personality (the mouth and lips symbolize the female genitalia).

GENITALS
146

A dream of GENITALS – if not a specifically sexual dream – may in a man be an allusion to general potency. What is he capable of in a universal sense? The allusion in women may be to menstruation, or to a desire to conceive. On the other hand, there may be a specific sexual allusion of which only the dreamer will be aware. A dream of castration (*see page 97*) reflects perhaps the most severe fear in men. The dream may be an allusion not merely to sexual virility, but to his whole sense of power and vigor. A woman dreaming of castrating a man clearly has a harsh desire to subdue him.

HAIR
146, 165

HAIR is an important sexual symbol for both sexes: in women, of their attractiveness to men; and in men of their virility. Being forcibly shaven in a

BALDNESS

dream – a symbol of castration (*see page 97*) – is a sign of subjugation – of being deprived of vigor, sex, or the very self. BALDNESS in both sexes may be seen as an anxiety dream – not only about losing your hair, but also about lack of intellect, or "bareness" of ideas.

BREASTS
BUTTOCKS

A man's dream of female BREASTS is most likely to be sexual, although perhaps maternal. Do you seek nurture or nourishment – not necessarily physical? For a woman, swollen breasts may be connected with a desire to bear children. A dream of breast-feeding is probably wish-fulfillment (*see page 150*); although you should consider who your baby may represent. A dream of being kicked in the BUTTOCKS is a clear signal of disapproval – perhaps self-disapproval. Dreams in which you are beaten or whipped can be straightforward sexual dreams, the result of a conscious or unconscious sexual appetite. This is an expression of your own inner nature, and perhaps one that should be explored. But who was beating you? Could this be an allusion to an ambitious colleague?

TEETH
95, 165
TOOTHACHE
STOMACH
BLISTER
95

Dreams in which you lose your TEETH, or they drop out, are among the most common. Almost everyone has such a dream at one time or another, and it is almost always associated with a concern with self-image; although it may sometimes reflect a fear of having spoken out of turn. Dreaming of a TOOTHACHE may, of course, be a signal that you need to visit your dentist. A dream of a STOMACH-ache may refer to your having to "stomach" something, and failing to do so. What is upsetting you or "giving you a pain"? If you dream that you have a BLISTER, consider which irritant may have raised it. If you burned yourself, have you gone too close to the fire – perhaps emotionally?

Sometimes we wake gasping from a dream, or seem unable to catch our breath. This can be a medical problem, and if it recurs you should consult your doctor. A dream about difficulty in

BREATHING BREATHING, unaccompanied by physical difficulty, may be an allusion to problems with life in general. In women it is sometimes an allusion to the animus or male part of their personality, in men to their maleness. Or do you simply need more air, space, or freedom?

DEFORMITY
94

A dream of having some sort of **DEFORMITY** is probably a self-critical dream, and its interpretation will depend on the form taken by the disfigurement.

PARALYSIS
155

In what way, in mind or body, are you at present disabled, or presenting a repugnant or frightening view of yourself to others? A dream of someone else's deformity may be showing you some repugnant aspect of their personality of which you have not been aware – or perhaps that you see in yourself. **PARALYSIS** in a dream is a symbol of disability, and may be a reference to an area of your life in which things have come to a standstill.

—◆— HEALTH —◆—

DREAMS IN WHICH our general well-being and health are a major theme may be commenting not only on our physical state, but also on our emotional condition. Such dreams also sum up our present condition and can help us achieve a more balanced personality.

KEEPING FIT A dream that you are KEEPING FIT by working out in some way may be commenting on the fact that you are under- or over-weight. Is there a perfect body inside you crying to be let out? If so, is your dream giving you the

necessary encouragement to do something about it? Obviously, you should also consider other elements in the dream. In your dream, were you trying to lift weights that were too heavy, or were you able to use them with

THE WORLD OF NATURE

FANTASY & FABLE

ARTS & SCIENCES

THE HUMAN BODY

BUILDINGS & INTERIORS

EVERYDAY THINGS

HUMAN EMOTIONS

HUMAN ACTIVITIES

HUMAN CONDITIONS

RITUALS & RELIGION

THE DREAM THESAURUS

THE WORLD
OF NATURE

FANTASY &
FABLE

ARTS &
SCIENCES

THE HUMAN
BODY

BUILDINGS &
INTERIORS

EVERYDAY
THINGS

HUMAN
EMOTIONS

HUMAN
ACTIVITIES

HUMAN
CONDITIONS

RITUALS &
RELIGION

THE DREAM
THESAURUS

considerable ease? Such a dream may be commenting on your psychological and emotional ability to face up to a task or project. It may also allude to the "weight" of the project itself.

DIET
106

A dream of a **DIET** may be referring to restriction of some kind in waking life. Food may have played a part in your dream (*see page 106*). In your dream, you may have been carefully measuring out the amount that you were allowing yourself to eat and drink, and perhaps longing for forbidden foods. In waking life, have you been measuring out your affection, or restricting the extent to which you are allowing your emotions to show? Are you holding back in the expression of your feelings? Conversely, if you broke your dream diet (with disastrous consequences) have you been allowing your feelings to run away with you in waking life?

HYGIENE
CLEANLINESS

In your dream, what were you trying to be **HYGIENIC** or **CLEAN** about? What made you feel dirty in the first place? Your dream may be commenting on your attitude toward sex, or perhaps on an unpleasant past experience, the memory of which you want to exorcise. It may also be making a statement about your physical condition. Do you have a build-up of toxins in your system, or are you suffering from constipation? Do you feel spiritually unclean in some way? Do you want to make a fresh clean start in life? (*See also Dirt, page 119.*)

DEFORMITY
93
CRIPPLE

It is disconcerting for a normally physically healthy person to dream that they are **DEFORMED** or have become **CRIPPLED** in some way. The most likely interpretation of such symbols is that you have been "crippled" by an emotional injury and are probably not in a position to do anything about it. Has someone in your waking life seriously hurt you? You should also be considering your self-esteem. Do you have a low opinion of yourself and your actions at present? Do you feel psychologically deformed? Perhaps your opinions or outlook on life

are somehow distorted. Remember that another crippled or deformed person in the dream could also represent you.

VITAMINS

If you dreamed that you were taking a large amount of **VITAMIN** pills, your dream may be commenting on the state of your health. Does your vitality need boosting? There is also a suggestion that you have been overindulgent. You may have dreamed that you were in a health shop and were trying to decide which vitamin would be best. If so, the choice probably represents a variety of possibilities facing you in waking life.

OXYGEN
48

If you were in need of **OXYGEN** in your dream, you were either too far under the blankets, or your dream was suggesting that you need more actual or metaphorical fresh air in your waking life.

SMOKING
CIGARETTE
136

If you are trying to give up smoking, it may be the case that many apparently unrelated dream symbols are focusing on your progress – or lack of it. It may be useful to consider this when interpreting your dreams during this period of your waking life. Perhaps you were having an escapist dream, in which you were **SMOKING** and enjoying your **CIGARETTE**. On the other hand, if you stubbed your dream cigarette out with determination or if it suddenly seemed repulsive to you, you are making good progress. The cigarette is also often a phallic symbol, and it could well be so in your dream.

CANCER
69

If you dream that you have **CANCER**, it is unlikely that you actually have the disease. However, if you are at all apprehensive you should have a medical checkup. It is far more likely that the cancer in your dream is representing a person or a problem that is "eating away" at you and gradually lowering your resistance. Try to work out what – or who – it may be. Alternatively, you may be aware of the characteristics of the Sun sign, Cancer (*see The Zodiac, page 69*), or you know someone who is a Cancerian. If so they – or what they represent – may be influencing your dream.

ILLNESS

A DREAM OF ILLNESS is often symbolic of other areas of our waking lives. However, dreams that emphasize certain areas of our bodies may herald symptoms that are not yet physically apparent. If you dream that you are in pain or have injured yourself, you should consider mentioning it to your doctor.

RASH
SORE
ECZEMA

RASHES, SORES, and ECZEMA are all unpleasant ailments that give discomfort and embarrassment without – usually – being too serious. What are you feeling uncomfortable about? What is causing you embarrassment or irritation? Are you "sore" about the way someone has treated you? Have you behaved without due consideration to other people?

COLD
BRUISE
BLISTER
92
STROKE

The most logical explanation of a dream COLD is that you awoke having kicked off your blankets and were literally feeling cold. A dream BRUISE may be reflecting some emotional hurt, although it may also indicate an emerging health problem. If your dream was of a BLISTER, you may need to rid yourself of an emotional problem. If you or someone else was having a STROKE in a dream, it may refer to an area of your life in which you feel frustrated, or are being prevented from taking action.

BLOOD
91
TRANSFUSION

Many women dreaming of BLOOD wake to discover that they have started menstruation. Otherwise, are you being bled financially or working so hard in waking life that you are under a great deal of stress, and your vitality is weakening as a result? If so, this is a dream warning not to be ignored. Receiving a dream blood TRANSFUSION may be suggesting that you are being revitalized in some way – perhaps by a new relationship or friendship.

VACCINATION
INJECTION
INOCULATION

Dreams of VACCINATION, INJECTION, or INOCULATION may relate to your sex life. The dream may be stating that you are being sensible and taking the necessary precautions, since both vaccination and inoculation are preventative measures.

Alternatively, is your dream warning you to be more cautious and take extra precautions? Against what? An injection, like a blood transfusion (*see above*) may signify someone or something new coming into your life.

DISEASE

Your dream of DISEASE may refer to some discomfort or uncertainty in your waking life. Someone in particular may be causing this condition. Is there someone in your life who is exerting too much power over you?

ANESTHETIC

To dream you are having an ANESTHETIC may be suggesting that you are trying to escape from reality. Even if it was administered by a doctor, refer to escapism (*page 136*). There may be something in your life that you want to get away from or forget – at least for a while. Are you in need of a vacation?

DENTIST
HOSPITAL
TEETH
92, 165
DOCTOR
NURSE

Many people fear visits to the DENTIST, and knowing one has to go into the HOSPITAL is often even more traumatic. When these symbols emerge in your dreams, they may be advising you to face up to reality and bravely take whatever is coming to you. As is the case with so many dreams that feature health (*see opposite*) or illness, they may be signaling the onset of a physical complaint, so it may be well for you to have a dental or medical checkup. Any dream featuring TEETH may have a variety of possible meanings and associations with waking life. Dentists and doctors are authority figures in dreams, so you should take the advice they offer. If you are attracted to your dream DOCTOR or NURSE, an element of wish-fulfillment (*see page 150*) may be entering into your dream.

THE WORLD OF NATURE

FANTASY & FABLE

ARTS & SCIENCES

THE HUMAN BODY

BUILDINGS & INTERIORS

EVERYDAY THINGS

HUMAN EMOTIONS

HUMAN ACTIVITIES

HUMAN CONDITIONS

RITUALS & RELIGION

THE DREAM THESAURUS

—EROTIC DREAMS—◆

OPENLY EROTIC DREAMS were a source of great anxiety to many 19th-century men and women, who believed them to cause physical and mental illness. Today, they are usually regarded as expressions of wish-fulfillment (*see page 150*) or as a means of releasing sexual tension.

PERVERSION PORNO-GRAPHY SADISM

It would be an oversimplification to suggest that all openly erotic dreams are the products of wish-fulfillment or sexual frustration. Some people find openly sexual dreams disturbing, especially when they seem to express a desire or PERVERSION of which we are not conscious in our waking life. For example, someone who dislikes the idea of homosexuality may find themselves aroused, in a dream, by a member of the same sex; puritans of either sex may find themselves enjoying PORNOGRAPHY; or someone who abhors the idea of SADISM may be involved, in a dream, in some kind of sadistic behavior. It is important to remember that our dreams are not inflicted upon us by anyone else – they are our *own* dreams. If, in a dream, we find ourselves enjoying some kind of sexual activity that is anathema to our waking selves, then there may be an implication that there is a small part of our being that is not as repelled by such behavior as we believe. Such a dream may be an appeal for understanding and a greater degree of relaxation about different types of sexual behavior than we may think ourselves capable of.

Unless erotic dreams are seriously disturbing (when psychiatric help should be sought) there is no reason not to enjoy them like any other sleeping fantasy.

—◆—NUDITY—◆—

DREAMS OF APPEARING NUDE or semi-nude in a public place are extremely common. They rarely have anything to do with sex; the emphasis is almost always on embarrassment, although occasionally there is a feeling of freedom from care.

EXPOSURE

The major question to ask yourself is why you were so EXPOSED in your dream. In what way, in waking life, are you too naive, too open, or not open enough? If your main feeling in the dream was one of embarrassment or horror, then you are obviously concerned that in some way you are too exposed. If, on the other hand, you were enjoying your freedom from clothes, you may need to be more open or more free from convention than you generally are in waking life, or you may long to be free of social formality. Nudity may also have some reference to complete honesty and truthfulness. You are concealing nothing in your dream, and perhaps you need to

NAKEDNESS

be equally forthright in waking life. You may dream that you are the only NAKED person in a crowd, but other people seem not to notice the fact. This may express the feeling that you are worried about being in some way "found out" – seen as you really are. Dreams that underline a feeling of embarrassment at appearing in public without clothes may reflect nervousness about communicating with other people. Men who dream of appearing in public without their trousers may be expressing doubts about their own sexual capability. Dreams of nudity may also be practical: a dream that you are naked in an airport may be reminding you to check your vacation suitcase.

THE WORLD OF NATURE

FANTASY & FABLE

ARTS & SCIENCES

THE HUMAN BODY

BUILDINGS & INTERIORS

EVERYDAY THINGS

HUMAN EMOTIONS

HUMAN ACTIVITIES

HUMAN CONDITIONS

RITUALS & RELIGION

THE DREAM THESAURUS

—◆— THE SHADOW —◆—

WE FREQUENTLY DREAM that someone is trying to break into our
home: they may be rattling the windows or battering at the door.
Very often the figure in the dream (who we hate or who frightens us)
is our Shadow – an important character in our dreams.

Humans are usually reluctant to recognize their own faults. We may be prepared to admit some venial defects – occasionally lying or losing our temper – but our deepest sins of character are buried so deeply in our unconscious that we almost automatically deny them. Jung believed that they are nevertheless shown to us, in our dreams, by a Shadow figure who represents everything about ourselves that we hate. In waking life, it is sometimes possible to identify someone's Shadow simply by asking them what sort of person they really despise.

Because our own deepest prejudices and vices are so thoroughly concealed, we are reluctant to recognize our Shadow even when he (or she, but the Shadow is usually in a male disguise) is presented to us in our dreams. We often displace responsibility by placing the traits we dislike on others' shoulders.

In Jungian analysis, dreamers are encouraged to find out more about their Shadow, to come to terms with him, and even to befriend him. He may well be someone you know in everyday life, or perhaps a well-known personality (we frequently recognize in prominent people personality traits that we despise but know we possess). We can, however, strive to know ourselves through the figure whose purpose seems to be to reflect all the worst aspects of our characters. This is a painful process, and one that is best done in analysis.

—◆— CASTRATION —◆—

AN OVERT DREAM OF CASTRATION will be extremely disturbing to any
man who has it; equally, any woman who dreams of castrating a man
is clearly expressing powerful emotions. Such dreams may be
sufficiently disturbing to be regarded as nightmares.

There are many possible symbols for the phallus: for example, one man may dream of someone cutting his necktie off, another of someone demolishing a spire, or of losing an arm-wrestling competition. It is important to consider the context of these dreams: who was "attacking," and in what way? Your own feelings as the dreamer are also highly significant: were you apprehensive, terrified, confident, or fearless? You should then consider what the waking problem might be. Sometimes the dream may relate to impotence or fear of it, and sometimes to a man's anxiety that he might not be able to satisfy a particular woman. The dream may also refer to a fear that someone wants to emasculate you – and not necessarily in a sexual context. The attack may be on your virility, or on your success at work or in sport, or allude to your apprehension that a colleague or rival may be "more of a man" than you and will show you as deprived of your pride and masculinity.

Although such a dream may be extremely significant, it may merely reflect a waking anxiety. Your feeling about the dream can be relied on to "place" it.

THE WORLD
OF NATURE

FANTASY &
FABLE

ARTS &
SCIENCES

THE HUMAN
BODY

BUILDINGS &
INTERIORS

EVERYDAY
THINGS

HUMAN
EMOTIONS

HUMAN
ACTIVITIES

HUMAN
CONDITIONS

RITUALS &
RELIGION

THE DREAM
THESAURUS

THE SPORTS CAR DREAM

" *I was driving an open sports car very fast along narrow, winding country roads. Although I was sitting in the car, I could see it from above at the same time. Ahead of me lay many sharp bends, busy crossroads, and traffic lights, but as the driver I was unconscious of these, and kept my foot hard down on the accelerator. I enjoyed skidding around the bends, and laughed as I crossed other lines of traffic and almost crashed. The atmosphere of the dream was enjoyable, and I did not really think that I could be hurt.*

After a while, I drove into a service station and filled up with gas, but instead of taking my hand off the lever of the pump when the car was full, I held on to it and the gas spilled all over the ground. There was someone smoking a cigarette nearby, and I thought 'I hope he doesn't drop a match.'

Instead of simply having an office, the service station was a house. I realized that it was my own house, and that the front door led straight into the bedroom. A mechanic came out of the bedroom; he was very macho, wearing overalls unbuttoned to the waist and a lot of cheap jewelery. I said, 'It's going to start raining. Put the convertible top up.' He replied, 'Don't be such a wimp — a little rain won't hurt you. Besides, this make of car doesn't have a top.' He then turned his attention to another car, and began to chat up the girls in it.

I started driving again, but as I tried to steer through difficult traffic it began to rain stones. They rattled onto the hood of the car, and some fell inside; I was afraid that one of the stones would hit me. From above, I saw the car heading for a T-junction and a cliff. The car was going too fast, and I thought, 'I can't possibly stop in time.' and woke up covered in perspiration. "

FRANK FILLS
CAR WITH
GAS

FRANK
ALMOST
CRASHES

FRANK DRIVES
VERY FAST

ROAD IS
NARROW AND
WINDING

MAN SMOKES
NEAR SPILT
GAS

MACHO MECHANIC
TALKS TO GIRLS

CAR HEADS FOR
T-JUNCTION

IT STARTS TO RAIN
STONES

INTERPRETATION

The car is an obvious sexual symbol in many ways: the man was in the driver's seat, the car's hood projected in front of him, and the engine was strong and powerful. Frank had a healthy sexual appetite, and had failed to take warnings about safe sex seriously; his attitude was "I've always been all right before." In the dream, his frequent philandering was represented by fast driving, but the fact that he unconsciously knew of the dangers was reflected by his overview of the narrow road with many hazards.

At the service station there was another symbol of Frank's devil-may-care attitude: he willfully spilled gas, regardless of danger (although he was conscious of the danger of fire – another symbol of sexual passion). In dreams we are not necessarily only ourselves: anything

or anyone in a dream can represent us. It is fairly clear that the macho motor mechanic was Frank's image of himself (he came out of Frank's bedroom), and even though he was a businessman – more at home in a suit than in overalls – he had secretly thought of himself as a more forceful character than he actually is.

It is not difficult to see that the convertible top of the car represents a condom, which the macho half of Frank believes to be unnecessary, and which he usually does not carry. Stones threatened him, which the top would have deflected, and he saw an accident ahead.

This is a typical "warning" dream: Frank is aware that the lifestyle he is leading is potentially dangerous. There may be a hint (when the mechanic chats up the girls) that he realizes the potential danger to others.

— BUILDINGS —

BUILDINGS IN DREAMS often represent the body or personality of the dreamer, or of the lovers or family of the dreamer. A building may also represent the intellect or understanding: people about to begin new work may dream of exploring new, unfamiliar rooms in a well-known house. These rooms represent unexplored potential.

In many cases, dreams about exploring buildings are encouraging us to start a journey of exploration into our own personalities or to resolve an ongoing psychological problem. Above all, our unconscious is telling us that we must make more of our attributes and talents. In other words, our dreams are probably informing us that we are ready to develop in some way – perhaps creatively or physically. This is particularly appropriate when, in a dream, we are exploring a building we know well, but in which we find unfamiliar rooms.

DOOR
101, 103, 153
WINDOW
101
**BALCONY
HOUSE**
101, 161

Buildings in dreams contain certain obvious symbols. For example, they have openings that may represent the openings of the body: a **DOOR** may signify a mouth, **WINDOWS** may symbolize eyes, and breasts may be represented by **BALCONIES**. A dilapidated **HOUSE** may suggest a

personality or body in search of better health; while a fine house may signify someone that holds themselves in proper self-regard. A house under attack may suggest a body or mind under threat (who or what was trying to break in?). If the house in your dream is familiar, the reference may be to the building itself, and have a literal application: so if you dream of an electrical fault in your own house, you could check the wiring.

**CAFE
CHURCH**
180
**ABBEY
CHAPEL**
180
**MANSION
PALACE**

The kind of building that appears in a dream will be significant. A dream of a **CAFE** may have a bearing on your diet (was food being delivered or rejected?). A **CHURCH**, **ABBEY**, **CHAPEL**, or other religious building suggests that religion or morals lie at the heart of the dream. If you are at home in a **MANSION** or **PALACE** and you are conscious of its grandeur, you are clearly interested in your status – as you may be if your home was a

THE WORLD
OF NATURE

FANTASY &
FABLE

ARTS &
SCIENCES

THE HUMAN
BODY

BUILDINGS &
INTERIORS

EVERYDAY
THINGS

HUMAN
EMOTIONS

HUMAN
ACTIVITIES

HUMAN
CONDITIONS

RITUALS &
RELIGION

THE DREAM
THESAURUS

BUNGALOW
CASTLE
HOTEL

less imposing place. Did you feel content or discontent in your dream? If you were living in a **BUNGALOW** in your dream, there may be a suggestion that your life is being lived too much on one level, practically or emotionally. Was your **CASTLE** under siege, and if so by whom? A **HOTEL** is open to everyone: are you being sufficiently hospitable? Consider carefully how you reacted to your surroundings. Were you intimidated by them, or did you feel at home? If the former, your dream may be telling you to restrain yourself a little – that ideas or projects in your waking life are beyond your present ability. The latter reaction is reassuring.

FACTORY
116
BARRACKS
CANTEEN

The building in your dream may not be a domestic house; it may be a **FACTORY**, for instance. What reference may this have to your work or workplace, or what you are making of your life? A dream of being confined in a **BARRACKS** may be a warning that your life is too restricted, and that you are too much under the influence of authority. Being in a **CANTEEN** immediately suggests a connection with food (*see page 106*) and probably a reference to your emotional life.

BRIDGE
CAMPER
CONSER-
VATORY
LIGHTHOUSE
121

A dream of a **BRIDGE** may suggest that you should be bridge-building in waking life; for example, mending a relationship. If you were crossing a dream bridge, it may signify that you are moving from one phase of your life to the next. A dream of living in a **CAMPER** may suggest that it is time to move on in waking life, or it may reflect a worrying temporary aspect of your life. A **CONSERVATORY** may imply that you have something to hide, or even that you are being too frank and open. Perhaps some light has been thrown on a particular problem, or an idea has suddenly become "as clear as day." If you dream that you are living in a **LIGHTHOUSE**, to whom should you send an urgent message or warning? Dreams in which you are wandering around in a house have another significance. If you are thinking about or starting a new project, you may dream of exploring previously unknown rooms. The

ANNEX

discovery of a previously unsuspected room (*see page 103*) may indicate the discovery of a new idea. Planning or altering a house, or building an **ANNEX**, may refer to a change to your lifestyle or your approach to life.

HOUSE
100, 161

HOUSES can be forbidding places; being worried by a dream of foreboding (especially in a house that you know) suggests that something is troubling you about your body or personality. Consciousness of a particular part of the house may provide a clue (*see above*). It is fairly common to dream of returning to a house that you knew in the past. Your reaction to the house in your dream and your waking feelings about it are crucial; the dream may be a nostalgic reminder, or it may reflect your wish to return to childhood innocence. If you dreamed of leaving home, the message may be that you are ready to move on in your waking life – perhaps in your career.

STAIRCASE
PASSAGE
SPIRE
OBELISK
ENTRANCE
CHIMNEY
DOOR
100, 103, 153
WINDOW
100
WALL

Dreams of ascending or descending a **STAIRCASE** are often found to have a sexual basis, especially for men; however, there could also obviously be a reference to ambition or general progress in life. A dream of a **PASSAGE** may suggest transition (perhaps private or secret); dreaming of a **SPIRE** may indicate pride or aspiration; an **OBELISK** in a dream is likely to be a phallic symbol; while a secret room (*see page 103*) or **ENTRANCE** may be a female sexual reference. A **CHIMNEY** in a dream may be a phallic symbol, particularly if it was a tall factory chimney. Was it being felled or standing upright? Dreaming of a blocked **DOOR** may signify the repression of speech or expression; and blocked **WINDOWS** the denial of sight – or a determination not to see. What is being hidden from you, or are you hiding from others? **WALLS** support the whole fabric of a building; if they were unsafe or falling down, there may be a serious comment on the fabric of your waking life.

CELLAR

Dreams of a **CELLAR** are often trying to deliver significant messages about the deepest regions of your unconscious.

THE WORLD
OF NATURE

FANTASY &
FABLE

ARTS &
SCIENCES

THE HUMAN
BODY

BUILDINGS &
INTERIORS

EVERYDAY
THINGS

HUMAN
EMOTIONS

HUMAN
ACTIVITIES

HUMAN
CONDITIONS

RITUALS &
RELIGION

THE DREAM
THESAURUS

—✦— HOME —✦—

A DREAM OF HOME often relates to our sense of emotional or financial security. You may be nostalgic for the past, and from such dreams you may learn how to relate the past to your present life, or life in the future. It is common for elderly people to dream of their childhood home, especially if their early family life was happy.

FURNITURE A dream in which you were moving FURNITURE around, or trying to make it fit into a small space, may be reflecting on the way you are trying to cope with the many problems in your waking life. You may be attempting to "fit everything in." If in your dream you arranged things to your liking, the chances are that you have your everyday life under control. Perhaps you dreamed of a favorite piece of furniture? If so, who uses it most frequently? That particular piece of furniture may symbolize that person, or what they represent in your mind.

CUSHION A dream of a CUSHION may be suggesting ways of protecting yourself – but from what? Is there something unpleasant that you have to face up to in waking life? On the other hand, if you simply relaxed into a beautiful cushion, you may be feeling secure – in your relationship or in a more material sense. The color of the cushion may be significant (*see page 75*).

CURTAINS DRAPES Closing the CURTAINS or DRAPES in a dream may mean that you do not want to face up to a problem, or that you simply do not want to know what is going on. Alternatively, it may indicate that you are being secretive and do not want other people to know how you are feeling or reacting. Try to think about the view outside, or what was facing you when you turned around from the curtains. How did you feel about these things in your dream?

GUEST *175* If you dreamed that you had GUESTS in your home, much of the analysis will depend on how you felt about them. Did you welcome them with open arms, or

— DREAM ANALYSIS —

"I constantly dream that I am moving the furniture around in my tiny room to make a proper space for my word processor. I am not usually successful."

Glynys, a novelist, has less space than she would like in her home. This dream, however, is actually referring to the difficulties she has when she must divide her time equally between her home and domestic commitments and her writing career.

were you reluctant to let them in because they frightened you in some way? Did they cross your doorstep? The welcome guest may represent the beginning of an important and fascinating new project; the dream may be suggesting that you are now ready to begin work. The unwelcome guest may be something – or someone – you do not want to face up to. However, having decided what the guest represents in your waking life, consider whether you should accept this unwanted responsibility. You may soon receive more help from other dreams.

NEIGHBORS In waking life, NEIGHBORS can either be a tremendous help or a total nuisance. Your dream of them may simply be practical and helpful, hinting at what you can do to help them or – if they are noisy or nosy – to shut them up. You should also consider whether there is someone or something important to you that requires some attention.

RENT MORTGAGE If you dream of worrying about being unable to pay the RENT or MORTGAGE when this is not a problem in waking life, your dreams may be focusing on a heavy burden that is troubling you.

◆ ROOMS ◆

DISCOVERING A NEW ROOM in your home is a particularly
interesting dream symbol, since it is often a powerful
indication of the state of your whole personality. It is
more common for women to dream of discovering a new
room than men – particularly when they have
reached times of change in their lives.

If you dreamed that you opened a
cupboard door, not to find the usual
contents but that it opened out into an
empty room or a room you were not
aware of, you have experienced a
common but important dream image.
Your dream is implying that you are
ready for new experiences, and that you
should accept fresh challenges. There
may be something you have always wanted
to do – perhaps start a small business or
learn a new skill. If so, your dream may
be suggesting that the time is right.

DOOR
100, 101, 153

In a dream featuring DOORS, whether
they were opening or closing is the most
important factor. It is, therefore, easy to
relate such a dream to your waking life.
It is important to consider whether you
are shutting something out of your life
or whether you are being warned by
your dreams to "shut up." Perhaps as one
dream door is closing, another is
opening. Does this have any bearing
on your present situation? It may be
particularly relevant if you were
changing jobs, for instance. If you were
the door and it was in a poor state, does
this reflect your physical condition?

DINING ROOM

You may have dreamed that you were
setting the table in the DINING ROOM. The
accent on preparation may be reflecting
some kind of important preparation for a
special event, or your reaching a decision
in your waking life. If you were eating a
meal in the dream the accent will be on
food (*see page 106*).

OFFICE
116
KITCHEN

The OFFICE and the KITCHEN are places of
work and activity, where a great deal of
energy – physical and emotional – is

spent. If your dream features either of
these rooms, is your unconscious
focusing on your lifestyle and your
concerns? In your dream, are you being
told to "get out of the kitchen"? If so, you
may be interfering with things that are no
concern of yours. You should think about
your routine and the pace of your life;
these may well need reviewing.

**LIVING
ROOM
BEDROOM**

The LIVING ROOM and the BEDROOM are
rooms in which we need to feel
comfortable, relaxed, and secure.
Dreaming of either of these rooms may
be a reflection on how secure and
comfortable we are feeling with
ourselves and with life in general. The
bedroom is also the place where we
make love most frequently, therefore
your dream may be commenting on your
sex life. Perhaps you were making your
bed in the dream? If so, and you are not
enjoying a rewarding
relationship or sex
life, there may be
an element of
wish-fulfillment
(*see page 150*) in
your dream.

THE WORLD
OF NATURE

FANTASY &
FABLE

ARTS &
SCIENCES

THE HUMAN
BODY

BUILDINGS &
INTERIORS

EVERYDAY
THINGS

HUMAN
EMOTIONS

HUMAN
ACTIVITIES

THE WELL DREAM

"*I was peering down, fascinated, into a well. I was frightened but knew that I had to dive down into the deep, clear water. I undressed, left my clothes on the ground and plunged into the well. I was driven by a desire to swim down into the depths of the well. However, what I thought was simply dark, deep water was actually a heavy, sticky substance — like molasses or black treacle — and I was unable to penetrate the surface.*

Eventually, I was able to dive, and with considerable difficulty swam further and further down below the surface. What had been a vertical well now became a horizontal tunnel, and after a while I discovered that my feet were on the ground, although I was still forcing my way through the heavy, tacky liquid. This liquid gradually became shallower and less sticky, and I eventually waded out of the tunnel and found myself in a huge underground cavern, with stalactites hanging from the ceiling. I touched one of the stalactites and it melted away. Then I saw stalagmites growing up from the floor and being fed from the ceiling with drips of water and blood. The stalagmites were firm to the touch. I was aware of three doors in the curved wall of the cavern. Over the top of each door was a dog's head. A voice said 'Open the doors.' I first opened the door above which was a dog's head turning to the left, where I saw a child crying. I did not want to have anything to do with him. Then I opened the door underneath the dog's head turning to the right. Beyond it was blue sky that dazzled me, and I found it frightening, so I closed the door quickly; but I could still see light shining through the portal. I went to the central door — underneath the dog's head that faced forward — and upon opening it discovered a vast space. I walked through the door. In one corner was a pile of bricks. The voice said 'Build a house.' I replied that I did not know how. 'Yes, you do!' was the answer.

I mixed some cement, but it melted like ice cream. 'Put some nuts in it,' said the voice. I tried again and seemed to be more successful. I became hungry, so I ate some of the gritty, nutty ice cream and felt satisfied. Then a woman appeared carrying a tiny prefabricated roof. 'It won't fit,' I cried. 'It's up to you to make it fit,' she replied. Then I woke up."

DEEP WATER IS
LIKE MOLASSES

WOMAN APPEARS
CARRYING ROOF

CEMENT MELTS
LIKE ICE CREAM

INTERPRETATION

Terry was already into analysis when he had this dream. It has a great many interesting and relevant symbols, some of which are repeated – an indication that an important message was communicating itself. Terry had had a restricted and unhappy childhood, and as a result had encountered sexual problems. He was a lonely and emotionally unfulfilled man who found it difficult to relate to either men or women. He had been apprehensive but willing to go into analysis, so at the outset of the dream he sheds his clothes (he was ready to "bare all") and is about to plunge into the well of his unconscious. He soon realized that the process of analysis was more difficult than he had imagined. The water (representing emotion) that he thought was just deep and dark, turned out to be almost impenetrable. He was being held back in the process of analysis, but the situation eased as the analysis progressed, and this was depicted by the way he waded out of the treacle.

Terry then found himself in the large cavern. Here, we find a different kind of water symbol – that of the melting stalactites. This was probably a phallic symbol

describing impotence. However, this was at once followed by the more positive stalagmites, suggesting that he would probably overcome this problem. Terry eventually realized that the dogs' heads were of mythological origin. Although the three heads were not attached to one dog, they were a depiction of Cerberus – whose heads looked to the past (the left), the future (the right), and the present (straight ahead). The child was himself; he had turned his back on the past, and although he was not ready to face the future, he entered through the door representing the present.

The voice in his dream was that of authority – in this case representing his female analyst. Emotions were depicted by the symbolic ice cream, and while it melted he was shown that he needed greater inner strength – as shown by the addition of the nuts.

The last sequence of the dream, the presentation of the roof for his house by the woman (again his analyst), told him that he must develop further in order to be in a position to put the roof on his house. In other words, to grow in confidence and psychological wholeness.

STALACTITES HANG FROM CEILING

BLUE SKY IS DAZZLING

—◆— FOOD AND DRINK —◆—

SINCE FOOD AND DRINK are so important to us, it is not surprising that we are often engaged in eating and drinking in our dreams. This may simply be because we are hungry, but more often these dreams present us with symbols — often comforting ones — referring to other appetites, for example sexual, spiritual, or intellectual.

EATING DRINKING

Whatever we are EATING and DRINKING in a dream may represent something that we want to possess. It may represent a need for affection, or for nourishment of the senses or the mind. The symbolism may be almost blatant — particularly where sexual needs are concerned.

The type of food that featured in the dream is important. Was it enjoyable? Was it soft, warm, and comforting, or acidic, tart, and stimulating? Was it poisonous? Why do you think you were eating it? Were you being forcibly fed, and protesting, or was the food being withheld from you? Recognizing the context, you must then attempt to relate the particular type of food or drink to an appetite or desire in waking life.

CEREAL CROISSANT CASSEROLE STEW

There is quite frequently an important significance. CEREAL or a CROISSANT, for instance, may refer to breakfast, and so to a "beginning" of some kind; while a CASSEROLE or STEW may represent a pool of ideas, or some plans that have been quietly cooking away.

FIG
54
MANDRAKE SUCKING LICKING

Dreams of eating often seem to have a sexual implication, and the very actions of love also reflect the allusion. The ancients believed certain types of fruits and vegetables to be aphrodisiacs simply because of their shapes, and these associations have lasted through the ages. In art, the FIG has often been used to symbolize the vagina, and the MANDRAKE the male genitals; these two symbols inevitably also appear in dreams. Your physical actions in the dream will also be significant: generally, both SUCKING and LICKING are more likely to imply a sexual

BITING CHEWING

background to the dream than BITING and CHEWING. Freud insisted that dreams of fruit were always dreams of women's breasts, although they may allude to "the larger hemispheres of the female body" — the buttocks.

HUNGER
130

Dreams of desperately seeking or eating food, even of yourself being food for some animal, may emphasize an unspoken statement that you have voracious appetites, or that you have more to give than others may realize. HUNGER may be literal: for example, prisoners deprived of food have told of dreams of luscious feasts. The hunger may be a symbolic cry for love, or power or status; the context of the dream should provide a key.

ABSTINENCE DIET
94
GLUTTONY

The following are clues to the possible interpretation of dreams of food, but it is important to remember that your dreams are your own, and no one can provide an infallible reference. A dream of ABSTINENCE may suggest that you have been overdoing things. In waking life, have you been trying to "take in" too much or cope with too much work? If you dream that you are on a DIET, you may be telling yourself to limit an emotional involvement, or pare away unnecessary anxieties. A dream of GLUTTONY may well hint that you are expending too much emotion in a particular situation, or simply overdoing

THE WORLD OF NATURE

FANTASY & FABLE

ARTS & SCIENCES

THE HUMAN BODY

BUILDINGS & INTERIORS

EVERYDAY THINGS

HUMAN EMOTIONS

HUMAN ACTIVITIES

HUMAN CONDITIONS

RITUALS & RELIGION

THE DREAM THESAURUS

LEFTOVERS

things in waking life, either emotionally or physically. Perhaps you are showing too much fervor where a rather more moderate approach would be more productive. A dream that you are eating **LEFTOVERS**, on the other hand, may well suggest that you are losing out in some way. In waking life, are you subsisting on the "leftovers" of someone's affection? Similarly, are you accepting a smaller salary than you feel you deserve?

APPLE
54
LEMON

In dreams, the **APPLE** is often seen as a symbol of wrongdoing, dating back to the apple offered to Adam. In waking life, who, or what, has tempted you? A dream of sucking a **LEMON** may be a bitter experience. What are you being forced to tolerate in your waking life?

BANQUET
DINNER

Dreaming that you are attending either a **BANQUET** or a **DINNER** may be a reference to comfort or luxury. Were you enjoying the occasion, or were you thinking guiltily of those less fortunate than you?

SAUCE
CUSTARD

Rich **SAUCES** and **CUSTARD** enhance food, and dreaming of them may imply that you are in special need of nourishment in

BUTTER
CREAM

waking life. **BUTTER** and **CREAM** in dreams contain similar meanings. However, if the food was cloying and nauseating to you, there may be a suggestion that your life is too full of emotional affluence.

BREAD
EGGS
OMELETTE

Bread is traditionally the most basic of foods – a symbol of life itself. A dream in which **BREAD** features may well be a reference to money, particularly to your income (which supplies your family's needs). In Christian mythology, bread plays an important role – your need may be for spiritual nurture. **EGGS** are also important symbols of life, and for some women there may be a reference to conception. A dream of breaking eggs (perhaps making an **OMELETTE**) may be one of necessary sacrifice, although the eggshell can represent a skin of falsehood through which you must break to get at the truth of a situation or emotion.

ICE CREAM

Dreams of **ICE CREAM** may be telling you to keep cool, to "cool it," or that some situation is "cool." You must therefore consider what proposed actions of yours may need restraint, or what situation may be less threatening than you think.

THE WORLD OF NATURE

FANTASY & FABLE

ARTS & SCIENCES

THE HUMAN BODY

BUILDINGS & INTERIORS

EVERYDAY THINGS

HUMAN EMOTIONS

HUMAN ACTIVITIES

HUMAN CONDITIONS

RITUALS & RELIGION

THE DREAM THESAURUS

THE WORLD OF NATURE

FANTASY & FABLE

ARTS & SCIENCES

THE HUMAN BODY

BUILDINGS & INTERIORS

EVERYDAY THINGS

HUMAN EMOTIONS

HUMAN ACTIVITIES

HUMAN CONDITIONS

RITUALS & RELIGION

THE DREAM THESAURUS

**JAM
CURRY
GINGER
OYSTER
MUSSEL**

Sweet or spicy foods such as **JAM**, **CURRY**, or **GINGER** may imply that you need more sweetness or stimulation in your life; while someone dreaming of **OYSTERS** or **MUSSELS** may feel that their libido is in need of stimulation.

MENU

To dream of studying a **MENU** could indicate that you have multiple choices in some areas of your waking life. Were you decisive, confused, or worried in the dream situation? This may be a comment on your waking attitude toward the decision you must make.

COFFEE

While food may well refer to both the physical and emotional aspects of waking life, drink seems most often to refer to the emotions. A dream of a sweet drink may imply that you yearn for more affection and love in your waking life; while dreaming of a strong drink such as espresso **COFFEE** may suggest a need for

**TEA
ALCOHOL
HANGOVER**

additional energy, or else for a stronger approach to a situation or problem. For many people, a dream of a cup of **TEA** could indicate a need for relaxation. Dreams of **ALCOHOL** can be difficult to interpret; much will depend on whether your attitude toward it in waking life is one of approval or disapproval. There could be a warning to take it easy; or, conversely, a suggestion that in some way your waking life needs some stimulation. Alcohol is a stimulant, so there may be a suggestion that you need rather more excitement in your waking life – unless you had over-indulged. Were you drunk with success? A dream of a **HANGOVER** may well be a comment on overindulgence.

MILK

Like bread and eggs, **MILK** is a very basic food, and a dream of it may contain a reference to some deep-seated need. For women, a dream of feeding milk to a child may refer to a desire for children.

—◆—CONTAINERS—◆—

WE KEEP THINGS SAFE in containers. They may be secret places, or they may be used when we want to move from one place to another. Such dreams often comment on hidden areas of our psyche, and sometimes on personality traits that we would like to deny.

BAG
109
BAGGAGE

Your dream **BAG** or **BAGGAGE** may be making a comment on your burdens and responsibilities in waking life. Perhaps you picked up your dream bag and then discovered that it was either lighter than you expected or so heavy that you were unable to lift it. If the latter, you should ask yourself whether you can carry on your present lifestyle, which may be becoming too much for you. In your dream, you may have been putting things

into your bag, or even stealing a bag. In waking life, are you being avaricious or taking too much from other people and not contributing your fair share?

JUG
POT
73

A cracked **JUG** or **POT** was for centuries a symbol of lost virginity, and although you may not have been at all conscious of the allusion, it could still appear in your dreams complete with its very ancient significance. If liquid was spilling from the jug, your dream may be suggesting that you are wasting your emotion, or else that your feelings for someone are overwhelming you. If, on the other hand, the contents were safe in your pot or jug, your dream may be reassuring you that you are in control of your emotions. A woman dreaming of creating a pot may be thinking about having a child.

TRUNK
51
BOX

A trunk is used to store large items, or may be packed to send away. Because your dream **TRUNK** is likely to be a part of you, whether you are opening or closing the lid is important. In either case, you may be on a voyage of self-discovery: you may be unfolding as yet undeveloped potential, or disposing of unwanted or undesirable elements in your waking life. A similar interpretation can apply to a dream of a **BOX**, but the mythological Pandora's box must also be considered. When Pandora opened the box, evil was released into the world. Your dream box may be encouraging you to be more self-controlled, to accept things as they are, and to resist temptation.

CAR TRUNK
BAG
108

A dream that you are packing a **CAR TRUNK** may be making a statement about your sex life. It may also refer to a secret that you are intent on keeping. If you were filling a **BAG** in a dream, there could be a suggestion that you should dispose of some garbage in your waking life. However, was the garbage in the dream to be recycled or simply thrown away?

LUGGAGE

Dreaming of **LUGGAGE** may relate to burdens you must carry in waking life, although there may be a reference to a vacation you may need – especially if, in the dream, you leave the luggage behind.

HANDBAG
WALLET

The **HANDBAG** and **WALLET** – and their contents – represent items that are personal and important to us. A dream featuring either item may, for women, be a sexual symbol (representing the vagina), so a dream of losing your wallet or handbag may be a warning. Wallets contain money and credit cards, and such symbols may sometimes relate to the way we express our love. Are you letting your love "go down the drain," or are you being overly possessive?

ENVELOPE

If you dreamed of an **ENVELOPE**, did you open it carefully or apprehensively, or did you tear it open, anxious to read its contents? It is difficult to separate an envelope from its message. Were you the envelope in the dream, about to tell someone something, or do you want to keep your secret?

—◆— UTENSILS —◆—

MANY EVERYDAY UTENSILS are essential to the smooth running of our lives, so dreams that feature them may be concerned with whatever we have on hand in our waking lives.

BROOM
52
SCISSORS

If you were using a new **BROOM** in a dream, you may be attempting to make a "clean sweep" in your waking life. The dream may be telling you to rid yourself of a particular part of the past, which may be symbolized by what you were sweeping up. If, in your dream, you were cutting something cleanly with **SCISSORS**, it would seem that you are in good control of your present situation in waking life and you are being decisive. The scissors may represent an extension of your own personality, since they are the utensil you were actually using in your dream. You should then try to consider what you were cutting and what that symbol represents.

FORK
115
SPOON

If both a **FORK** and a **SPOON** appeared in your dream, they may well represent the masculine and feminine elements of your personality, and your dream may be referring to your sexuality and how you express and keep in balance these two contrasting areas. If the fork appeared in the dream on its own, perhaps you are trying to probe, or to get to the root of, a tricky problem in your waking life. If a spoon was featured in the dream and you were looking into it and perhaps seeing a distorted picture of yourself or some object, you may have a distorted view of yourself or your opinions. If you were spooning up some liquid (consider your present emotional state) or some other

THE WORLD OF NATURE

FANTASY & FABLE

ARTS & SCIENCES

THE HUMAN BODY

BUILDINGS & INTERIORS

EVERYDAY THINGS

HUMAN EMOTIONS

HUMAN ACTIVITIES

HUMAN CONDITIONS

RITUALS & RELIGION

THE DREAM THESAURUS

THE WORLD
OF NATURE

FANTASY &
FABLE

ARTS &
SCIENCES

THE HUMAN
BODY

BUILDINGS &
INTERIORS

EVERYDAY
THINGS

HUMAN
EMOTIONS

HUMAN
ACTIVITIES

HUMAN
CONDITIONS

RITUALS &
RELIGION

THE DREAM
THESAURUS

substance, you may be able to relate your dream spoon to something or someone in waking life that you want to protect, cherish, or hold on to. Did the spoon contain some unpleasant medicine? If so, you may be accepting an unpleasant or difficult situation in waking life, or you may have to swallow your pride.

SCREW If you were using **SCREWS** in your dream, you may have been involved in mending or making something. This dream could be referring to some creative work or to a certain project you are planning. Did everything in the dream fit together neatly? If so, you are obviously making good progress in your waking life and your dream is reassuring you.

PIN
114
NEEDLE
115
If a **PIN** appears in your dream, you may be trying to "pin down" a specific problem or person in your waking life. Alternatively, are you confused about a particular issue? If the pin in your dream fell out, you may be feeling insecure about something in waking life. A pin or a **NEEDLE** could also be a phallic symbol in a dream. If we prick ourselves we may bleed, so lost virginity or a physical or emotional injury caused by a partner in our waking lives may also be the object of these symbols.

RAZOR When we shave we get rid of unwanted hair. A dream featuring a **RAZOR** could be suggesting that you should dispense with something in your waking life – perhaps an unattractive characteristic. If, in your dream, you were trimming your beard or tidying the short hair at the back of your neck, there may be an element of fear of castration.

—✦— MONEY —✦—

MONEY GIVES US SECURITY, but generosity or meanness with it may reflect on our ability to give and express love for our fellows. When money and its associations emerge in our dreams we should consider whether they are commenting on our waking attitudes.

CHECK
COIN
Writing a **CHECK** is a deliberate and calculated action, so your attitude in such a dream is important. If you wrote a check in your dream, knowing that your account was empty, you may be nursing some guilt feelings in waking life. These may relate to money or perhaps to your recent actions toward your partner. Were **COINS** running through your

fingers in the dream? Are you being extravagant or silly in waking life? Are you wasting time and love on someone who is not worthy of it? Your dream may be warning you to be more prudent.

MISER If your dream features a **MISER**, that character could well be you. You should ask yourself whether you are being at all miserly in waking life, always taking from others and not giving in return. The

BEGGAR

BEGGAR in your dream could also be you, and the focus will be an area of your personality or sphere of your life that is in some way deficient. Perhaps there is an emptiness in your emotional life. Do you lack intellectual challenge?

DEBT

What was the DEBT in your dream? In waking life, it may represent something that you owe yourself; for example, more time to yourself. It may also be a symbol that your loved ones owe you something; for example, more consideration, respect, or love. Conversely, are you in debt to your friends or family?

ADMISSION

A dream in which you were refused ADMISSION to a place because you did not have enough money to pay for your entry, may signify frustration in waking life. You may be unable to move forward because of an obstructing circumstance or someone's interference. You may also like to consider whether you are blocking your own way forward, whether some deep-rooted inhibition is holding up your progress. In that case, your dream may be suggesting that you need more money (here, money may symbolize self-confidence) to "get through."

WAGE SALARY

Dreaming of a WAGE or SALARY may represent your potential in waking life. How you spent your wage or salary in the dream may be a reflection on how you are developing your abilities in waking life, and may be suggesting how you can improve and further develop your attributes. The income may represent the work itself, or else the achievement toward which you are battling. Wages are also tokens of a job well done; your dream may be reminding you that you have cause to feel satisfied with what you have already achieved.

BANK

In your dream, if you were going into a BANK and depositing money, you are probably feeling secure in waking life. Your dream may be reassuring, but it may also be highly influenced by wish-fulfillment (*see page 150*). There is also a possibility that what you were banking represents something that you are storing within yourself. Are you withholding emotion? Should you confront someone?

INVESTMENT

Making an INVESTMENT in a dream, as in waking life, suggests an outlay of some kind, in which there is always an element of risk involved. It should not be difficult to interpret this particular symbol; you may be taking a risk in waking life – probably of the emotional kind. On the other hand, you may be investing in your own potential and starting a new interest or enterprise. Your dream may well be guiding and warning you, and summing up your present attitude and situation.

THE WORLD OF NATURE

FANTASY & FABLE

ARTS & SCIENCES

THE HUMAN BODY

BUILDINGS & INTERIORS

EVERYDAY THINGS

HUMAN EMOTIONS

HUMAN ACTIVITIES

HUMAN CONDITIONS

RITUALS & RELIGION

THE DREAM THESAURUS

THE BALLOON MAN DREAM

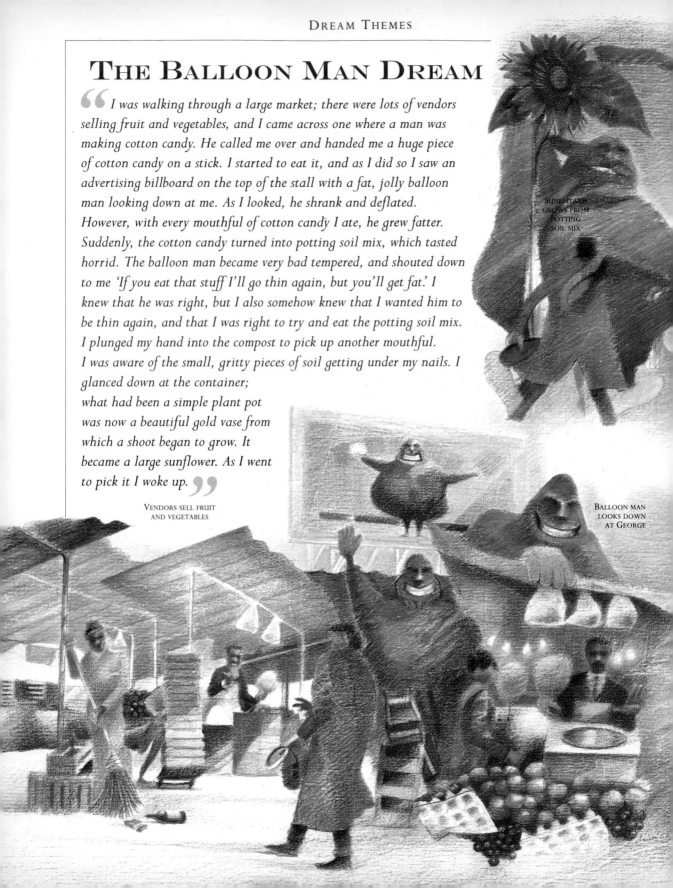

I was walking through a large market; there were lots of vendors selling fruit and vegetables, and I came across one where a man was making cotton candy. He called me over and handed me a huge piece of cotton candy on a stick. I started to eat it, and as I did so I saw an advertising billboard on the top of the stall with a fat, jolly balloon man looking down at me. As I looked, he shrank and deflated. However, with every mouthful of cotton candy I ate, he grew fatter. Suddenly, the cotton candy turned into potting soil mix, which tasted horrid. The balloon man became very bad tempered, and shouted down to me 'If you eat that stuff I'll go thin again, but you'll get fat.' I knew that he was right, but I also somehow knew that I wanted him to be thin again, and that I was right to try and eat the potting soil mix. I plunged my hand into the compost to pick up another mouthful. I was aware of the small, gritty pieces of soil getting under my nails. I glanced down at the container; what had been a simple plant pot was now a beautiful gold vase from which a shoot began to grow. It became a large sunflower. As I went to pick it I woke up.

SUNFLOWER GROWS FROM POTTING SOIL MIX

VENDORS SELL FRUIT AND VEGETABLES

BALLOON MAN LOOKS DOWN AT GEORGE

INTERPRETATION

COTTON CANDY
TURNS INTO
POTTING SOIL MIX

BALLOON MAN
GROWS FATTER

George had great difficulty in maintaining relationships. He had been on the lists of several dating agencies, to no avail, because when he met a woman he would brag, show off, and pretend to be someone quite other than himself. This tendency was due to a lack of self-confidence, resulting from living in the shadow of an older brother who was smarter and better looking than he. George was in fact a nice, practical, reliable person, with many down-to-earth qualities. The accent on food in his dream represented the love and affection that he craved. George being in a dream market reflected the fact that he was "shopping around" for a partner. It is interesting, however, that he ignored the delicious fruit, vegetables, and meat that would have given him real sustenance; he was, instead, attracted to the sweet, ephemeral cotton candy.

The man who offered it to him was a symbol of his brother. This was summing up George's problems in relation to his brother very clearly.

The balloon advertisement man was George himself, and his comments to George were showing him that he was simply an inflated bag of air that could become deflated at the slightest provocation. If he continued along his unproductive path of trying to find a partner, his odds for meeting with success were not at all good. George wanted to discover a new way to true love – hence his dislike of the balloon man, and his equal dislike, but awareness of, the message. The dream was telling him to come down to earth and be more sensible. In the dream he did this by making himself eat the unpleasant-tasting potting soil mix, which got under his nails and irritated him as much as it nauseated him.

The sunflower in its pot that turned to gold also represented George – the new George. It was a powerful symbol of hope and rebirth, showing him the potential rewards of becoming more true to himself.

This dream seemed meaningless at first, and George had to work hard to believe that the balloon man did, in fact, represent himself. However, once he recognized the salesman as symbolizing his brother, the dream began to make more sense to him; and the moment he associated himself with the balloon man, the word "deflated" came into his mind, and the connection became even clearer.

JEWELRY

MOST DREAMS INVOLVING fine jewelry are pleasant and reassuring, and often have a basis in wish-fulfillment (*see page 150*). The gift of jewelry can encourage confidence, especially if you receive an accolade. Loss of jewelry could be a practical warning: you should check the clasps and settings of your favorite pieces.

THE WORLD OF NATURE

FANTASY & FABLE

ARTS & SCIENCES

THE HUMAN BODY

BUILDINGS & INTERIORS

EVERYDAY THINGS

HUMAN EMOTIONS

HUMAN ACTIVITIES

HUMAN CONDITIONS

RITUALS & RELIGION

THE DREAM THESAURUS

MINING DIGGING *48, 148* **GOLD SILVER**

Dreaming of MINING or DIGGING for GOLD may suggest that in waking life you are desperate to make more money. Your confidence in being able to make money may relate to how successful you were in the dream, and to the level of difficulty of the process. The same is true of SILVER, and because we associate silver with coinage, it is more likely to have a direct association with your day-to-day living expenses, or with taxation. Silver has the properties of a mirror when it is clean and highly polished. If you were looking at a reflection in a piece of silver, your dream may be suggesting that you need to reflect on your waking situation.

CORAL CRYSTAL CRYSTAL BALL

CORAL has a significant meaning as a dream symbol, since it comes from the depths of the sea. It may relate to your deepest and most instinctive emotions, those which you inherited. In many countries, coral is worn by young children as protection against illness – is your dream suggesting that you are in need of greater protection of some sort? If you dream of CRYSTAL, your dream may be commenting on how clearly or otherwise you see your present situation in waking life. Were you looking into a CRYSTAL BALL? What did you see in it? You should not assume that your dream is in any way predictive – it is more likely to indicate a wished-for symbol.

DIAMOND GEMSTONE

Whether or not you are in a relationship, your dream DIAMOND may well be commenting on your attitude toward this sphere of your life, perhaps hinting that you should look at the various "facets" of a problem. If your dream was of another GEMSTONE, try to work out

DREAM ANALYSIS

"I dreamed that I was being crowned by a very old archbishop. Before the crown was put on my head I saw it; it was beautiful — made of gold and all kinds of gems. Once it was on my head, however, I knew that it had turned to lead, and I had to struggle to keep my head upright under its immense weight."

The dreamer had just been appointed to a new and responsible position in his company. He had been told about it by the elderly chairman. At first he was delighted, but he soon realized the burden of his new responsibilities. The dream was reassuring him and telling him that he could cope with the job.

SEMI-PRECIOUS STONE

what that stone means to you. Was it your birthstone, or the birthstone of someone you know? You should also consider its color. If your dream was of a SEMIPRECIOUS STONE, its texture and any associations or myths connected with it should help you in your interpretation.

BROOCH PIN *110*

If the BROOCH in your dream was one that you own, your feelings about how you acquired it, or from whom, and what the feelings mean to you, should be your first consideration. If it was being admired in the dream, you may be pleased with yourself. Similarly, if you were receiving a medal for some achievement, your dreams are hinting that you are on the right track in waking life, and that you will "win." A brooch is often called a PIN: in that context, someone may be trying to "pin" something on you, or to blame you unfairly.

RING

A ring can be a symbol of sexuality, and your dream of a RING may be suggesting that you are in need of greater sexual fulfillment. Perhaps you are ready to

EARRINGS
NECKLACE

advance a relationship through marriage. If your dream was of a lost ring, you should take this as a practical warning and check that your rings are not loose on your fingers. Dream **EARRINGS** may be drawing attention to your ears. In waking life, are you "getting the message" – whatever or from whoever it might be? Wearing a beautiful **NECKLACE** in a dream suggests wish-fulfillment (*see page 150*), but if it was a chain or if it was heavy to wear you may feel restricted in waking life. Are you being dragged along in a direction that is contrary to your wishes? Do you have heavy responsibilities?

CROWN
KING
162
QUEEN
65, 162

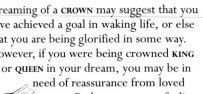

Dreaming of a **CROWN** may suggest that you have achieved a goal in waking life, or else that you are being glorified in some way. However, if you were being crowned **KING** or **QUEEN** in your dream, you may be in need of reassurance from loved ones. Perhaps you were feeling neglected in waking life, so you escaped into a different world in your dream. However, with a crown comes responsibility. Are you about to take on a new and demanding job? Is Christ's crown of thorns significant to you?

—✦—TOOLS—✦—

WHEN WE HAVE A DREAM in which machinery features, or in which we are using an implement, it is particularly important to remember that any symbol in a dream can relate to us in a vast number of ways. We may be the bulldozer, sweeping everything before us. The crutch on which we lean may be our partner. The needle we are desperately trying to thread may be an intractable problem.

BULLDOZER
PLOW
DREDGER
ENGINE
117

If you dream of a **BULLDOZER**, think about what it was clearing away. Similarly, what was the dream **PLOW** or **DREDGER** revealing? The dream may be referring to a psychological block or nagging problem in waking life with which you must come to terms before it can be resolved. In your dream, were you having difficulty in starting or fueling the **ENGINE**? If this was the case, the reference may be to actually getting a project under way in your waking life and having or building up the necessary motivation.

CORKSCREW

It is not surprising that our dreams often refer to familiar objects that are part of almost every waking day. However, you should look for the indirect association; for example, a **CORKSCREW** is useful, but if it is "crooked" or "bent" it does not go straight to the

CUTLERY
KNIFE
118
FORK
109

point. In waking life, are you being particularly devious in performing an apparently straightforward task? Because food is often associated with emotion, a dream of using **CUTLERY** that was old and rusty, or inadequate or wrongly used (for example, eating peas with a **KNIFE** or soup with a **FORK**), may imply that you are attempting to satisfy your emotions in an inappropriate manner.

DRILL
163
HAMMER
NAIL
NEEDLE
110
LEVER
SPADE

Many tools have sexual inferences: for example a **DRILL**, a **HAMMER**, a **NAIL**, and a **NEEDLE** are all seen as phallic symbols. The work you were doing with the tool may provide a clue to the dream's meaning – as may its level of efficiency. For example, the symbol of a needle being threaded has often been used to suggest the loss of virginity. The action of the tool in your dream is important: a **LEVER** is used to enhance one's strength, and a **SPADE** both to dig things up and cover them over.

WORKPLACES

WE SPEND MUCH OF our time at work, and the place where we
work is of considerable importance to us – often emotionally.
If we are comfortable there it may become a symbol of
reassurance, stability, and reward; if uncomfortable, or
irritated by our colleagues, it may be a symbol
of obstruction and dismay.

OFFICE
103
FACTORY
101
WAREHOUSE

If you work in an **OFFICE** or a **FACTORY**, it
is likely that your workplace will at some
time appear in your dreams. Sometimes
these dreams will indeed be connected
with your work, but the images of your
workplace may represent another aspect
of your waking life. This may well be a
particular problem or, on a general level,
your emotions or your attitude toward
life. In your dream, there may have been
a crowd of people, perhaps colleagues,
around you, or you could have been
surrounded by busy typewriters or
computers. If so, the dream may be
indicating a "crowd" of problems, none
of which necessarily relate to your
working life. However, an office or
factory that was suddenly closed or
deserted in your dream may reflect an
emptiness or vacuum in your waking life.
Has a phase of your life ended? If your
dream featured a **WAREHOUSE**, the allusion
may be to the experience of life that is

**STOCK-
TAKING**

stored up in your mind. If you were
STOCK-TAKING in your dream, you may be
taking stock of your present situation in
waking life. If goods are being carried
out of the warehouse, your dream may
have been telling you that your resources
in waking life are being emptied in some
way – probably emotionally.

SHOP

We go into **SHOPS** to buy things, and have
to hand over money in return, thus a
dream of shopping is often a dream of
something we want or need, in relation
to what we have to pay, or give, for it.
Emotion is often represented in the
dream: someone paying too much for
an item of underwear may feel they are
having to pay too much – emotionally or
physically – to impress a lover or partner.
The article in question is important, of
course – look this item up as a separate
symbol. The kind of shop in which you
found yourself will also be important.

VEHICLES

MALE DREAMS OF CARS are almost invariably associated with sex. For
women, however, dreams of a car often seem to be connected with
feelings of self-respect and ambition, and may also be related to
antagonism toward male chauvinism.

CAR
134, 135, 162

When women dream of **CARS** there often
seems to be a reference to ambition,
assertion, and perhaps even a desire to
"overtake" the male. But women seem to
dream relatively rarely about their cars,
while men often dream of theirs. Almost
universally, psychiatrists assent that such
dreams always represent men's sexual
drive – with power, mobility,

dexterity, and carelessness as possible
references. There are, however, many
other things to be considered. Were you
alone in the car? Did the car belong to
you, or to a parent or friend? Was it a
convertible? Was it reliable and slow, or
was it a sports model? It is important
to consider what part of the car was
emphasized in the dream, since this may

THE WORLD
OF NATURE

FANTASY &
FABLE

ARTS &
SCIENCES

THE HUMAN
BODY

BUILDINGS &
INTERIORS

EVERYDAY
THINGS

HUMAN
EMOTIONS

HUMAN
ACTIVITIES

STEERING
HEADLIGHTS
FUEL
FLAT
GEAR
ACCELERATOR
ENGINE
115
ANTIFREEZE
IGNITION
BACKSEAT
DRIVER

be related to your situation in waking life. Were you having difficulty with the **STEERING** (your self-control) or with the **HEADLIGHTS** (can you see where you are going)? Were you short of **FUEL** (running out of energy) or did you have a **FLAT** (has something deflated you)? Was it impossible to engage the correct **GEAR** (are you struggling with an intractable problem)? How were you using the **ACCELERATOR**? Were you attempting to go faster than the **ENGINE** would allow? Was the accelerator unresponsive, or too responsive? In waking life, the reference may be to your energy level. If **ANTIFREEZE** featured in your dream, it may well relate to your emotion. Do you have a desire to prevent a relationship from cooling down? The failure of the **IGNITION** in a dream is fundamental: something is failing to strike a vital spark. In your dream were you using tools to repair a car? (*See page 115.*) Most cars carry more than one person, so your dream may refer to a partnership in waking life. Was there a **BACKSEAT DRIVER** trying to persuade you to take a particular road? Sometimes a dream of a car that is not your own may suggest that you are in some way stealing a reputation: you may look dashing and sporty, but all of the energy you are displaying in waking life belongs to someone else.

Dreams of other kinds of vehicles may also refer to your sexuality, but (as is true of cars) can apply to other areas of your

DREAM ANALYSIS

"I was driving my sports car along an empty road, but I gradually began to slow down, and then stopped with a bump. I got out, and looked at my car, which had run into a hole in the road. I got back into the car and managed to drive it out of the hole, but I knew that it would never race again. I drove off, quite enjoying a more leisurely progress."

Victor had been having a life of sexual freedom, but had run into a problem when he fell in love. He regretted his loss of freedom (the car "would never race again") but was relieved that he could slow down.

BICYCLE
144
WHEEL-BARROW
TRUCK
VAN
LIMOUSINE
STREETCAR
TRAIN
121, 135

life. A dream of a **BICYCLE** may allude to your own private means of progress in waking life: it can carry no one else and is sensitive to balance, and problems with it may relate to your own sensitivity. A **WHEELBARROW**, a **TRUCK**, and a **VAN** all carry loads. If you dream of these vehicles, think about the nature of the load. It may be unwanted clutter from your emotional life. Were you merely moving the load from one place to another, or were you on the way to the garbage dump? A **LIMOUSINE** is luxurious, so a dream ride in one may be a positive image, but how did you pay for it? Who was the driver? A **STREETCAR**, like a **TRAIN**, runs on rails; dreaming that you are under way, you will be unable to deviate from the route. A dream of a train entering a tunnel symbolizes coition.

—◆— WEAPONS —◆—

IT IS IMPOSSIBLE TO BE dogmatic about the significance of any symbol
in a dream, and when weapons appear – either used by or
against the dreamer – it may be that they are associated with
physical violence. More often, however, there are other
associations, sometimes with hatred or antipathy, but also
in the context of sexual or sensual love.

ATTACK
120, 155, 159

It was Freud's view that almost every weapon is a phallic symbol, and most psychiatrists agree. For some men there may be an unconscious association between lovemaking and physical assault. However, there is a difference between this and a man's dream of **ATTACKING** a woman with a weapon. The apparent allusion to rape is too close for comfort, and any man who has a recurring dream of attacking women needs professional counseling. Even an occasional dream of such a nature may well reveal an equivocal attitude toward women. A dream of "hunting" women, while it may simply reflect the fun of the chase, can also reflect a waking perspective in which women are prey rather than companions. A woman who dreams of being attacked may be expressing sexual insecurity, or a more imprecise fear of the male.

ARROW
72, 127 133
DAGGER
KNIFE
115
SPEAR
GUN
BULLET

The type of weapon in the dream may certainly be significant: an **ARROW** may simply be Cupid's arrow, and a pleasing rather than frightening symbol; a **DAGGER** or **KNIFE** will appear more threatening, although the knife has many harmless domestic uses. A dream of a **SPEAR** is symbolic rather than actually harmful, while a dream of a **GUN** or **BULLET** may contain a more immediate and real warning. The atmosphere of the dream will be the best clue to analysis.

POISON

A dream of **POISON** – of either poisoning someone or being poisoned yourself – may refer to some venomous action we are taking or which is being taken against us. It may be a plant or an animal that is being poisoned; look for clues in the dream as to what it represents. Its color or another association may connect it to someone you know in waking life. Then consider your attitude toward that person. There may be a warning that someone or something is poisoning your life without your being aware of it. You may, of course, simply be acting "poisonously" yourself, in some way; or your favorite food or drink may be doing your health no good. In any event, this is a potent symbol that is worth taking note of for any future analyses.

THE WORLD OF NATURE

FANTASY & FABLE

ARTS & SCIENCES

THE HUMAN BODY

BUILDINGS & INTERIORS

EVERYDAY THINGS

HUMAN EMOTIONS

HUMAN ACTIVITIES

HUMAN CONDITIONS

RITUALS & RELIGION

THE DREAM THESAURUS

DIRT

THE PRESENCE OF IMAGES of dirt in our dreams will almost certainly refer to something distasteful in our waking lives, and the strength of the dream's allusion may relate to the degree of nausea we feel. However, such a dream need not be entirely negative – after all, we use manure to encourage growth.

FERTILIZER MANURE
73

A dream of spreading **FERTILIZER** or **MANURE** is likely to be very positive. We are using something that appears unpleasant to persuade crops to grow. The allusion may be to some action you are persuading yourself to take in waking life – or are perhaps being forced to take – that may be disagreeable, but may have excellent results. The dream is therefore an encouraging one.

EXCREMENT FECES POLLUTION

EXCREMENT or **FECES** in a dream may have a different meaning: you are more likely to be disposing of something unpleasant. Are you purging yourself of someone or something in your waking life that would poison your system if you clung to it? A dream of **POLLUTION** also refers to something that may damage you – either emotionally or physically – if you do not dispose of it thoroughly.

REFUSE

REFUSE IS SOMETHING that we want to dispose of. It may be something we no longer want or something foisted upon us by others. Dreams in which we are disposing of refuse are usually positive indications that we should clear our lives of "garbage."

GARBAGE DRAIN PUDDLE SOOT

The dream image of draining away waste, or dumping **GARBAGE** or other unwanted material, may be a symbol of clearing waste from your waking life. This may be emotional or material waste. Try to work out what the dream is referring to and dispose of it. You should remember that although a **DRAIN** may dispose of excess water (and a dream of this action may be suggesting that you are in some way being drained of emotion), some action must be taken to dispose of garbage. If, in a dream, your garbage was being dumped for you, it may be that someone is carrying a burden for you in waking life, or helping you to dispose of it. There may also be a suggestion that you need help to rid yourself of something – even a particular attitude. A dream of splashing through a **PUDDLE** or getting dirty – being covered with **SOOT**, for instance – may refer to some mild irritation in your waking life.

DREAM ANALYSIS

"I was walking in the country and saw a beautiful bird that was sitting on top of a tree and grooming itself. As I approached I saw a large notice saying 'Do Not Feed the Phoenix.' I realized that if I could get hold of the bird I could make a lot of money. I saw a shotgun leaning against a rock, and thought that if I could not capture the bird I should shoot it. I picked up the shotgun and pulled the trigger, but the pellets simply trickled out of the end of the gun. The bird immediately began to laugh. I took a revolver out of my pocket and aimed it, but this time the barrel seemed to melt and just drooped from my hand. I heard the bird laughing again, and when I looked up it was gone."

This is an incoherent dream, but clearly refers to the dreamer's attitude toward women, and toward one woman in particular. She seemed mysterious, and so was represented by a mythical bird. He had approached her, but she had rejected him. The dream may have been warning him against "coming on too strong," and implying that the woman found such advances amusing rather than seductive.

THE WORLD OF NATURE

FANTASY & FABLE

ARTS & SCIENCES

THE HUMAN BODY

BUILDINGS & INTERIORS

EVERYDAY THINGS

HUMAN EMOTIONS

HUMAN ACTIVITIES

HUMAN CONDITIONS

RITUALS & RELIGION

THE DREAM THESAURUS

—✦— FEAR —✦—

DREAMS THAT PUT US in a state of fear by their content are usually
described as nightmares, but some dreams express our waking fears
in images that can haunt us for days, weeks, or even longer. They
can, however, be valuable in putting our anxieties into perspective,
and even showing us how to deal with them.

THE WORLD
OF NATURE

FANTASY &
FABLE

ARTS &
SCIENCES

THE HUMAN
BODY

BUILDINGS &
INTERIORS

EVERYDAY
THINGS

HUMAN
EMOTIONS

HUMAN
ACTIVITIES

HUMAN
CONDITIONS

RITUALS &
RELIGION

THE DREAM
THESAURUS

"Physical" nightmares (*see page 154*) – in
which we dream we are being drowned
or crushed – usually occur during the
first ten or twenty minutes of sleep. They
are similar to the familiar dream of
falling, which some analysts explain by
saying that we are simply "falling asleep."
There seems to be a physical rather than
psychological reason for such dreams, as
for others – of being chased or captured
– that occur most frequently in the last
hours of sleep (indeed, they often wake
us). There is no explanation as to how
they arise, although some analysts have
suggested that they seem to occur after
we have done something of which we are
ashamed, or that we know to be wrong –
almost as though we invoked the dream
as punishment. Other analysts believe
that they are the result of the suppression
of hidden or forbidden desires. No one
has yet been able to suggest a reliable
way of ensuring that they do not recur,
although work is continuing in dream
laboratories, and there is some evidence
that discussing your nightmares with
other sufferers can help to resolve them.

ATTACK
118, 155, 159

If you have a dream in which you are
being attacked or pursued, you should
try to identify the person on the **ATTACK**
or in pursuit (*see page 147*). If this is a
recurring dream it may have a serious
root problem in waking life. Try to turn
and face your demon, since recognition
of the fiend and what it represents is a
large part of the solution. In a one-shot
dream, the "monster" may be something
as simple as a problem pursuing you at
work, or a tax demand.

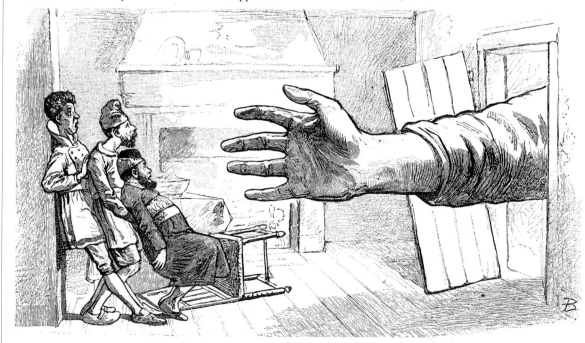

ANIMAL
127, 144, 155

ANIMALS in dreams represent our animal nature, which it is usually necessary to keep under control. Dreams of being threatened or attacked by animals may be telling you that you are spending too much time repressing your instincts – perhaps you are simply being too "civilized." You should try to loosen up and be more natural.

A dream of someone intruding into one's home is fairly common. It can be prompted by some kind of intrusion in waking life – not necessarily by a person.

INTRUDER

It may be that you cannot stop worrying about a particular problem or task in waking life. It is important for you to identify the **INTRUDER** in your dream; it may be your shadow (*see page* 97), and you should be able to understand the reason for the invasion.

INSANITY

Irrational fears in dreams become more rational when you examine them. For example, a fear of **INSANITY** may be a reflection of a quandary in your waking life. Make the connection, and take the advice of your dream.

—◆— INSECURITY —◆—

THE MOST SELF-ASSURED people have areas of insecurity in their lives, of which they are often unaware or which they have taught themselves to ignore. However, repression of any emotion can be damaging, and it is better to recognize and acknowledge it. Our dreams often see this as a strengthening process, and can assist us.

BUS
TRAIN
117, 135

A dream of missing a **BUS** or **TRAIN** may be a simple "prompting" dream. If you have an appointment to keep or a journey to make, the dream may be reflecting your fear of missing it. It may also be suggesting that you are unconsciously insecure and uncertain in a particular area of your waking life. If something obstructs you and makes you miss the bus in your dream, it may represent a person or factor in waking life on which you are prepared to blame any inefficiency on your part. If you are simply furious that you missed the bus in your dream, you may be angry with yourself about something in waking life.

STORM
49, 158
EARTHQUAKE
48, 158, 161

If you dream of being adrift in a **STORM** at sea, blown around by the wind, and unable to hold on to anything, in waking life you may be worried about loss of control – almost certainly in the sphere of your emotions. A dream of any phenomenon that threatens your physical stability – an **EARTHQUAKE**, for instance – may be a sign of insecurity in waking life. Look for clues to uncover the hints the

ANCHOR
LIGHTHOUSE
101
LIFEBOAT

dream may be giving you. Was your **ANCHOR** dragging? In waking life is someone on whom you depend showing signs of being less dependable than you thought? Was there any sign of hope, such as a **LIGHTHOUSE** or a **LIFEBOAT**? What or who could these represent in waking life? Did the building you were in resist the earthquake?

ABROAD
58, 135

A dream of talking to someone whose language you cannot understand, or of being "**ABROAD**" in a country with which you are unfamiliar, may reflect insecurity about a new person or task materializing in your waking life.

AUCTION
152

You may dream that some treasured possession is up for **AUCTION** but no one is bidding, or that you are bidding for something but are continually being outbidded. If so, there may be a suggestion that you are unsure of being able to accomplish a task in waking life. The identity of the object under the hammer should reveal what particular task is worrying you.

THE WORLD OF NATURE

FANTASY & FABLE

ARTS & SCIENCES

THE HUMAN BODY

BUILDINGS & INTERIORS

EVERYDAY THINGS

HUMAN EMOTIONS

HUMAN ACTIVITIES

HUMAN CONDITIONS

RITUALS & RELIGION

THE DREAM THESAURUS

THE WORLD
OF NATURE

FANTASY &
FABLE

ARTS &
SCIENCES

THE HUMAN
BODY

BUILDINGS &
INTERIORS

EVERYDAY
THINGS

**PSYCHIATRIST
PSYCHO-
LOGIST
ASTROLOGER
63
FORTUNE-
TELLER**

A dream in which you are consulting a **PSYCHIATRIST**, a **PSYCHOLOGIST**, an **ASTROLOGER**, or a **FORTUNE-TELLER** may have nothing to do with any particular problem you have in waking life but perhaps to a feeling that you are not as thoroughly in control of the course of your waking life as you feel you should be. Though many people believe that a psychologist or an astrologer can help them, there is still a general feeling of doubt about this. Your dream may be hinting that you need help of some kind in your waking life but that you are not entirely sure who to turn to for reliable or useful assistance.

— DREAM ANALYSIS —

"I was in an auction room, and people were bidding for a vase decorated with roses. I kept raising my hand, but the auctioneer would not look my way. A red-haired man bid double the amount that I had bid, and the vase was sold to him. However, as the auctioneer brought down the hammer he hit the vase, which shattered."

The dreamer was strongly attracted to a young woman who, he knew, had many admirers. He saw her regularly both socially and at work, but had not been able to summon up the courage to approach her. He was sure she was attracted to a colleague and believed that if she had a relationship with him it would prove disastrous. The woman's name was Rose, and the man was called Mr. Redcap.

—◆— HOSTILITY —◆—

WE OFTEN HARBOR hostile feelings toward people, and in waking life we frequently refuse to rationalize our feelings. They are often based, not on the behavior of the person we feel hostile toward, but on our own character or behavior.

ABUSE

In waking life, verbal **ABUSE** may relieve our feelings, but rarely has any direct result other than making a situation worse. A dream of verbal abuse may be a warning that you are wasting your energy. If someone is abusing you in a dream, the inference may be that you have provoked someone. However, the abuse may contain an element of truth. If you are accused of something in a dream, you should consider whether you are accusing yourself.

If you use weapons (*see page 118*) in anger in a dream, it may suggest that you are in the sway of strong emotion. Many weapons also have sexual connotations in a dream, so consider whether it is a particular aspect of your sexuality or sexual behavior that has provoked the dream. The person you are threatening or attacking in the dream may be a person toward whom you feel antagonistic in waking life. In this case, the dream is a literal translation of your feelings. However, it is more likely that the victim in the dream represents you, and that your anger is the result of some action or emotion in waking life that you have failed to control. You should think about the weapon you were using, and what it might represent in waking life.

ARGUMENT QUARREL

There are two sides to an **ARGUMENT** or **QUARREL**, and such a dream may relate to an actual dispute. This may not necessarily be between you and another person, but between one side of your own personality and another. In waking life, you may be faced with a difficult decision, and the opposing facts may be difficult to balance. So who won the dream argument, or how was the quarrel resolved? Think about the winner, since they may present you with a clue to the course you should take in waking life.

THREAT

If we threaten someone, we are warning them. This is usually because we are angry at an action or opinion, or else dissatisfied with someone's behavior. Whoever made the **THREAT** in your dream, the subject may be you. Were you accusing yourself of something? The threat may be pointing out the consequences of some unwise action of yours in waking life. You should also note the attitude taken to the threat – the dream may be showing you that you should hold your own under intimidation.

—◆— ANGER —◆—

ANGER IS ONE OF the strongest of our emotions, and it can express itself in our dreams – either by physical action or by using symbols such as weapons (*see page 118*). Dreams are unlikely to stop until the source of your dream anger is discovered and dealt with.

ASSAULT RAPE

A man dreaming that he is **ASSAULTING** or **RAPING** a woman may have a deep-rooted sexual problem that requires treatment. Certainly, if such dreams frequently recur he must realize that he needs professional help to deal with it. A single dream in which a certain degree of aggression occurs, sexual or otherwise, is not so serious and is actually quite common. Such a dream may be expressing strong (probably unconscious) feelings in the dreamer. It may be that sexual hostility (if the dream is sexually oriented) is based on rejection (not necessarily by the victim in the dream, who may symbolize all women). Alternatively, the dreamer may envy the woman's charm, beauty, or social graces and wants (consciously or unconsciously) to degrade her. The female side of men is susceptible to criticism of this sort from within the unconscious. A man dreaming of being raped may be suffering from acute feelings of dishonor and embarrassment in waking life.

ASSASSINATION MURDER

Dreams of **ASSASSINATION** or **MURDER** have a similar implication. Strong images in dreams demand close attention, and an effort should be made to understand them and consider their messages.

EVICTION

A dream that you are planning to **EVICT** someone – either from their home or from your home – suggests that there is something you want to dispense with in your waking life. This may be a person or an unattractive characteristic of yours. Concentrate on the identity of the person at the center of the dream: it may be that you see in them the type of

THE WORLD OF NATURE

FANTASY & FABLE

ARTS & SCIENCES

THE HUMAN BODY

BUILDINGS & INTERIORS

EVERYDAY THINGS

HUMAN EMOTIONS

HUMAN ACTIVITIES

HUMAN CONDITIONS

RITUALS & RELIGION

THE DREAM THESAURUS

THE WORLD
OF NATURE

FANTASY &
FABLE

ARTS &
SCIENCES

THE HUMAN
BODY

BUILDINGS &
INTERIORS

EVERYDAY
THINGS

HUMAN
EMOTIONS

HUMAN
ACTIVITIES

HUMAN
CONDITIONS

RITUALS &
RELIGION

THE DREAM
THESAURUS

AMBUSH behavior that you despise but are conscious of exhibiting from time to time. A dream of **AMBUSHING** someone may have a similar meaning, but it may also mean that you want to capture something representative of the victim in the dream. You may want to possess some of the victim's valuable (good) qualities in waking life, so your motive for the ambush is important.

LIBEL A dream in which you are vilifying someone may be implying that in waking life you want to spread harmful information – or that someone else is doing so. The nature of the **LIBEL** will be important, but you should not take it literally. Remember that dreams usually speak in symbolic and allegorical terms.

FEUD REBELLION As with most dreams of hostility, a dream that you are conducting a **FEUD** with someone, or **REBELLING** against authority, may be inward- or outward-turning. The dream may reflect a disagreement that you are having with someone in waking life. Conversely, your feud may be with yourself; you may be rebelling against a trait that is mirrored in the character with whom you are arguing in your dream. Younger people at variance with their parents or older relatives often have dreams in which they give vent to their hostility. These may take the form of a literal feud. Such dreams may not only be expressing your emotions but saying something about them, so you should pay attention not only to the events but also to the atmosphere (*see page 33*).

—◆— GUILT —◆—

PART OF THE DUTY of dreams is to allow us to admit to things that our waking selves would rather deny. So it is not surprising that our dreams are often concerned with guilt; they remind us of our offenses against others, and offenses against our own true nature.

It is not unusual to wake from a "guilty" dream, in which you may believe that you have committed a crime (*see page 140*), and suspect that you are going to be found out. The dream could be commenting on your whole way of life, and focusing on repression of some kind. It may be suggesting that you should feel guilty because you are concealing the crime of repressing your true self.

ADULTERY BIGAMY A dream of committing **ADULTERY** or **BIGAMY** may be one of wish-fulfillment (*see page 150*). Someone who is in a marriage that is emotionally and sexually cold is not unlikely to have such a dream. However, the atmosphere in the dream is important, and it may be an expression of guilt – even if you have only thought about adultery. Because your dream may be more honest about your feelings than your waking self, you should pay it some attention; you may not find deceit as easy or guilt-free as you anticipate.

ALIMONY DIVORCE A dream that you are paying **ALIMONY** may not relate to any thought of **DIVORCE**, but may simply refer to the fact that, in one way or another, you are paying for a misdeed in waking life.

CRIMINAL *170* **BEATING HANGING PRISON** *169* **FINE** A dream in which the dreamer is a **CRIMINAL**, or is conscious of having committed a crime (*see page 140*), is most likely to relate to some misdemeanor in waking life. If a penalty is being exacted from you, it may be based on guilt in waking life, and the severity of the penalty may reflect your true feelings about the offense. They may not match with your waking feelings, since we are capable of self-deception where our own shortcomings are concerned. So if you are being **BEATEN** or **HANGED**, or else sentenced to **PRISON**, somewhere in the back of your mind there may be a strong regret for some recent action or thought. A **FINE** may refer to a minor wrongdoing in waking life. The action that has made

JUDGE
162, 164
LYNCHING
171

you feel guilty may relate to one particular person, in which case there should be a clue in the dream. Who was the JUDGE, or the jury foreman? Or was there simply someone in the court who seemed particularly interested in your case? You may have been condemned in your dream by society at large; this is likely to be the case if the judge was a famous person (a television interviewer, for example). If, in a dream, you were being LYNCHED by an angry crowd, it will almost certainly be society in general rather than an individual that you have offended in waking life.

ALLERGY

An ALLERGY is the body's reaction against something we feed it, put on it, or do to it. A dream of having an allergy may express guilt that lies very close to home.

PULPIT
180
PREACHER
CONFESSION

Even for people who are attached to no particular religion, religious symbols are remarkably potent. A dream of being condemned from the PULPIT by a PREACHER (a common authority figure in dreams) may suggest that you are an anathema to someone in waking life. If you are CONFESSING in your dream and eager for absolution, you may need to rectify a situation in your waking life. You may then dream of being absolved, which would be extremely comforting.

GALLOWS
170
GUILLOTINE
171

Death rarely has a literal meaning in dreams. To dream of yourself, or someone else, being on the GALLOWS or the GUILLOTINE does not mean that anyone is about to die. There is the possibility that such a dream would represent the ultimate condemnation of some action or thought of yours in waking life. Alternatively, it may also mean that you are going to dispense with some or all of your present habits in waking life. These are usually reassuring dreams. An execution in a dream may be conducted by someone else (perhaps representing the law or a superior at work) or ourselves. Through such a dream we may undergo a sort of resurrection, with the offer of a new start in waking life.

PROCESS
SERVER
COLLECTION
AGENCY

In dreams, money is often related to emotion, and to be pursued by a PROCESS SERVER or COLLECTION AGENCY may be a suggestion that you owe someone something. Have you failed to return someone's affection?

SHOP-
LIFTING
THEFT

SHOPLIFTING is regarded by many people as a petty crime: it is morally less reprehensible to steal from a large organization than an individual. If you dreamed that you were shoplifting, your conscience may be rebuking you for a petty crime in waking life. A dream of engaging in a more serious crime of THEFT may mean that your subconscious is aware of some action of yours in waking life that may have serious results if you are found out. The action may be anything from actual theft of some kind to a moral lapse. For example, in cheating on your partner you are "stealing" something to which they have a right: your affection and faithfulness.

BLACKMAIL

If you dream that you are BLACKMAILING someone – demanding money with menaces – in waking life, are you trying to obtain affection by threatening to leave someone, or gain respect by some less than admirable action?

BEREAVEMENT
87

It is extremely common, in situations of BEREAVEMENT, to feel guilty about one's behavior toward the dead. We often think that we should have spent more time with them, written to them more often, or loved them more. A dream may show us such a person in tears, or rebuking the living. Such a dream may be the result of your conscience nagging you, and you may resolve the problem by thinking about your waking experience with the dead person, and perhaps admitting your fault to yourself.

THE WORLD OF NATURE

FANTASY & FABLE

ARTS & SCIENCES

THE HUMAN BODY

BUILDINGS & INTERIORS

EVERYDAY THINGS

HUMAN EMOTIONS

HUMAN ACTIVITIES

HUMAN CONDITIONS

—◆— LOVE —◆—

DREAMS FROM WHICH we take advice about our love-life can take many forms, and are often more difficult to decipher and translate than overtly sexual dreams, since almost any symbol can be associated with this area of our life. In our dreams we can see our partners and potential lovers – and our emotions – for what they really are.

THE WORLD OF NATURE

FANTASY & FABLE

ARTS & SCIENCES

THE HUMAN BODY

BUILDINGS & INTERIORS

EVERYDAY THINGS

In less sophisticated times, young women used "magic" to show them visions of the man they would marry. They would peel an onion, wrap it in a handkerchief, put it under their pillow, and then recite a particular rhyme. They would then expect to see in a dream the face of their true love. And no doubt many of them did, for they were invoking the power of their unconscious, which presented to them a picture of the young man to whom they were most strongly drawn. Our dreams often react swiftly to a (perhaps irrational) attraction to a person we have met in waking life. This, however, does not necessarily mean that you will dream of the actual person; you may find the object of your interest heavily disguised. One girl, who found a man she had met extremely sexy, dreamed not of him but of the spire of Salisbury Cathedral. He had told her that he came from Salisbury, and the rest is obvious. It is always worth looking for a sexual symbol in such dreams, if only because our initial attraction to others is often sexual in nature. However, there will be other symbols: look especially for puns on your new friend's name or occupation. In such dreams there will rarely

be a strong promise of anything to come; a dream of lovemaking is more likely to be one of wish-fulfillment (*see page 150*) than prophesy.

BELLS If our dreams often tell us things that we do not particularly want to know, they can also tell us things that we have not yet realized. Since our emotional life is often confusing, it is worth taking note of any hints that come to us in sleep. If we are undecided about making an emotional commitment to another person, there are often signs that may either encourage or discourage us. If you dream of a chime of BELLS, you may be receiving a strong hint in the direction of matrimony. Dreams have been known to suggest this by the ringing of a doorbell, and when the door was answered the prospective spouse was on the doorstep. However, such dreams are not always so literal; symbols may represent the ~~person~~ about whom you are concerned – perhaps through an image associated with them in your mind. Decision-making can also be helped in a remarkable way. A dreamer who was unable to make up his mind about a potential partner dreamed that he was making bread, and kneading the dough. It took him some time to realize that he "needed" the young woman who was on his mind.

The emotional tensions within a home often make relationships between parents and children, and between siblings, difficult. If dreams often remind you of family ties, they may tell you that the time has come to express your dislike of the actions of another family member, to sever relations with them, or to let them go their own way. A parent's dream of the loss or breakage of a beloved object may relate to the need to "lose" a child – only in the sense of allowing them more freedom. Such dreams are not always forthright in their imagery, but a dream of anything closely related to home life, or a favorite object, may be worth relating to a family member.

BEACH
59, 150

Your dreams may hint that you are not getting as much pleasure out of life as you could. They may show you the way to increased periods of relaxation, or to new hobbies or pastimes. They may also suggest that you take more interest in your work so that the daily grind becomes less of a trudge and more of an adventure. The symbols in dreams can be many and various. Straightforward dreams of lazing on a tropical **BEACH** or walking in your favorite landscape (*see page 58*) may be reflections of the pleasures you most enjoy. These are dreams of wish-fulfillment (*see page 150*).

Other symbols may be less easy to interpret and more exciting. For example, someone whose leisure pastimes are entirely sedentary, and who dreams of flying (*see page 147*) over an exciting landscape of mountains and rivers, may be incited to explore new landscapes of interest and adventure – not necessarily physical. On the other hand, someone whose recreation is sports-oriented may have a dream indicating that they are neglecting the adventures of the mind. In each case, the dream is suggesting that your love of life is restricted because of narrow interests.

ADOPTION

A dream of **ADOPTING** a child may reflect an element of wish-fulfilment (*see page 150*), but on the other hand, the idea of taking care of someone is strongly associated with the idea of love, and may reflect the wish to take care of a loved one. As with other areas of mythology (*see page 64*), to dream of shooting

ARROW
72, 118, 133
CANNIBALISM

ARROWS may recall the myth of Cupid. Who were you shooting at, or who was shooting at you? The arrow in certain contexts may also be a phallic symbol. Was it aimed correctly? Did it hit the bull's-eye? Food (*see page 106*) often has sexual connotations in dreams. A dream of **CANNIBALISM** – of actually eating a person – may have stronger and stranger significance and should be considered carefully. Cannibalism is one of the most powerful symbols in dreams, and while it will undoubtedly be important, it will not necessarily have murderous overtones. Cannibals used to devour the flesh of their enemies in order to acquire their power, and in dreaming of consuming someone we may be craving the potency we recognize in them. The basic image is of assimilating something, almost certainly some property of the person you are eating.

ANIMAL
121, 144, 155

Your lover may be represented as an **ANIMAL** in a dream – for example a puppy. In waking life does your lover need to be cuddled or protected in some way?

DREAM ANALYSIS

"I was in a supermarket, hesitating before picking up a brand of coffee that I had never tried. I thought the packaging was elegant, and it had a brand name on it. I wondered whether the contents would be as good as the packaging. I picked it up and noticed that the packet was leaking, and I thought that I would just have a taste. But as I was about to take one, a manager came along and said, 'Oh no, you don't, not without paying,' and I woke up."

John had been introduced to a new colleague during a coffee break, and had immediately felt attracted to the young woman. On the rebound from a relationship that had fallen to pieces rather unpleasantly, he began chatting with her. On the way home, however, he wondered whether he really wanted to become embroiled in another romance just yet. The dream appeared to be reflecting his feelings, and was reminding him that he still had to pay for his previous mistake.

THE CLAWS DREAM

" I was alone in an open desert. I knew that it was a desert, because there was shifting sand under my feet that made it difficult for me to walk; but I knew that I should walk. I knew that I was not on a beach, because I was not able to hear the sound of waves. In fact, I could not hear any sound, and there was a very dense, murky fog, so I could not see where I was going. I tried to part the fog by waving my arms in front of me — almost as if I was swimming — but my effort had no effect. Suddenly, two huge claws grabbed my arms and hands. I could not see the creature to whom they belonged. I was terrified: my arms and hands were bleeding from deep gashes made by the claws. The claws eventually released their grip, and I saw two eyes — bright green — that were shedding tears. Still terrified, I ran away and discovered a hole in the sand. I was very grateful for the hole and climbed down into it. Inside, it was warm, wet, and sticky. I nursed my bleeding arms and hands, and as I did so I became very angry. I arose from the hole and found that I was surrounded by a ring of fire that began to clear the fog. I was fraught with anger. I picked up pieces of burning coal and was about to throw them at the claws, but they were nowhere to be seen. Then I woke up. "

SHIFTING SAND MAKES IT DIFFICULT TO WALK

SHIRLEY PICKS UP BURNING COALS

RING OF FIRE CLEARS FOG

SHIRLEY CLIMBS INTO HOLE

INTERPRETATION

Shirley had been maltreated as a child, and at the time of this dream was being regularly molested by a vicious husband. For years she had lived with his cruelty, not daring to do anything about it. The opening of the dream suggests her insecurity (the soft, slippery sand) and confusion (the thick fog).

The claws were those of her husband, although she did not see the whole creature. The dream seemed to be implying that Shirley did not see or understand her husband's problems, which were also serious. She had unconsciously realized that he needed help, for not only did the claws suddenly stop injuring her, but the green eyes were weeping. She had described her husband as being insanely jealous, crafty, evasive, and deceptive, becoming mawkishly sentimental, feigning sorrow, and craving pity after he had beaten her. These characteristics seemed to be evident in the incomplete dream monster: it suddenly and for no reason stopped clawing her, and then shed maudlin tears.

Shirley responded with gratitude to falling into the hole. She was glad to climb down into it, since it symbolized a place where she could be free of her husband's cruelty. The conditions in the hole suggest very vividly that she was displaying a desire to retire to the womb. It was in the hole that she gained strength and became ready to express her suppressed anger.

For centuries, a ring of fire has been a symbol of protection, occurring in many myths and legends. The fact that the dream ended in Shirley picking up pieces of burning coal to throw at her monster was extremely positive: the dream was not only demonstrating the need for her to take action against her husband, but assuring her that she had the inner strength to do so. It is also interesting to note that in her dream, although Shirley picked up hot coals, she was not burned by them. This was another way of telling her to express her anger, but warning her that she must be cautious, especially since the claws and eyes had disappeared.

SHIRLEY TRIES
TO PART FOG

BRIGHT GREEN
EYES SHED TEARS

CLAWS MAKE
DEEP GASHES

—·— EMOTION —·—

IT IS EXTREMELY IMPORTANT to consider the emotional atmosphere of a dream when we try to work out its meaning. When a specific dream symbol triggers a burst of emotion we often have a powerful hint of an emotion we need to release or suppress in our waking lives.

THE WORLD OF NATURE

FANTASY & FABLE

ARTS & SCIENCES

THE HUMAN BODY

BUILDINGS & INTERIORS

EVERYDAY THINGS

HUMAN EMOTIONS

HUMAN ACTIVITIES

HUMAN CONDITIONS

RITUALS & RELIGION

THE DREAM THESAURUS

YAWN BOREDOM

Sometimes the obvious implication of a dream can be exactly right, and a dream YAWN may be indicative of overtiredness or boredom in your waking life. Let the symbol prompt you into taking some positive action, since the dream may be summing up your present lifestyle.

SADNESS

We sometimes awake from a dream with an overwhelming feeling of SADNESS. Sometimes you may not be able to remember the dream event that has made you so sad, but at other times there may be a strong symbol – perhaps the death of a friend or a reflection of a national or international tragedy. However, the real cause of our sorrow may lie in a powerful emotional response to something or someone in waking life. If the dream recurs, you should consider taking professional advice, especially if you are feeling generally depressed.

DEAF BLIND
92

If you dream that you are DEAF or BLIND, it is probably not a comment on your physical shortcomings. Are you "turning a deaf ear" to a problem or someone's comments or advice in waking life? Are you blind to what is going on around you? Think of such dreams as powerful warnings, suggesting that you change your attitude. There is also a chance that the dreams could be the precursors of trouble with your eyes or ears, and if you are even slightly concerned about this it will be wise to have them tested. However, as with a dream of death or dying (*see page 86*), such symbols are rarely predictive.

LAUGHTER

When we awake LAUGHING from a dream we often realize that what we are actually laughing at is stupid and not particularly funny. To reveal the real meaning of the

—— DREAM ANALYSIS ——

"I awoke in floods of tears, but surprisingly felt happy and elated. In my dream I had been watching the most beautiful performance of Tosca – the singing and staging were quite perfect. The tenor, Cavaradossi, came down from the stage and held me in his arms, but then he returned to the stage."

The dream summed up Ruth's present situation. She had just been parted from her husband, who had left to take up an important position with a thriving company in Italy. While she was sad at his leaving, she knew that it would be marvelous for their future. The opera *Tosca* is set in Rome.

JESTER

dream you will have to study the symbol causing this emotion. A JESTER appearing in your dream may represent someone who would be a wise adviser in waking life. On the other hand, if you were the jester, are you criticizing and mocking someone else in waking life? Or is someone mocking you?

REFRIGERATOR THAWING ICE
172
HEAT

A perception of heat and cold in dreams, unless we have too many or too few blankets, represents the extremes of emotion. For example, if a REFRIGERATOR appears in your dream there may be a reference to your emotional coldness or sexual frigidity in waking life. In the future, you may have dreams that are indicative of THAWING, in which case your feelings may be changing and you may be taking a more relaxed attitude to the area of your waking life that has been giving you concern. On the other hand, perhaps you have put some project on ice in waking life. Are you unable to make progress with it? Remember that ICE is also water (*see page 46*). When the feeling of HEAT is evident in a dream, the reference may be to passion, to sexual feelings, or to some waking cause that is important to you. How you control your dream heat is important (*see Fire, page 45*). You should also consider your mood: did you feel angry in the dream? (*See page 123.*)

REJECTION

If you have a dream **REJECTION**, you should seriously consider what you need to reject in your waking life. A great deal depends on how you felt and coped in your dream. Such an important symbol needs a very careful building of the interpretation of the elements in a dream. Your dream may be suggesting that there is clutter in your life that you need to reject or dispose of. The clutter may be of worn-out ideas and opinions, or old objects or garments.

TREASURE
PET
42
TOY

If, in your dream, you were being robbed of a valued **TREASURE** or **PET**, or even of a childhood **TOY**, it may be warning you that someone in waking life is draining you emotionally. If you were actually loving and treasuring such things in a dream, it may be suggesting that you are too acquisitive or possessive in waking life. If you were taking stock of what you own, your dream may be referring to your talents and potential in waking life. Are you developing and making enough use of your abilities? Are you acting possessively toward loved ones?

PARTING
ESCAPE

If you dream of a **PARTING** or an **ESCAPE**, you may feel either tremendous relief or considerable sadness. Even a parting can bring relief – the result of a job well done, for instance – and with it, inner satisfaction. The dream may also be referring to a phase of your life that is now over, and focusing on your actual reaction to it. What did you escape from in your dream? Have you at last resolved a problem that has been bothering you in the form of dreams of being chased (*see Pursuit, page 147*). If so, you may have resolved a deep-rooted psychological problem and made some progress.

HUNGER
106

A dream of **HUNGER** may be making a powerful comment on the lack of love and affection in your life. Perhaps you are feeling rather lonely, or there is a certain emptiness in your life. This may be particularly true if you have recently suffered bereavement or been divorced, or have just left home.

EXPLOSION
158
FUSE
73
DEMOLITION

If you have recently exploded with rage or happiness in waking life, you may realize that your dream **EXPLOSION** is a pun on your actual feelings. However, if you are bottling up anger, resentment, or jealousy, your dreams may be saying that the time is right to express yourself in no uncertain terms. If you were lighting a **FUSE** in the dream that triggered your explosion and led to a **DEMOLITION**, you may have a desire to destroy some aspect of your waking life. There may be an allusion to your current relationship, but your dream may also be centering on a negative aspect of your personality that needs to be destroyed and perhaps replaced by a more positive quality.

SUNSET
SUNRISE

A dream of a romantic **SUNSET** in a landscape such as a tropical island, with someone you love, may contain elements of wish-fulfillment (*see page 150*). There may also be a feeling of inner satisfaction and contentment, with a certain overtone of finality. Your dream of a **SUNRISE** may indicate that you are feeling hopeful and positive about the future.

THE WORLD OF NATURE

FANTASY & FABLE

ARTS & SCIENCES

THE HUMAN BODY

BUILDINGS & INTERIORS

EVERYDAY THINGS

—◆—GAMES—◆—

MOST PEOPLE ENJOY either playing or watching games: admiring
skill, scoring goals or points for our teams, protesting against
cheating, or cheering on our own teams or favorite players. Dreams
themselves are great game-players, and it is not surprising that
they often use symbols from games played by people in waking life,
to convey their messages.

THE WORLD
OF NATURE

FANTASY &
FABLE

ARTS &
SCIENCES

THE HUMAN
BODY

BUILDINGS &
INTERIORS

EVERYDAY
THINGS

HUMAN
EMOTIONS

HUMAN
ACTIVITIES

HUMAN
CONDITIONS

RITUALS &
RELIGION

THE DREAM
THESAURUS

REFEREE If you dream of a **REFEREE**, you are
invoking a strong authority figure. The
dream referee may represent someone
who has the power to alter or affect your
waking life, or is offering advice that they
are able to enforce. If you were ignoring
the referee in your dream, or protesting
a decision that was made during a game,
you may do well not to take the same
course in your waking life – unless the
dream merely reflects your disgust at
some ruling that has affected you. But
dreams are rarely that simple.

BALLS
BILLIARDS
72
SNOOKER
LAWN
BOWLING
MARBLES

If a man dreams of a game in which **BALLS**
are obviously the chief objects, he may be
receiving a message about his sexuality or
sexual prowess, or about his physical
power or courage. There are, however,
many other possible interpretations to
such dreams. **BILLIARDS** and **SNOOKER** are
games requiring great skill: in a dream,
concentration on such skills may refer to
concentration on a problem or a series of
problems in waking life. Should you be
dealing with problems in a particular
order? Is someone attempting to obstruct
you by interfering with your plans for
problem-solving? One of the aims of
LAWN BOWLING is to obstruct the course
of your opponent's balls. A dream of
games involving obstruction by an
opponent will sometimes contain this
kind of reference, whether the game is as
sophisticated as billiards or as simple as
MARBLES. The dream of such a childish
game, however, may hint at something
immature, or too simplistic, in your
behavior in waking life.

PLAYGROUND Your dream of playing one of the games
you played as a child will probably deal
with basic emotions, as dreams of
childhood (*see page 88*) often do. If other
children were involved in the dream,
they may symbolize adults in your
waking life, or the child in you. Were
you being selfish, or were you cheating
or making too much noise? Anything that
happened in the dream **PLAYGROUND** or
on the street corner may have its parallel
in your waking life. In dreams, we can
return to the emotional state of children,
since our childlike selves are still within
us, and all too often emotionally control
our actions in waking life.

FOOTBALL
SOCCER
BASEBALL

Dreams of team games almost inevitably refer to our waking attitude to "teams" of one sort or another. This may be the team in which we work, or the team that is the family. Anything that happens in a dream of **FOOTBALL**, **SOCCER**, or **BASEBALL**, for example, may allude to your relationship with a number of colleagues or family members. Petty jealousy, envy, friendship, joy, and dejection will all have a parallel in waking life, but the dream will not simply present these emotions – it will present the reason for them. In your dream, did you score a goal or block a goal? Did you foul an opposing player or display bad temper?

PITCHER
UMPIRE
TENNIS

The other characters in the dream will be worth thinking about: in baseball, the **PITCHER** may be someone wanting to strike you out, and the **UMPIRE** may have the same significance as a referee (*see opposite*). A dream of playing **TENNIS** will usually only involve two players, so the identity of your dream opponent will be worth examination. It is also important to remember that in your dream you may in fact be playing against yourself; your

---

DREAM ANALYSIS

"I was practising at a billiard table when I suddenly realized that the balls had turned into football players, and I was watching a match from the grandstand. Instead of nets, however, the pockets of a billiard table were at each corner of the football field. I then found myself to be the referee, and ordered several players off the field, but they had to go and jump into one of the pockets. When I looked, I saw that the pockets had no bottoms, so the players simply fell out and vanished. I stopped sending men off when they committed an offence, but instead simply told them to behave themselves. The crowd was aware of the change, and everyone cheered for me."

Martin was conscious of keeping control of the staff in the department of which he was the head. One man was particularly troublesome, and always complained abut Martin's authority, which he alleged was misused. "You've got us all in your pocket," was a phrase he used. Martin had become self-conscious abut the accusation, but could not understand it. His dream was suggesting that he should relax his authority and persuade his colleagues to agree with him, rather than ordering them around.

GOLF

opponent may represent one side of your character, or one side of an argument that you are having with yourself. The same applies to a dream of playing **GOLF**, but you should also think about the skill involved in hitting the ball. The score, in any game (and the method of scoring) may also be important. Were either you or another person cheating? If so, the implication may be that whatever the game you are playing in your waking life, there are chances of miscalculation.

CHESS
BRIDGE
CROSSWORD
173

Dreams of more cerebral games, such as **CHESS** or **BRIDGE**, may refer to your intellectual life. Although there may be the same element of competition as in dreams of physical team games, the implication will be somewhat different. There may be some reference to your thought patterns, to the way in which you think, and in particular to any complex plans you have (perhaps plans you are laying to compete with others in business or in emotional matters). The identity of your opponent, and your behavior toward each other, will be important. The clues in a **CROSSWORD** may be significant, as will be the word you are seeking.

DARTS
ARROWS
72, 118, 127

In a dream of playing **DARTS**, the emphasis will probably be on the darts themselves. There may be a similarity to a dream of **ARROWS**, and this – together with the ambition to "score" – may have a strong sexual association. Clues to the meaning of the dream should be evident. Who was your opponent in the dream darts match? Who won the game? What color was the board? How high did you score? Were there any spectators?

BOWLING

In a game of bowling, the aim is to knock down as many pins as possible. Therefore, a dream of **BOWLING** may be about ambition. Or is it a warning that someone is going to get hurt?

THE WORLD OF NATURE

FANTASY & FABLE

ARTS & SCIENCES

THE HUMAN BODY

EVERYDAY THINGS

HUMAN EMOTIONS

HUMAN ACTIVITIES

HUMAN CONDITIONS

RITUALS & RELIGION

THE DREAM THESAURUS

SPORT

DREAMS OF SPORT and games (*see page 132*) are commenting on our lifestyles and our attitudes toward challenges. Like all dream symbols, they suggest many possibilities, but they will usually aim to increase our self-confidence and self-esteem.

Sports require dexterity, planning, caution, and physical and emotional energy. To be successful in any sport it is also necessary to be dedicated. So your dream may be emphasizing these characteristics; there may be a suggestion that you should develop these traits further, in order to become more successful in waking life.

ATHLETICS
JUMPING
148
RACE
167

your dream was drawing your attention to some deep-rooted anger that you need to release. If you were engaged in karate or judo in your dream, your problem may have intellectual implications; are you trying to outwit your rivals in waking life? If in your dream of **ATHLETICS** you were **JUMPING** high or winning a **RACE**, there may be a positive comment on your ambition in waking life.

BOXING
WRESTLING
178
KARATE
JUDO

If the sports of **BOXING**, **WRESTLING**, **KARATE**, and **JUDO** are not part of your waking routine, but you dream of them, you may be facing opponents of some sort in your personal or professional life. How well you performed in the dream may be summing up your progress. You may be wrestling with a difficult problem. However, think about whether

SKATING
145, 148
CYCLING
RACING
140

If you were confidently **SKATING** or **CYCLING** in a dream, you were probably feeling exhilarated; so your waking mood is probably enthusiastic and hopeful for the future. However, you could encounter bumps in the dream – which may represent problems in waking life. Did you simply skate or cycle over the bumps? If so, in waking life are you ignoring difficulties? If you were **RACING** in your dream, consider whether you were winning. Is your dream suggesting ways in which you could improve your performance in waking life?

TRAVEL

TRAVEL IS OFTEN a means of escape – of getting away from the realities of our daily lives in order to refresh our bodies and spirit. We talk of that "dream vacation" and we work hard to take it. We can daydream about exotic locations, and indulge in armchair travel.

Your dream of travel will be representing many interesting possibilities. Was the road smooth and the way ahead clear? If this was the case, you appear to have your waking life under control and are making good progress. What sort of landscape did you see along the way (*see page 58*)? What was the weather like (*see page 49*)? If you were traveling in your

CAR
116, 135, 162

CAR, the dream may have sexual overtones, especially if you are male. On the other hand, if the dream was vague and you were only conscious of a need to travel, you should consider whether you want to move on in some way in your waking life. Perhaps you need to change your job, or to end or cement a new relationship. You may also require

THE WORLD OF NATURE

FANTASY & FABLE

ARTS & SCIENCES

THE HUMAN BODY

BUILDINGS & INTERIORS

EVERYDAY THINGS

HUMAN EMOTIONS

HUMAN ACTIVITIES

HUMAN CONDITIONS

RITUALS & RELIGION

THE DREAM THESAURUS

ABROAD
58, 121
VACATION

challenging intellectual stimulation; to learn a new language perhaps, especially if you were **ABROAD** in your travel dream. If you were on **VACATION** in your dream, you should seriously consider whether it was suggesting that you may actually need one in waking life.

PASSPORT
BORDER

If your **PASSPORT** featured in your dream, your unconscious may be giving you permission to "go ahead" with a project in waking life. However, if you lost your passport in your dream, or it was invalid, there may be a suggestion that you are not ready to make a particular move or make a certain decision. If you arrive at a **BORDER** in your dream and the officials allow you to go through, the same interpretation is possible. However, if you are not allowed across the border, you should also consider what, or who, is frustrating you or holding you back in some way in your waking life.

ATLAS
MAP

Referring to an **ATLAS** or a **MAP** in a dream may indicate that you are either looking for the way ahead or you are being shown it. You should decide whether you have a good sense of direction in waking life.

In your dream vehicle (*see page 116*), was the speed and the way it was moving more important than the vehicle itself?

AIRPLANE
162
CAR
116, 134, 162
TRAIN
117, 121
AIRPORT
RAILROAD
STATION

Were you about to take off in your dream **AIRPLANE**, or start up your **CAR** engine? If so, you may be ready to start a new project in waking life. If you were in a **TRAIN** leaving a station, the symbolism is similar. However, if the train was long, does that represent a long train of events or tasks that you are leaving behind you in waking life? A dream of being in an **AIRPORT** or **RAILROAD STATION** may indicate how secure you feel at the beginning of a new project or situation.

ADVENTURE

IF YOU EXPERIENCE SOME sort of adventure in a dream, this may
be a reflection on your waking life, which may have recently
become more adventurous. In this type of dream, your mood
and emotions will be particularly significant.

If you experienced an overall feeling of danger (*see page 158*), your dream may be giving you a warning. You may be taking a risk in waking life. Were you actually enjoying the dangerous situation – was it appealing to your sense of adventure?

HERO
65
HEROINE

If your dream **HERO** or **HEROINE** was someone you admire, you may be able to enjoy your dream in retrospect. This is

particularly true if you are attracted to the person, and in the dream you were making love. However, this sort of dream is unlikely to be predictive. You should take notice if the hero or heroine was giving you words of warning or advice. You should also consider what characteristics you

admire in that particular person, and whether you can emulate them. On the other hand, you may be the hero in the dream. If so, you may be more successful in waking life than you actually realize. Such dreams are endeavoring to inspire us and increase our self-confidence.

LEAPING
148
FALLING
147
BUNGEE-JUMPING

You may dream that you are taking a **LEAP**; you should not confuse this symbol with **FALLING**. It may be that you are about to take a leap in real life, and the dream is a pun. Perhaps you were **BUNGEE-JUMPING** in your dream. If you had confidence in the equipment, it may be an indication that all will be well in your waking enterprise. But were you terrified in your dream? Was it dark? If so, you should think again about your present situation, and decide whether in your dream you were overly confident, as that too may convey a warning. Are you looking before you leap?

ESCAPISM

TRAVEL IS ONE FORM of escapism, but there are many other forms.
There are escapist activities that can ruin our health, or even kill us,
such as cigarettes; and there are others, like going to the movies,
that simply give harmless pleasure.

CIGARETTE
94

Messages heavy with sexual innuendo were sent between couples during the first half of the 20th century as they lit each other's cigarettes, and to smoke a cigar was to exude an atmosphere of prosperity and opulence. Now we know that smoking can damage your health, and your dream of **CIGARETTES** may have been pleading with you to give up the habit. Our dreams often know better

CIGAR

than our waking selves, and it may be wise to take their advice. A dream **CIGAR** may symbolize someone in your waking life who is prosperous, showy, and perhaps dogmatic. Or does this identify with your behavior in waking life?

DRUGS

If you take **DRUGS** – even medically prescribed ones – or drink alcohol before going to bed, the proportion of "dream

ADDICT
HALLUCIN-
ATION
OVERDOSE

time" to mere sleeping time diminishes sharply. This reduces the amount of "help" you get from your dream. However, if you dream that you are a drug **ADDICT**, your unconscious may be warning you not to fall into this highly dangerous form of negative escapism. In waking life the drug may be more innocent: you can become addicted to work or to another person – anything can become a "drug." All dreams are in a sense hallucinations, but a dream of **HALLUCINATING** may suggest that you are losing touch with reality in your waking life. A dream of taking an **OVERDOSE** may equally mean that you are "overdosing" in waking life; you may be working too hard, seeing too much of someone, or being too possessive.

MOVIES
76

For generations, movies have been the most popular form of escapism. A dream of going to the **MOVIES** these days may contain similar symbols to dreams of communication (*see page 137*). The image in the film that your unconscious chooses to insert into your dream will have been carefully chosen: it will not be there simply because you particularly noticed it during the film. If romance colored your dream, you should give some thought to your waking life and your relationships. Is your life lacking in romance or color, and are you bored or restless? (To dream of a color film seen in black and white sends this obvious message.) If you come to the conclusion that this is the case, do all you can to rectify the situation, or ask your dreams to give you suggestions (*see page 33*).

—✦— COMMUNICATION —✦—

COMMUNICATION IS THE BASIS of dreaming, since dreams are messages
from ourselves to ourselves. However, when it emerges in a
recognizable form our unconscious seems to be making an effort to
convey a message in a way we should find easy to understand.

CORRESPON-
DENCE
LETTER

In a dream, your reaction to a piece of **CORRESPONDENCE** or a **LETTER** is important. You may have discovered the letter and heaved a sigh of relief, or felt resignation or anxiety. How you opened the letter in the dream will confirm your reaction: did you do so with eagerness or care; or did you put it aside, not wanting to open it? Your dream would seem to be advising you, in no uncertain terms, that there is something in your waking life that needs attention; if you put your correspondence aside, you are not facing up to your problem. Other symbols in the dream may help you reach a final decision. In waking life you may be awaiting examination results or the result of a job interview, for example. If in your dream you receive the news that you hoped for, there are two possible interpretations. Your dream may be one of wish-fulfillment (*see page 150*), or if in waking life you know that you did your best, your dream may be reassuring. If you are writing letters in a dream, it may be indicating that there is some message you want to communicate to another person in waking life.

BUILDINGS &
INTERIORS

EVERYDAY
THINGS

HUMAN
EMOTIONS

HUMAN
ACTIVITIES

HUMAN
CONDITIONS

RITUALS &
RELIGION

THE DREAM
THESAURUS

FACSIMILE TELEGRAM CABLE

The receipt of a FACSIMILE, TELEGRAM, or CABLE in your dream suggests urgency, and it would seem that you are being drawn to some element of your life that requires your immediate attention. The content of your correspondence may seem unrelated to your waking problem or concern, and in its simplest form your dream may be an instruction to take action at once, or to be decisive. There is a difference between the old-fashioned cable and telegram and the modern fax machine, and the one that emerged in your dream probably relates to your particular age and generation. If you are elderly, and have unpleasant memories of receiving a telegram, try not to be too apprehensive about a dream telegram.

GREETING HANDSHAKE

If you were GREETING someone or being greeted in your dream, assuming that you welcomed the greeting and that the experience was pleasant, it would seem that your dream is suggesting that you are open-minded and ready to start a new project or challenge in waking life. If, on the other hand, you spurned what was being offered, you should ask yourself whether you are facing up to a problem in waking life. Then you will have to decide if the dream was advising you to reassess your attitude. A dream of a HANDSHAKE may have a similar connotation, but the pressure of the handshake is important. If the hand offered was weak and clammy, do you think your attitude in waking life may be lacking in enthusiasm, or that a concern or idea is being received in a half-hearted way? If the hand was firm and friendly, it would suggest that you have a balanced attitude in waking life, but if the hand grasped yours so hard that you felt physical pain, you may be under pressure to accept your waking situation.

LANGUAGE *173* **MORSE CODE**

Dreams in which someone is trying, unsuccessfully, to communicate to you in a foreign LANGUAGE, or in which you are receiving indecipherable MORSE CODE, involve complex symbols. You should ask your dreams for an understandable symbol (*see page 33*), but either you

INTERPRETER

are not putting across your thoughts, ideas, or feelings coherently to other people or you are muddled or confused at present. Try to calm down if you are at all upset, try to analyze your problems, and hope to get assistance, rather than aggravation, from your dreams. Perhaps help was at hand in your dream and an INTERPRETER appeared. This figure would probably represent the more rational and organized part of you, and would be a positive symbol. Did the interpreter translate satisfactorily for you?

TELEPHONE *158*

A TELEPHONE is the classic "message" dream symbol. In your dream, who was on the end of the line? Consider what this person means to you, and what they stand for in your waking life. If you were making the call, your dream may be concentrating on a message that you are trying to convey to someone in your waking life. You must ask yourself what that message is and at whom it is aimed. If in your dream you were desperately trying to get through to someone and had difficulty in doing so, you are probably being frustrated in waking life. In your dream you may have been crying for help. Do you need help in reality? Do not forget that you could be the telephone itself, trying to convey a message.

INTERVIEW

Dreaming of attending or giving an INTERVIEW may mean that you are questioning yourself about your motives and actions, and possible decisions you may be facing. If in your dream you heard the result of the interview, you may discover how successful you are being in real life with solving problems and making decisions. If you are facing an interview in waking life, your dream was either reassuring you or warning you of the possible outcome.

MESSAGE NOTICE

If you dream that you receive a written MESSAGE or read a NOTICE, your dream may be telling you to "take notice" of something in your waking life. The dream message may be suggesting that you are less observant than you should be. However, even if your message was

PRESCRIPTION of a spiritual or religious nature, you should realize that it is still from you to you. If any type of god enters your dreams it will probably represent an authority figure, who may be part of your own personality or may be someone who is influential in your waking life. If you dream that you are handling a **PRESCRIPTION**, you may be receiving advice on how to rectify a particular situation in waking life.

TALK
SPEECH If you were giving a **TALK** or delivering a **SPEECH** in your dream, in waking life you may be volubly stating your opinions. How your efforts were received in your dream will tell you just how effective, or otherwise, you are. If you were inhibited

STAMMER
INTERFERENCE by a dream **STAMMER** you may at present be hesitant about making certain decisions or taking a particular action. Or, if you were talking too much, your dreams may have been dropping a hint. This seems most likely if you suffered **INTERFERENCE** from other characters that were present in the dream.

VISITOR You should give a great deal of thought to a **VISITOR** that appears in your dream. Was the visitor a stranger or someone you know and admire? If it was the former, you may be searching for new interests or adventure; if it was the latter, you may want to embrace the admirable characteristics or skills of the person concerned.

—◆— GAMBLING —◆—

DREAMS IN WHICH YOU are trying your luck at the gaming tables, backing a horse in a race, or simply taking a risk, have one thing in common — you have an aim, and there is a chance that you may not achieve it. The situation will in some way be reflected in waking life.

CARDS
ACE
ROULETTE
140 A dream of staking money — perhaps at **CARDS** — may have something to do with your emotions. In waking life, are you investing too much, emotionally, in the result of a risky situation, or in someone who may prove to be unreliable? If you dream that an **ACE** turns up in your hand, or a particular number at **ROULETTE**, consider who it may represent in waking life. What color and suit was the ace? What significance does the number (*see page 80*) have?

POKER
CASINO If you were playing **POKER** in your dream, the emphasis may be on concealing your hand, or on not showing your feelings in waking life. Playing at a **CASINO** in a dream may suggest that a number of people are involved in the situation or event under discussion.

Games of pure chance, rather than those that have at least an element of skill, are likely to refer to "fate" rather than to anything over which you have control. If you dreamed that you were buying

THE WORLD OF NATURE

FANTASY & FABLE

ARTS & SCIENCES

THE HUMAN BODY

BUILDINGS & INTERIORS

EVERYDAY THINGS

HUMAN EMOTIONS

HUMAN ACTIVITIES

HUMAN CONDITIONS

RITUALS & RELIGION

THE DREAM THESAURUS

LOTTERY
RAFFLE
BINGO
ROULETTE
139
DICE

tickets for a **LOTTERY** or **RAFFLE**, you may be involved in some situation in waking life that has become out of control. Or, the dream may be pointing out that you cannot always predict the results of your actions. There may also be an element of wish-fulfillment (*see page 150*). Winning a game of **BINGO** or **ROULETTE** in a dream has little to do with anything other than luck, and it would be unwise to gamble a huge amount on such a dream being accurate. If you were throwing **DICE** in your dream, are you "dicing with death," or taking a chance in waking life?

HORSE RACE
RACING
134
BOOKMAKER

A dream of betting on a **HORSE RACE** may allude to your emotional life (it is common for humans to feel close to horses). If you are a regular gambler and follow **RACING** keenly, a dream that alludes to a particular horse may be worth following up, since your unconscious may be better at choosing a winner than your waking mind, with its various distractions. A **BOOKMAKER** may represent a rapacious friend in waking life, but is also someone who takes a chance: are you relying on someone whose advice may be selfish?

⸻ CRIME ⸻

A DREAM OF COMMITTING a specific crime – whether it is murder or petty theft – should be carefully considered. Who was the victim? Think about how you felt in the dream.

THIEF
BURGLAR

Were you a **THIEF** in your dream? If so, what were you stealing, and from whom? Remember that nothing in our dream world is what it seems, so an object that you steal from someone may represent something quite abstract. For example, someone dreaming of stealing money from a colleague may envy their position at work, and may be seeking promotion over them, while a woman who steals another's makeup may envy her beauty. **BURGLARS** break in, and the action can

POACHER
ACCESSORY

have a sexual connotation in a dream: a man dreaming of burgling a woman's home may be contemplating (consciously or not) stealing something other than her possessions. A **POACHER** steals living things; as with a burglar, there may be an association with someone else's lifestyle. If, in your dream, you were an **ACCESSORY** to a crime, in waking life you may have been persuaded to help someone else in an action that you know to be wrong (*see also Guilt, page 124, and Fear, page 120*).

⸻ WAR ⸻

PEOPLE WHO HAVE BEEN in a war situation may later be plagued with dreams of their ordeals, but during the crisis their dreams are often of peace and hope. For those who have never seen war, such dreams usually refer to private battles they are waging either with themselves or with other people.

Aggression, anger, sorrow, or pity are usually to be found in a dream of war. Whatever the emotion, it will be important, because it will show your attitude to whatever feeling or action in waking life has provoked the dream. The clue to the dream's real subject may be

ARMY
SOLDIER
BATTLE

found, for example, in the identity of the opposing **ARMIES**, in the landscape (*see page 58*), or the **SOLDIERS'** clothing. The progress of the **BATTLE** (who won, who lost, the maneuvers, and the tactics) will be equally important in suggesting a possible course of action in waking life.

REGIMENT	
176	
INVASION	

REGIMENT
176
INVASION

If, in your dream, you were part of a **REGIMENT** involved in a war, the suggestion seems to be that there is safety in numbers. Sorrow or pity may be an aspect of guilt (*see page 124*), or may simply reflect your attitude to an event in waking life. A dream of an **INVASION** seems likely to refer to interference of some kind. It may be symbolic of an invasion of someone else's space in waking life, either real or psychological.

GUERRILLA
HELMET

Taking part in **GUERRILLA** action suggests clandestine plans in waking life, while a preoccupation with a **HELMET** and protective clothing may mirror a desire to "take cover" in some waking circumstance. (*See also Weapons, page 118.*)

—◈— SERVICE —◈—

AT THE BEGINNING OF the century, to be a "good servant" was no ignoble aim; today, giving good service is rarely a matter for private pride, and is more often good business. So a dream of being in service may be about your self-presentation to the world.

BUTLER
CHAMBER-MAID
CHAUFFEUR

A dream of being a **BUTLER** or **CHAMBERMAID** offers the idea of subservience, and also has an old-fashioned air about it. At work, are you expected to be subservient to your employer? If you are a housewife and mother, do you see yourself as a "skivvy"? Were you being complimented or denigrated in your dream? Were you pleased that while appearing to be the polite servant, you were really scheming behind your employer's back? You may have been driving with extreme skill in a dream that you were a **CHAUFFEUR**; are you proud of your skills in waking life?

PORTER

If your dream features a **PORTER**, think about your burdens in waking life. If you were unloading your burdens onto a dream porter, are you putting your responsibilities in waking life onto someone else's shoulders? Did you tip the porter generously, or are you being mean to someone who has done you a

DOORMAN

service? A dream of a **DOORMAN** may mean that you are opening doors for someone in waking life. Alternatively, is someone doing the same for you?

THE WORLD OF NATURE

FANTASY & FABLE

ARTS & SCIENCES

THE HUMAN BODY

BUILDINGS & INTERIORS

EVERYDAY THINGS

HUMAN EMOTIONS

THE GAME DREAM

I was playing a board game with my friend Mary. I picked up a card on which was written: 'Go to jail, move directly to jail, do not pass Go, do not collect two hundred dollars.' I felt frustrated at this point because Mary seemed to be winning all the time. Then I picked up the 'Get out of jail free' card, and Mary landed on a square where I had a hotel and had to pay me a lot of money. As she gave me the money she said, 'You'd better have this, too,' and gave me the card that read 'Advance to Go.'

I then found myself walking up a steep, narrow path in a thick, humid jungle. There were jungle noises, thick and exotic vegetation, and trees all around me; it was very exciting, but I felt extremely nervous. I picked up a twig and it broke in my hand, but something inside me told me to be brave and carry on, and that I would enjoy the view from the top of the path. I then realized that I was at the top of a large hill, looking across a valley at a huge cliff where some people were rock climbing. 'Come on, join us,' they shouted across the valley.

Then I was with the group of climbers, but I was wondering what would happen if I broke the twigs. Then I was descending the cliff with a rope, feeling free and happy. At one point — about halfway down — when I was against the cliff side, I grabbed a handful of twigs. They all snapped in my hand but I did not care that I had broken them. It was a marvelous sensation and I woke up, feeling extremely positive, from the best dream I ever remember having.

TWIG BREAKS

PERCY SEES CLIMBERS

TWIGS SNAP IN PERCY'S HAND

MARY IS
WINNING
GAME

PERCY PICKS UP
"GET OUT OF JAIL
FREE" CARD

INTERPRETATION

Percy suffered from brittle-bone disease and had always been confined to a wheelchair. He was an extremely talented calligrapher, but he would often break a finger while holding a pen. At the time of his dream, his father had been offered a new appointment in Africa, but the country where his parents were going had inferior medical facilities to those in Chicago, and the climate would prove trying for Percy. He was an adult, and the decision must be his own.

Mary was Percy's nurse and a close friend in his waking life. The board game clearly pointed to his dilemma. The cards relating to jail represented Percy himself, trapped inside his weak body; their message was of restriction, but also of security. The fact that his fortunes in the game changed and he had the chance to get out of jail, and to advance to "Go," conveyed a message that he should take a risk. The transformation to the exotic jungle was giving him some idea of how he would react to his new life.

Percy had always longed to see some of the world he had only read about in books. The move was a challenge to him, which most people told him not to accept. While he was excited in his dream, he also felt apprehensive and nervous, as shown by his reaction to the broken twig. He was brave enough to go to the top of the hill, and to join the rock climbers. His elation at descending the cliff, and not caring any more about the twigs (representing the snapping of his brittle bones) helped him come to a decision to go to Africa.

One of the most interesting elements of this dream was the fact that Percy was walking up the jungle path; something that he would never be able to do in waking life. The confusion of the jungle, the plants, and the noise surrounding him, represented the problems that such a move would create; but it also demonstrated Percy's adventurous spirit. While there is a great deal of escapist wish-fulfillment (*see page 150*) in this dream, it was a positive experience for the dreamer.

—◆— ACTIVITIES —◆—

WHEN SPECIFIC ACTIVITIES enter our dream world we should ask ourselves whether we are filling our waking hours in a rewarding way. It may be that we need to do more physical exercise, or accept a new challenge. Some dream activities, however, draw our attention to our personal characteristics and hint that we may be expressing them too forcibly – or not forcibly enough.

CLIMBING
HILL
58
MOUNTAIN
58, 172
DIGGING
48, 114
EXCAVATING

You may have dreamed that you were CLIMBING up a HILL or a MOUNTAIN. Whether you were climbing with ease or difficulty, the dream may be reflecting on your ambitions, progress, and ability to face up to challenges in waking life. If you were DIGGING or EXCAVATING in your dream, it may suggest that you are trying to dredge up facts, or get to the root cause of a problem in waking life. More important (especially if you have a recurring dream that involves either of these symbols), your dream may be saying that you need to work on your personality and resolve deep-rooted problems. If you are really concerned about such a dream, you might consider seeking professional advice.

EXERCISE
73

If you dream that you are doing EXERCISE, you must decide whether you need to be more energetic in waking life. However, you should also consider whether the sort of exercise your dream mentioned is, in fact, physical. You may need to exercise your mind, your common sense, caution, or tact. If for some reason you are unable to do physical exercise, although you would like to, you may have

WEIGHTS
73

to resign yourself to the fact that your dream is a matter of wish-fulfillment (*see page 150*). If you were training with WEIGHTS in your dream, you may need to lose or gain weight in waking life. In either case, you should take your dream hint seriously.

RIDING
HORSE
42, 170
MOTORCYCLE
BICYCLE
117
ANIMAL
121, 127, 155

A dream of RIDING a HORSE may be connected to your sex life. If you were fearless and enjoying yourself, it would seem that you are enjoying a rewarding relationship in waking life. On the other hand, if you were apprehensive or nervous about falling, consider taking action to improve this sphere of your life; you may be suffering from some inhibition, or unable to commit yourself to a partner. The inference is similar if you were riding a MOTORCYCLE or BICYCLE, but if your ride was bumpy or uphill, do you think these obstructions represent frustration and problems in waking life? If you were riding another ANIMAL, think about who or what that animal represents in waking life. It may be a zodiac animal: a bull or a lion, for instance; in which case, do you know a Taurean or a Leo in waking life? An easy ride suggests that there are no real problems – provided that you are not "riding high," taking people for a ride, or conversely, being taken for one.

WALKING
73
RUNNING
73
JOGGING
148

The dream activities of WALKING, RUNNING, and JOGGING are probably all commenting on the pace of your waking life and how you are coping with your various commitments. If you were walking in your dream, it would suggest that you are in control of your life, and taking everything in your stride. Your stress level is also probably low. If you dreamed that you were jogging, you appear to be taking your waking life at a steady pace. Are you, however, bored with some aspects of your daily life? You may have dreamed that you were running, and provided that you were keeping up with the others in the dream, this is quite positive; but you may be under more stress than is good for you. If you were falling behind rival competitors in the dream, or trying to win a race and failing, you should attempt to rearrange your schedule in waking life, so that some of the pressure is relieved. You should treat this as a dream warning. You might like to think of where you were walking, jogging, or running to. What was the goal? What sort of landscape were you passing through (*see page 58*)? What was the dream weather like (*see page 49*)? This should tell you about the prevailing atmosphere in your waking life, and hint at the achievement or otherwise of your objectives.

SKATING
134, 148
DANCING
148

Dreams in which you are **DANCING** or **SKATING** are usually dreams to be enjoyed. Nevertheless, they do have special significance, even if they are often to be accepted as mere wish-fulfillment (*see page 150*). The symbols in both dreams are similar, and from one perspective it would seem that you are enjoying life. If you were performing steps or movements that you know you could never do in real life, your dream may be suggesting that you are ready to "take off" in some way in waking life. In such cases the symbol is related to dreams of flying (*see page 147*). If you were on skates in your dream, and out of control, consider whether you are acting recklessly or emotionally in waking life. Alternatively, are your dreams telling you to "get your skates on" – to speed up the pace of your life and put

DANCING SHOES

more activity into it? Wearing **DANCING SHOES** that caused you pain in your dream may be indicative of a physical problem with your feet in waking life.

Dreaming of playing games (*see page 132*) may be drawing your attention to how you cope with rivals in waking life, and whether you are a good or a bad loser. In your dream, were you helping your team mates, or were you cheating – knowing that you were doing wrong and feeling guilty about it? Your dream may, for example, be commenting on a mental game you are playing in waking life to try and win a partner in romance. Or, it may be reflecting on your business life and your attitude toward your rivals in this area. Is your dream suggesting that you should take life more or less seriously than you usually do?

WEAVING KNITTING CROCHETING SEWING

A dream of **WEAVING**, **KNITTING**, **CROCHETING**, or **SEWING** may be making a strong statement. You should consider whether you are bogged down in a repetitive routine in waking life. Your dream may be suggesting that you need to broaden your horizons, for when we occupy ourselves with these crafts, although they can be rewarding and may satisfy a creative instinct, they call for constant attention to detail and much of the work is repetitive. Does this reflect your waking lifestyle, especially if it centers around home, family, and loved ones? If you were sewing and perhaps joining pieces of fabric, are you bringing certain aspects of your waking life together? If your dream involved weaving, you may be plotting or planning something in waking life. If you were knitting or crocheting, these symbols may (like the others) simply be indicative of similar waking action. For example, if you dropped a stitch in the dream, have you been tactless recently in your waking life? If there was a break in your yarn, have you had a quarrel with someone? Whether you were successful in rejoining the yarn or not may give you advice on whether you should patch up your differences.

THE WORLD OF NATURE

FANTASY & FABLE

ARTS & SCIENCES

THE HUMAN BODY

BUILDINGS & INTERIORS

EVERYDAY THINGS

HUMAN EMOTIONS

HUMAN ACTIVITIES

HUMAN CONDITIONS

RITUALS & RELIGION

THE DREAM THESAURUS

THE WORLD OF NATURE

FANTASY & FABLE

ARTS & SCIENCES

THE HUMAN BODY

BUILDINGS & INTERIORS

EVERYDAY THINGS

HUMAN EMOTIONS

HUMAN ACTIVITIES

HUMAN CONDITIONS

RITUALS & RELIGION

THE DREAM THESAURUS

—◆— CLEANSING —◆—

IT IS FAIRLY COMMON for people to dream of washing their hands compulsively – trying to cleanse their unconscious of the recollection of a deep sin or crime they have committed.

SCRUBBING
STAIN

A dream of washing oneself almost always relates to something that is worrying us or troubling our conscience, in our waking state. The harder we are **SCRUBBING** ourselves in a dream, the more compelling the instinct. Washing a **STAIN** from an article of clothing (*see page 84*) has a similar implication. You must decide to what trouble in waking life the dream symbol refers; in most cases this is either obvious or there are other clues offered in the dream (sometimes the dream may suggest that you should be conscience-stricken about something).

SHOWER
47
BATH
46
SHAMPOO
HAIR
92, 165
GENITALS
92

The part of the body involved in the dream may be significant. Standing under a **SHOWER** or being immersed in a **BATH** seems to indicate an all-embracing problem in waking life. A dream of **SHAMPOOING** your **HAIR** is often an allusion to your emotions. If you were washing your **GENITALS** in a dream, it may indicate that there is a sexual escapade in

waking life of which you are or should be ashamed. Alternatively, it may reflect a concern about disease.

A dream of cleaning your home (*see page 102*) or a particular room (*see page 103*) may relate to an unconscious desire to reorganize your waking life. You may need to dispose of some kind of "dirt" or "dust" that is perhaps slowing down your responses or clouding your judgment in waking life.

WASHING
MACHINE

The image in your dream may have been of a **WASHING MACHINE**. If you were simply watching the wash in the machine go around, the reference may be to your daily routine. Is it a boring and repetitive one? A dream of watching a television commercial for detergent may have a similar meaning, it may reflect a desire to upgrade your lifestyle – perhaps by buying a new washing machine.

—◆— MARRIAGE —◆—

A DREAM OF MARRIAGE may simply be one of wish-fulfillment (*see page 150*). However, such a dream may be about other forms of "joining," for example a marriage of ideas, activities, or opinions in waking life.

FIANCE
HUSBAND
90
WIFE
90
CUCKOLD

The folklore of many countries contains various ways of prompting someone to dream of a lover or a future **FIANCE** – placing a particular item under the pillow, for example. It is not surprising that this frequently works, since such prompting immediately before falling asleep will often have a positive result. A dream of a future **HUSBAND** or **WIFE** may nevertheless not be literal, but may be an expression of some other hope for the future. In the same way, a dream of being a **CUCKOLD**, although it may be an

HONEYMOON
151
INFIDELITY
POLYGAMY

expression of jealousy, may be about the stealing away of an idea. To dream of a **HONEYMOON**, while it may symbolize looking forward, may reflect a happy period in waking life. A dream of **INFIDELITY** may mean that you are accusing yourself of being unfaithful to an ideal or a principle in waking life – or indeed to a spouse. A dream of **POLYGAMY**, while also perhaps wish-fulfillment (*see page 150*), may be an accusation of trying to cope with too many activities or ideas at once.

FLYING

DREAMS OF FLYING are extremely common, and some people have been so convinced by the apparent realism of their dream that on waking they have fallen downstairs, attempting to defy gravity.

Dreams of flying vary from dreamer to dreamer, but in general it seems that very few of them involve long, high flights. More often, the dreamer only seems to be able to fly a few yards above the ground for between 20 to 100 yards (18–91 meters), usually with a springy motion. The simplest explanation offered for flying dreams was put forward by the English physician, and writer on sex, Havelock Ellis, in his book *The World of Dreams*. He suggested that the simple action of breathing in and out is enough to suggest the idea of flying, which the body then translates into the sensation of flight.

FALLING
136

There is also some comparison with dreams of **FALLING**, which can simply mean that we are "falling asleep." Freud supposed that dreams of flying were "nothing else but the desire to be capable of sexual activities," and several other psychologists support the view that flying dreams are connected with sex. However, like all dreams, those of flying can have a great number of interpretations – usually unique to the dreamer. You should consider the dream's atmosphere and context. Are you, in waking life, trying to "rise above" a problem, achieve promotion, or improve your life? Are you developing an idea or an ambition? You may be flying into a rage, flying in the face of fortune, flying off the handle, or quite simply "letting fly."

PURSUIT

DREAMS OF PURSUIT, like dreams of flying, are extremely common. Sometimes the dreamer is the pursuer, but more often the pursued – chased by (often unidentifiable) enemies or monsters.

It is important to identify the symbol that is pursuing you, but remember that it may not be what it seems. Perhaps it is an idea; for example, fear of unemployment. On the other hand, is it a lover, sexual insecurity, a house, or something you are planning to buy? You may either be the pursued or the pursuer – or even both – so your ambition may be chasing you and urging you on to success. Or you may be chased by an emotion, perhaps one that you are rejecting in waking life. It has been suggested that almost every dream

of this kind is one of conflict, and that the person or thing that pursues you is something that you unconsciously identify with, even if you consciously abhor it. You should work on such a dream: before going to sleep, imagine facing your pursuer and demanding to know why it is chasing you. It is important to discover the nature of the fear that is on your heels then you can face up to it and conquer it. The dream may be a disturbing nightmare (*see page 154*), or it may recur (*see page 36*).

THE WORLD OF NATURE

FANTASY & FABLE

ARTS & SCIENCES

THE HUMAN BODY

BUILDINGS & INTERIORS

EVERYDAY THINGS

HUMAN EMOTIONS

HUMAN ACTIVITIES

HUMAN CONDITIONS

RITUALS & RELIGION

THE DREAM THESAURUS

—◆— MOVEMENT —◆—

IT IS IMPORTANT TO RECOGNIZE that some inhibition prevents us from physical movement when we are dreaming of any physical activity, so we need not fear that we will throw ourselves from a window.

JIG
WALTZING
JUMPING
134
LEAPING
136
JOGGING
144

If you wake a sleepwalker, you will always find that he or she is in a dreamless sleep, just as people who toss and turn in bed are at a level of sleep where dreaming does not occur. Dreams of movement have other than physical significance: perhaps in waking life you need to move on, take another route, or speed up your progress. Dancing a JIG in a dream may refer to simple pleasure, as can dancing a WALTZ, although the emotions concerned will be different. JUMPING or LEAPING in a dream may signify ambition, or a desire to improve your status. Could this be a cry for promotion? A dream in which you are gently JOGGING seems to imply steady, unambitious progress, while dreaming of

DIVING
KICKING
DANCE
145
AEROBICS
BALLET
SKATING
134, 145

DIVING may signify the desire to throw yourself into something in waking life. You should remember that water almost always indicates that emotion is involved. To give or receive a KICK implies disapproval of some kind in waking life. If you were at a DANCE or AEROBICS class in your dream, there may be a suggestion that you should get more exercise. Dreams of BALLET dancing or SKATING may contain elements of wish-fulfillment (*see page 150*), but there is the underlying fact that both activities take years of dedicated hard work. Such a dream may be encouraging you to persevere with even amateur artistic skills, or there may be a general comment on your attitude toward work that demands discipline.

—◆— OCCUPATIONS —◆—

A DREAM IN WHICH the main symbol seems to be someone's occupation may be a comment on your own behavior. It is not necessarily that you see yourself as a cook or a barber, but that those occupations say something about your actions and attitudes.

ACTOR
DANCER

Were you an ACTOR or a DANCER in your dream, or were you watching some kind of performance? If so, your dream may be one of wish-fulfillment (*see page 150*), especially if you had thought of one of these activities as a career. However, the lives of theater people are not glamorous: they work hard and endure long periods without work. There may be a hidden message in your dream — especially if you think you are working long and hard for little or no return.

CAPTAIN
162

Your dream CAPTAIN may represent an authority figure in your waking life — perhaps part of your own personality. The captain may be giving you some kind of guidance or instruction, and may

represent someone known to you in waking life who has characteristics that you recognize in the dream. The dream may be reassuring you that you are in command — that you are steering your ship or piloting your airplane in exactly the direction you want it to go. However, you must decide whether the captain in your dream was doing the right thing, or was being indecisive, weak, or bullying. Compare the captain's actions and attitude in the dream to your present behavior in waking life.

PLUMBER
47

PLUMBERS often have to cope with unpleasant matter and very dirty water, and in dreams there is usually a relationship between water and our emotions. Have you been holding on to a negative emotion lately, such as jealousy or envy? If in your dream your plumber cleared a blocked drain, there may be a reference to your own blocked emotions. Should they be cleared away? Your dream plumber may be suggesting that you "plumb the depths" of your personality, and seek professional advice.

COOK
CARETAKER

If your dream featured a **COOK** or a **CARETAKER**, who were your dream characters "looking after"? Are you being overly protective toward someone close to you? Cooks are notoriously bad-tempered: does this reflect your own feelings at present? If you were the cook in the dream, there may be a suggestion that you are in need of affection and love in waking life – or that you should "serve it out" more generously than usual. If your dream was of a caretaker, do you think you are being too fussy or doing too much for loved ones?

GARDENER

Digging, planting, growing, and disposing of unwanted material are all themes related to **GARDENERS**. The symbol of a dream gardener is generally a positive one, and such a dream may reflect on your aspirations, goals, or expectations for the future. The planting of seeds may represent the planting of ideas, and picking fruit may signify gained experience. A dream of pruning roses may be connected with your love or sex life, particularly if you or your dream gardener suffered pricked fingers.

FISHERMAN
FISH

Since water is so frequently symbolic of our emotions, a dream featuring a **FISHERMAN** may signify your own search for an emotional element in your waking life that is missing, mislaid, or simply not being properly employed. Did the fisherman catch a **FISH**? Did you throw it back (reject it)? Did the fish get away, and if so, are you being too emotionally passive in waking life?

ARTIST
PHOTO-
GAPHER

If you own either a camera or a set of paints, you should consider a dream of an **ARTIST**, a **PHOTOGRAPHER**, or a

CAMERAMAN

CAMERAMAN on a practical level. Your dream may be saying that there is a photographer, cameraman, or artist within you and crying out for expression. Even if you think you are no good at such occupations, or you have been told that you have no talent, you may have underdeveloped potential. You should take notice of what the artist or photographer was painting or photographing, because it may hold an important message.

MISSIONARY

Was your dream **MISSIONARY** being helpful and inspiring, or simply misguided? If you were the missionary in your dream, you may be handing out excellent advice and spiritual leadership. However, you should also consider any other symbols that may appear in the dream; they may be signifying that you are actually misguided and overly zealous in waking life.

HUMAN EMOTIONS

HUMAN ACTIVITIES

HUMAN CONDITIONS

RITUALS & RELIGION

THE DREAM THESAURUS

THE WORLD OF NATURE

FANTASY & FABLE

ARTS & SCIENCES

THE HUMAN BODY

BUILDINGS & INTERIORS

EVERYDAY THINGS

HUMAN EMOTIONS

HUMAN ACTIVITIES

HUMAN CONDITIONS

RITUALS & RELIGION

THE DREAM THESAURUS

BARBER
165
HAIRDRESSER
BEAUTICIAN

For men, the dread of a visit to the **BARBER** in a dream is a classic indication of castration fear. Going to a dream **HAIRDRESSER**, on the other hand, suggests an improvement of your image – perhaps this is needed in waking life. If you were the hairdresser, your dream may have been commenting on your authoritarian behavior. Perhaps you are in a more powerful position than you realize in waking life. Dreaming of being pampered by a **BEAUTICIAN** may suggest that you need more relaxation or affection, or that you should improve your image; but conversely, you may be underestimating your appearance. If you were the beautician, it is possible that in waking life you are trying to help someone, improve their appearance, or restore their self-confidence.

SALESPERSON

A dream that you were a **SALESPERSON** may indicate that you are trying to sell something in waking life. Could this be an idea, a plan or project, or yourself? If you were buying something from a salesperson, were they shifty or trustworthy? Decide who that person represents in waking life. Consider your current emotional state: are you attempting to buy love and affection, or are you parting with too much, too often? Is this particular dream commenting on your emotional or financial security? Did you feel drained because you were forced to sell precious or sentimental possessions in a dream? If so, you may be making too many sacrifices in your life.

FARMER

FARMERS sow, plant, plow, and reap, but they also breed and herd animals, and eventually sell them to be slaughtered. Your dream of a farmer may be focusing on the rewarding and positive side of farming, or the less sympathetic. You should first decide which. In waking life you may now be reaping the benefit of a great deal of hard work, or you may be scattering seeds for the future. In your dream, you may have been driving a piece of farm equipment. Who does the machine represent in waking life? Someone who is big and powerful but whom you know you must control? If you were the farmer surveying your land, you may be feeling satisfied with your life. This is a positive dream.

◆— WISH-FULFILLMENT —◆

EVEN THE LEAST AMBITIOUS of us have our aspirations, hopes, and desires. We may learn to stifle these, because they seem unattainable; and we may even forget that we once had them. But in fact they remain deeply rooted in our subconscious, and together with less important desires, will be fulfilled in our dreams.

BEACH
59, 127
LAGOON
46
ADOLESCENCE

The most common dreams that are the result of our conscious or unconscious wishes reflect those wishes in an obvious way. If you are feeling tired and jaded, you may dream that you are relaxing on a sunny Mediterranean **BEACH** or by a calm **LAGOON**. If you are pursuing a member of the opposite sex in waking life, you may have dreams of success. Someone conscious of the passing of time may dream of being an **ADOLESCENT** again, or someone wanting a baby may dream

CRADLE
88
LUXURY

of a **CRADLE** and baby clothes. If you have financial worries in waking life, you may in your dreams be living in **LUXURY** surrounded by piles of money (*see page 110*). But it is important to remember that there may still be a complex system of symbolism at work in your dreams. A dream of currency for example, may seem to refer to your financial worries in waking life, but may instead mirror an element of sensual or emotional deprivation. So, however much a dream seems to be one of simple wish-fulfillment, you should still look at its imagery, and make sure that it is not (as it so often is) working in disguise.

BRIDE
177
BRIDEGROOM
177
HONEYMOON
146

There are many recorded examples of young men and women who dream of marriage (*see page 146*), of being dressed as a **BRIDE** or **BRIDEGROOM**, or of setting out on a **HONEYMOON**, and there is no doubt that in many cases these are actually straightforward dreams of wish-fulfillment. There may be a hint that your partner is in need of reassurance. A dream of a honeymoon may seem merely an anticipation of pleasure, but if your partner in the dream is someone with whom you are already living, it may be a suggestion that they need reassurance.

HAREM
PROSTITUTE
169
GIGOLO
169

A man dreaming that he is in a **HAREM** or is visiting a **PROSTITUTE** may be expressing his desire for sexual variety. A woman dreaming of being imprisoned in a harem or working as a prostitute is more likely to regard it as a dream of sexual subjugation; in her case it is extremely unlikely (although not impossible) to be a dream of wish-fulfillment. A man who dreams of being a **GIGOLO** may be expressing a secret notion of sex as a profit-making activity – the profit not

SHOPPING

necessarily being financial, but perhaps emotional. A **SHOPPING** spree is regarded as a great pleasure, but at a certain cost. A dream of buying something you want or need is simple wish-fulfillment, but it may be pointing out that satisfying your desires can be more costly than you think. If you were buying food in your dream, you may be buying someone's love and affection in waking life.

— DREAM ANALYSIS —

"I was dancing with my boss, and gradually as we danced we became amorous. I was not attracted to her, but I thought I had better respond. Then she said, 'I know you are not attracted to me, but why don't we go to bed? I can afford you, you know.' I said, 'I'm not for sale.' She said, 'What about $10,000 for ten minutes?' But she appeared ugly to me and I could not face the thought. Then I woke up."

Dave was uncomfortable at work because a woman had been appointed as the head of his department. He found her attractive, and she had made it clear that she needed his support at work, but he doubted whether he could work for her. He had been fantasizing about an affair with her – which would place her in his power to a certain extent. His dream was telling him that he should not offer himself in that way, since he would not be able to work with her. The fact that she was ugly to him suggested that she was not as impressive a leader as he had believed.

—◦— AMBITION —◦—

AMBITION IS OFTEN DISCUSSED in our dreams by symbolic reflections of our aspirations, which by the circumstances surrounding them reflect the ways in which we reach our goals. Our dreams may prompt us to raise our ambitions, or tell us that our objectives are unrealistic.

STAR
SKY

Humans have always aimed at the stars in the symbolic as well as the real sense. A dream of observing the night **SKY**, perhaps planning interplanetary or interstellar travel, may be a hint that you intend to reach as high as you can in your particular field. A dream of one bright **STAR** and your ambition to reach or capture it may refer to someone you desire to "capture" in waking life. A dream of mapping the skies may allude to

ASTROLOGY
MARS
65
VENUS
64
MERCURY
65

a number of ambitions in waking life, from which you should probably choose one – or perhaps are in the process of doing so. A dream of one specific planet may refer to **ASTROLOGY**: for example, **MARS** may be encouraging you to fight for your rights, **VENUS** to attend to your emotions, and **MERCURY** to communicate better with those around you. However, because the planets are far above us, the reference is likely to be to your

THE WORLD
OF NATURE

FANTASY &
FABLE

ARTS &
SCIENCES

THE HUMAN
BODY

BUILDINGS &
INTERIORS

EVERYDAY
THINGS

HUMAN
EMOTIONS

HUMAN
ACTIVITIES

HUMAN
CONDITIONS

RITUALS &
RELIGION

THE DREAM
THESAURUS

DREAM ANALYSIS

"I was at a sale, and bidding for an attractive porcelain model of the Eiffel Tower. The bidding was high, and when my money ran out I offered to give the auctioneer my house. He accepted it and handed me the ornament. However, I saw that it had one leg missing. I protested, but the auctioneer said, 'You bought it, and you're stuck with it.' I threw the object to the floor. It did not break, and a stranger picked it up and walked away. I was delighted."

Juliet was an ambitious minor executive in a travel firm, who wanted to head its Paris office. Her dream was telling her that she was too intent on the position, which might not actually suit her. Her subconscious had realized drawbacks about the post.

aspirations and ambitions. Or is the planet personified by someone you know in waking life?

ADVERTISE-MENT The purpose of **ADVERTISEMENTS** is to sell you something. A dream in which you were impressed by an advertisement or in which you created one, may be reminding you of an ambition or target. What the advertisement was displaying is vital, but so is its condition. Was it bright, well composed and impressive, or was it poorly spelled and in tatters? In the latter case, have you kept your ambitions clear, or have you allowed time to distort them? (*See Communication, page 137.*)

FISHING
169
ANGLING If you dream of **FISHING** or **ANGLING**, what are you fishing or angling for in waking life? Or is the dream telling you that extreme care and ingenuity is needed if you are to achieve your ambition?

AUCTION
121 If an **AUCTION** was featured in your dream, the ambition may be to possess something, and the major question is the identity of the object for which you were bidding. It may be a position at work. Was your bid too low, or did you pay more than the object was worth? If so, perhaps you should reevaluate your ambitions in waking life.

— DECEPTION —

SYMBOLS OF DECEPTION occurring in our dreams generally offer us a warning. They may not be easy to interpret, because we can deceive ourselves into believing only the least unpleasant of possible messages.

CHEAT Whether you were the **CHEAT** or the victim of cheating, your dream was certainly cautioning you. If you were cheating, for example, at cards, are you knowingly involved in some action in waking life in which you are deceiving another person? If so, you should face up to what your dream is telling you, and perhaps attempt to mend your ways. Alternatively, is someone trying to cheat you in waking life?

**FORGERY
FAKE** A dream of a **FORGERY** or **FAKE** may be suggesting that you are not being true to yourself, and that you are pretending to be what you are not. If the fake in the dream is antique, the reference may be to some deceit you have practiced in the past. If your dream fake was discovered, you may be in danger of being found out by other people. Do you have something to reveal in waking life? If so, did your dream end with feelings of relief or guilt? Being forced in some way to fake or forge something in a dream may suggest that you feel inadequate in some aspect of your waking life.

TRICK If you were performing a **TRICK** in a dream, did it impress people or were you a failure? This may be a dream warning that in waking life you are trying to be too clever, or that you are attempting to manipulate people.

PLOTTING If you were **PLOTTING** or scheming in your dream, the reference may be to plans you are making in your waking life. Subconsciously, you may realize that you have more in mind than you are revealing

---

to others. If so, your dream may be warning you of the eventual outcome of your – perhaps devious – plans.

SECRET

To dream of sharing a **SECRET** with another person may mean that there is something about your most private thoughts or behavior of which you feel you should be more consciously aware. We often "hide" things from ourselves, and pretend that they do not exist. Your dream may be pointing out that you should be attentive to a particular facet of your character, even if you are prepared to hide it from others. Such a dream may suggest that you are rather more secretive than is good for you.

CODE

In a sense all dreams are in **CODE**, but when a code occurs as a distinct symbol, you probably either found it difficult to decipher in your dream, or read its meaning immediately. If the former, you may be perplexed about some problem, person or aspect of your waking life. Are you attempting to be particularly tactful, and trying to tell someone something in such a roundabout way that

both you and the other person are confused? If you tried to read a message in code (*see Communication, page 137*) your dreams may be so obscure that you are unable to receive their message, in which case you will be advised to ask them for clarification (*see page 33*).

SAFE
STRONGBOX

A dream featuring a **SAFE** or a **STRONGBOX** may be commenting on your personal security: do you feel safe in waking life? In your dream you may have been locking up possessions and putting them into a safe. A dream such as this may be commenting on your attitude toward your partner or children. Are you treating them as your possessions? If in your dream you were locked up in a safe, are you living a claustrophobic life?

HIDING

Whatever you are **HIDING** from in your dream will represent some fear in waking life. As is the case in dreams of pursuit (*see page 147*), you will have to face up to your dream monster and come to terms with what it represents to you in waking life. You may be hiding from shame or because you lack self-confidence.

—◆— SECURITY —◆—

WHEN OUR SECURITY in waking life is threatened, our apprehension will often color our dream activity. When security appears as an emotion, or features in some other way in our dreams, we may need to make certain changes in waking life, or reassess how we feel.

DOOR

The opening of a **DOOR** in a dream, especially into a new room (*see page 103*) usually represents new opportunities or departures in life, but if the emphasis is on a door as a means of closing off the world, or closing yourself into your own environment, the emphasis is different. There may be a comment on how secure or insecure you are feeling in waking life. How secure was the door in the dream? Did it give you the protection you needed, or was it old and shaky? This kind of allusion could suggest that your sense of self is weak. The door's **LOCK** will be significant in much the same way.

GUARD

A dream of a **GUARD** may be advising you that something or someone needs protection, or it may be showing you that you have to guard against a certain possibility in waking life. If a guard in your dream blocked your path, are you being prevented from carrying out certain tasks in waking life? Did the guard warn you of dangers beyond? If so, there may be a general warning to be more cautious in waking life.

PENSION

Your dream of your **PENSION** may have been telling you not to worry about feeling old, since you will be looked

THE WORLD OF NATURE

FANTASY & FABLE

ARTS & SCIENCES

THE HUMAN BODY

BUILDINGS & INTERIORS

EVERYDAY THINGS

HUMAN EMOTIONS

HUMAN ACTIVITIES

HUMAN CONDITIONS

RITUALS & RELIGION

THE DREAM THESAURUS

after. However, the pension may represent your feeling of confidence, or your spiritual as well as financial, resources. If the pension check in your dream failed to materialize, it may mean that you are contributing to an unreliable fund, or that you may be feeling in some way insecure in waking life – possibly in a practical sense. Remember the association between money and emotion (*see page 130*): if your pension check or money was taken away from you, consider how emotionally secure you feel in waking life.

DREAM ANALYSIS

"I was in a theater, and a conjuror asked me to come up on the stage to help him with a trick. He whispered, 'You're on my side, aren't you? You'll pretend that the trick has worked?' I firmly replied that I would not, and ran out of the theater with him in pursuit. I slammed a door behind me and was dazzled by the bright afternoon sunlight."

A colleague of Kathy's had asked her to cover up for a serious error that she knew would cost her firm a great deal of money.

Kathy decided against deception, and the dream was suggesting that in doing so she had come out into the open.

—◆— NIGHTMARES —◆—

IN NIGHTMARES WE MAY feel as if we are being buried, stifled, or drowned, but without any "story" leading up to it. Or perhaps we are being chased or followed – often at the end of an ordinary dream.

INCUBUS ATTACK

The simplest nightmares are among the most mysterious of dreams, and are still not perfectly understood. These are dreams in which a feeling of horror comes over us for no reason, often accompanied by the sensation of being crushed or stifled. Such a dream is conventionally called an **INCUBUS ATTACK**, and the latest theory is that it is in some way physically produced – perhaps because we have difficulty in breathing during the dream. There is no modern connection with the traditional idea of an incubus – a dream sexual attacker (*see page 62*). Incubus attacks seem to be most common with children – although they are actually quite rare. If a child wakes, screaming, from such dreams, you should comfort them, and assure them that the dream will not happen again. Indeed, such dreams never seem to recur within a single night, and often do not return for some weeks, if at all. Although highly unpleasant, there is no record of incubus attacks

doing any damage – psychological or physical – to the dreamer. If they recur in adults, however, it would be worth getting a health check, and it may be wise to consider the "ordinary" dreams you have at the same time. Although it seems unlikely that incubus dreams have any meaning in themselves (there is never a "story" or narrative attached to them), there may be clues elsewhere as to what is producing them.

The second kind of nightmare is far more interesting than incubus attacks, and something can be done about it – although there are some mysterious elements. Dreams from which we wake with feelings of acute distress or worry usually happen toward the end of a night's sleep. There is no common element; we all have our own kind of nightmare, probably produced by our own psychological concerns or fears. Some analysts believe that these arise from our deepest frustrations, repressions, or self-condemnation. During analysis, these can often be brought to the surface, and the nightmare may then cease. One of the earliest students of nightmares, Ernest Jones, in his book *On the Nightmare*, suggested that "healthy people" never had nightmares. He believed that they were always the expression of "a violent conflict between a certain unconscious sexual desire and intense fear"; in men, he believed, this arose because they were unconscious of their homosexual inclinations and would have been disgusted to discover that they had any. Few people would accept such a simple explanation as the whole truth, but other suggestions also seem to be overly simple. Calvin Hall was of the opinion in *The Meaning of Dreams* that nightmares punish dreamers for some sin against their own conscience. In *The Dream Game* Ann Faraday supports this theory, confessing that she herself has had "many nightmares that were almost certainly self-punishment … These usually took the form of imprisonment or execution." She also recalls Jung's theory that nightmares, especially those in which there is a pursuer present, are concerned with the shadow (*see page* 97), representing unconscious cravings and desires that we suppress during the day. However, this class of nightmare can be dealt with. It may be difficult to do alone, and the help of a dream discussion group or a therapist may be needed to dispose of the most tenacious of them.

MONSTER

If you dream that you are haunted or pursued by a **MONSTER** of some kind, you should turn and face it. Mystery ceases to be horrifying when its nature is identified. When you look straight at it, your monster will seem less terrible; it may even appear comical. It is also likely to be entirely recognizable; it may be an animal – perhaps fierce and threatening, but something that can be dealt with. Once you have recognized your personal monster, persuade it to speak to you: ask it what it wants, and if necessary make use of the "two chairs" technique (*see page* 33). The monster in your nightmare may be trying to bully you into doing a certain task, or pleading with you not to do something.

ANIMAL
121

ANIMALS in dreams (*see page 42*) often represent the animal part of our nature, so if your pursuer is a lion, a tiger, or a boar, for instance, consider what it represents in you, and whether this element is in a healthy state. Are you threatening, restricting, confining, or subduing an important animal part of your nature? As you begin to understand this, the animal should become less fierce. Apart from a consideration of the symbol itself, you can help to reduce it to acceptable proportions by drawing it or writing a description of it.

PARALYSIS
93

One of the most frightening forms of nightmare is that involving **PARALYSIS** – when we dream that we are unable to move. Dreams of being paralyzed are a part of REM sleep, and during this (no doubt as a safety measure) we are immobilized. A person who is tossing and turning in bed is never in the throes of a nightmare. Part of the terror of the nightmare, indeed, is that we are unable to move. The obvious interpretation of such a dream is probably the correct one: seeming unable to move in our dream, we are in some respect unable to move in our waking lives. This will usually be an emotional paralysis, or a feeling of helplessness in a particular situation in our social or working lives. You may be caught between two opposing influences: for example, between your immediate superior and a colleague at work; between a spouse and a lover; or between two possible courses of action.

ATTACK
118, 120, 159
EARTHQUAKE
48, 121, 158, 161

It is true that we can recall in dreams, sometimes in the most traumatic detail, awful events that have happened in our lives, for example personal **ATTACKS**, **EARTHQUAKES**, or airplane or train crashes. Usually, while such dreams are extremely vivid and disturbing close to the time of the original event, they gradually become less intense. Like other dreams, these have a cause – the original event. In general, however, they have no "meaning" other than your own memory of it, and they may be helping to cleanse your mind of the original horror.

THE WORLD
OF NATURE

FANTASY &
FABLE

ARTS &
SCIENCES

THE HUMAN
BODY

BUILDINGS &
INTERIORS

EVERYDAY
THINGS

HUMAN
EMOTIONS

HUMAN
ACTIVITIES

HUMAN
CONDITIONS

RITUALS &
RELIGION

THE DREAM
THESAURUS

THE ROCK STAR DREAM

"I was watching a television disaster film in which a huge building collapsed. I was very frightened, but started scrambling over the rubble in the hope of saving some of the injured people; but I found no one I could help. Suddenly, I saw an enormously tall tree, at the top of which I saw a rock star performing. He smiled down at me, blew me a kiss, and asked me to come up and join him. I was elated, and at once put my foot onto the first branch. But at that moment my school principal appeared and blocked my path, saying 'You will not go to that dreadful man. Instead you will march round the playing field for ever and ever!' I was devastated; I wanted to be with the rock star because I knew that he wanted to make love to me. The principal pointed, and I had to turn around and start marching. As I did so, I saw all my friends playing hockey in the middle of the field. I tried hard to attract their attention, but they ignored me. Then I saw a huge billboard in the distance and wanted to read what it said. As I drew near I read the words, in enormous black letters, 'Keep Marching.' The billboard moved itself to the top of a very steep hill and I knew that I had to keep marching, as I had been told. Although I did not know why, I just had to get to the board, and as I did so it moved aside and revealed a tiny door locked with a huge padlock. The key was hanging on a string. I lifted the key, which was very heavy, and managed to put it into the lock and turn it. The small door sprang open, and I squeezed through it. On the other side was a large and very wild pony, which was leaping around. I went to stroke it, and it became a huge checkmark. Then I woke up."

BUILDING COLLAPSES IN MOVIE

KAREN SCRAMBLES OVER RUBBLE

INTERPRETATION

Karen (a 16-year-old schoolgirl) had disastrously failed several important examinations – hence the symbol of the falling building in the disaster movie. The fact that she then became part of the scene – scrambling over the rubble to try to find injured people – reflects her sorrow at her failure and her hope to make amends.

The sequence of the dream concerning the rock star is wish-fulfillment (*see page 150*). The appearance of the authority-figure (the principal) – and her threat has a double meaning: first, that Karen should concentrate on her schoolwork; and second, that she should curb her sexual activity. She had considerable sexual experience for a girl of her age, and the rock star symbolized sex for her. The marching symbolized the need for Karen to develop a more serious attitude toward work and life. The fact that her friends ignored her supported this theme, as did the message on the billboard. But she managed to squeeze through what seemed an impossibly small door, which suggested that she knew she could "get through." The pony was her natural self, representing the wildness with which she had to come to terms. When she stroked it, she was getting in touch with herself, and this provoked the appearance of a symbol of approval (the checkmark). Overall, her dream was reassuring her that if she could calm down and be more disciplined she would do well.

PONY TURNS
INTO
CHECKMARK

SIGN SAYS
"KEEP
MARCHING"

PRINCIPAL
ORDERS KAREN
TO MARCH

ROCK STAR
PERFORMS AT TOP
OF TREE

—◆— DANGER —◆—

A DREAM OF BEING IN DANGER may seem to be on the point of being a
nightmare (*see page 154*), but in fact it is likely to be much more
valuable. Nightmares generally have little or no meaning, while
dreams of danger are usually warning us about something in our
waking lives, and we should take notice of them.

AVALANCHE
161
Dreams featuring danger from some
natural hazard are not likely to be
prophetic. Although there are recorded
dreams to the contrary (*see page 62*), they
are not only rare, but also confined to
particular people. In addition, they are
often too generalized and vague to be
useful in any practical sense. A dream
in which you are in danger from an
AVALANCHE may refer to some oppressive
force in your waking life, which is
threatening to overwhelm you — an
avalanche of work, for instance. If in
your dream you are swept away by the
avalanche, the implication may be that
your life is actually out of control, and

EARTHQUAKE
48, 121, 155, 161
EXPLOSION
131
THUNDER
49
LIGHTNING
50
STORM
49, 121
HOLE
that you need to look for something or
someone to hold on to in order to regain
some kind of stability. A dream of an
EARTHQUAKE may represent insecurity in
waking life. If you dreamed that the earth
was shaking beneath you, and threatening
to demolish the building in which you
live or work, the threat may be mirrored
by insecurity at work or at home. A
dream of an EXPLOSION may refer to a
sudden alteration in your waking life, or
a sudden discharge of emotion. What
sort of damage was done in the dream?
If something was broken, you should
consider that as a symbol, or if someone
in the dream was relying on you, clinging
to you, or in similar danger, that may
also be significant. If you dreamed that
you were in danger from THUNDER and
LIGHTNING in a STORM, it may refer to
an emotional problem in waking life.
However, a dream of being struck by
lightning may also indicate a sudden
revelation. A dream of falling into a HOLE
can be frightening: in waking life are you
in some untenable position, or a situation
you cannot climb out of?

TELEPHONE
138
ALARM
Occasionally, if a car or burglar alarm
goes off during the night, you may have
a "mini-dream" that will lead to your
awakening. You may, for example, dream
that you are at your desk in the office and
the TELEPHONE rings. This sort of dream
probably has little significance. However,
a dream in which you are setting an
ALARM, or fixing one to your car or your
home, is another matter. Men's dreams
of cars frequently allude to their
sexuality, so a dream featuring a car
alarm may also be considered in that
context. Is there a reference to some
kind of rash behavior in that sphere of

THE WORLD
OF NATURE

FANTASY &
FABLE

ARTS &
SCIENCES

THE HUMAN
BODY

BUILDINGS &
INTERIORS

your life? A dream featuring a house alarm may allude to your family. Do they, or one particular member, need your protection at this time? Was the dream alarm a satisfactory one, and were you

confident of its efficiency? An alarm that fails to go off is an extremely pointed symbol. A dream of setting an alarm clock may refer to time (*see page 80*). For what event in waking life might you be too late? The dream may be reminding you to do something.

ATTACK
118, 120, 155
VIOLENCE

You may have dreamed that you were attacked, or threatened with **ATTACK**. If the **VIOLENCE** associated with the attack was not your main concern, but the threat of an attack was your chief fear, there may be a warning in the dream of an attack in waking life. This may not be a physical assault, but perhaps an attack on your character or integrity. The identity of your dream attacker is important; if you were unable to identify him or her, the dream may be underlining a vague apprehension in waking life that is in fact justified, and advising you to be careful.

—◆— WARNING —◆—

ONE OF THE MOST HELPFUL aspects of dreaming is the capacity we have to issue warnings to ourselves, and warnings of situations or phenomena that we may be unaware of in our waking lives.

**OVER-
SPENDING
ESCAPING**

When we examine our dreams in detail, we may often come to the conclusion that their main purpose is to warn us about something in waking life. These warnings may be psychological: for example, a dream of **OVERSPENDING** at the supermarket may be suggesting that you are expending too much emotion on a particular relationship. If you dream of **ESCAPING** from a locked room (*see page 103*) and walking happily through an unfamiliar landscape (*see page 58*), there may be a warning that you need to relax, and escape from your responsibilities.

There are other, practical, warnings that appear in dreams. You may dream that your dog's leash breaks, that the brakes on your car fail, or that a fire breaks out in your kitchen. In waking life, when you check up, you may find that the leash is worn, the brakes are faulty, and the

electrical wiring is defective. There is, however, usually a simple explanation for this: you may have unconsciously noticed the particular fault, and your dream has brought the fact to your attention. This kind of dream, therefore, should never be ignored.

It is a substantiated fact that dreams can sometimes diagnose sickness before we feel ill, and before a doctor would be able to see any symptoms. This should not, of course, be construed as an invitation for anyone who dreams of illness (*see page 95*) to rush to their doctor. However, a dream (especially if it recurs) of a pain or an ache in a particular area of your body, or of some kind of growth or discoloration — in fact anything that remains in your mind when you wake, and makes you uneasy — may be well worth taking note of.

THE WORLD OF NATURE

FANTASY & FABLE

ARTS & SCIENCES

THE HUMAN BODY

BUILDINGS & INTERIORS

EVERYDAY THINGS

HUMAN EMOTIONS

HUMAN ACTIVITIES

HUMAN CONDITIONS

RITUALS & RELIGION

THE DREAM THESAURUS

ACCIDENT

THERE HAVE BEEN A NUMBER of well-recorded dreams that have appeared to accurately foretell accidents. The safest theory about this (unless you believe in prophetic dreams) is that these dreams are cases of our unconscious having noticed things that we are not shrewd enough to note in waking life.

You may, for example, dream of a particular woman being knocked down at a particular crossing, and then it actually happens. The explanation is probably that the crossing in question is potentially dangerous, and the woman is a careless pedestrian. You may have unconsciously noticed both of these facts, and observed that the woman was likely to have an accident. However, the more subtle suggestions and clues we see around us all day are often subliminal.

If you dream that you have an accident, you should take note of how it occurred. This is particularly so if it was caused by something you use regularly, such as a piece of garden equipment. You should check that the equipment is in good order, and be careful when you next use it. However, the accident may not be what it seems, especially if someone else is involved in the dream (*see Dream Analysis, below*).

DREAM ANALYSIS

"I was cutting the grass in the garden with my electric lawn mower, when my neighbor greeted me over the fence. The sun was shining, and although only her head and shoulders were visible, I knew that she had been sunbathing in the nude. I went to switch off the machine to speak to her, when I was struck by a flash of lightning. I was not hurt, but it frightened my neighbor, and she vanished."

This could have simply been a dream warning the dreamer to check the electric connections of his lawn mower. In fact, although he was a happily married man, he had for some time admired his neighbor, and the dream was warning him of danger ahead if they became romantically involved.

DISASTER

DREAMS OF DISASTER are often extremely vivid. We may wake up in a terrified state, which can cause us to feel more frightened, worried, and apprehensive than is logical. Nevertheless, such dreams may be giving us a significant warning about our waking life, and should not be ignored or taken at face value.

To dream of any kind of disaster is always disturbing, but you should remember that it is unlikely that the dream was in any way prophetic. If your disaster dream involved something concerning your immediate surroundings – such as your home – it may embody a simple warning. For example, you may have unconsciously noticed a faulty electricity lead or a cracked wall, and failed to register the fact that a minor repair was needed to prevent a major rebuilding or plumbing job. Your dream may be drawing this to your attention.

A dream focusing on your home (*see page 102*) and showing it at the center of a disaster may be saying something about your personality and your attitude to life. It may be that you are ready to make

THE WORLD
OF NATURE

FANTASY &
FABLE

ARTS &
SCIENCES

THE HUMAN
BODY

BUILDINGS &
INTERIORS

EVERYDAY
THINGS

HUMAN
EMOTIONS

HUMAN
ACTIVITIES

HUMAN
CONDITIONS

RITUALS &
RELIGION

THE DREAM
THESAURUS

you should ask yourself whether you are fearful of life or whether you are being less assertive than you should be. If any of your colleagues or family members are experiencing difficulties, and you know you could assist them, your dream may be telling you to take a more active part in what is happening to them. In your dream you may have experienced an avalanche. Because **SNOW** is white (the color of innocence), you should consider whether you are disguising some action that is pricking your conscience. In waking life have you acted immorally, and as a cover-up are feigning innocence? A dream of an earthquake may be reflecting an insecurity in your waking life. It may be suggesting that the ground is giving way under your feet, and probably refers to materialistic insecurity. This may be true if you are about to lose your home or job.

SNOW
49, 172

If you dreamed that you were in a building (*see page 100*) that was falling down, consider whether your life is collapsing around you. Fighting for survival in your dream situation is a positive sign, since you are probably putting up a fight in real life. Such a dream in men may be reflecting on possible potency problems.

FLAMES
HOUSE
100, 101

The elements often have an important role in disaster dreams. Being consumed by fire (*see page 45*) may relate to the fact that you are being consumed by passion in waking life. Such a dream may be a warning – especially if you were trying unsuccessfully to smother **FLAMES**. The dream would be most reassuring if a **HOUSE** or room (*see page 103*) was catching fire and you could control the flames, for here is a symbol of controlled passion. The dream is reassuring you that you are in control of your life.

Water (*see page 46*) takes different forms in all dreams, but has its own place in disaster dreams. It is fair to assume that it is relating to our emotions when it so appears. If you dreamed that you were

HOUSE
100, 101

important changes in your waking life, which could involve destroying what you have built up over a long period of time. There may be a warning that your present or planned actions could prove to be disastrous in the long term. However, in your dream you may have watched your **HOUSE** fall down with a certain satisfaction, and your dream reaction was "thank goodness, that's over." Did you stride off happily, leaving the ruins behind you? If so, it would seem that you are ready to move on, and to dispense with the mayhem of your past life.

AVALANCHE
158
EARTHQUAKE
48, 121, 155, 158

In disaster dreams we may see a burning building (*see page 100*), people engulfed by an **AVALANCHE**, or an **EARTHQUAKE**. If you have such a dream you should first consider your reactions to it and your personal connection with the disaster – if any. If you were merely a spectator in the dream, standing by too terrified to move,

THE WORLD OF NATURE

FANTASY & FABLE

ARTS & SCIENCES

THE HUMAN BODY

BUILDINGS & INTERIORS

EVERYDAY THINGS

HUMAN EMOTIONS

HUMAN ACTIVITIES

HUMAN CONDITIONS

RITUALS & RELIGION

THE DREAM THESAURUS

SHIPWRECK
47

in a **SHIPWRECK**, and the water was overwhelming you, you are more than likely being overwhelmed by emotion — by your reaction to a situation in waking life that is very important to you. If this is the case, try to assess ways in which you can rationalize your powerful feelings and put them into a logical perspective. If you were attempting to save other people in your shipwreck, think about what they may represent in waking life. If a child was involved in the dream, it may represent an element of your waking life that you are trying to develop, that might act as a counter for your powerful emotional responses.

AIRPLANE
135

Your dream of an **AIRPLANE** disaster may be summing up your attitude toward an important project in your waking life. Ask yourself whether involvement in the project was premature, and whether you are now feeling apprehensive. You may be afraid of crashing financially, or of intellectual failure (especially if you are

being put to the test in some way or are about to take important examinations). You may also fear failure to achieve an ambition or objective. Have you been "aiming too high"?

CAR
116, 134, 135

A dream of a **CAR** crash may be warning you that you are "driving too fast" in waking life. Are you too eager to get ahead of rivals, overly ambitious, or out of control in some areas of your life. Driving cars usually relates to the sex life, particularly for men, so there may be another kind of warning: perhaps you are being careless in protecting yourself and your sexual partners.

FAMINE
DROUGHT

A dream concerning disasters such as **FAMINE** or **DROUGHT** may be suggesting that you are emotionally drained in waking life. Perhaps your partner is "draining" you and you are feeling worn out. Or the dream may be focusing on your humanitarian qualities and hinting that you could give more to charity.

—◆— AUTHORITY —◆—

OCCASIONALLY WE ENCOUNTER authority figures in our dreams. These are usually magisterial characters that appear in our dreams to instruct and guide us, and try to impose their will on us.

PRIEST
JUDGE
124, 164
KING
115
QUEEN
115, 162
HEADMASTER

Generally, the earliest authority figures we recognize are our parents, and some of the authority figures that appear in our dreams will stem from deeply ingrained memories of our mothers and fathers. They may, however, manifest themselves in our dreams as characters such as **PRIESTS**, **JUDGES**, **KINGS**, **QUEENS**, or **HEADMASTERS**. The authority figures in our dreams may sometimes remind us of responsibilities we would rather forget: such as our responsibility to society.

You are unlikely to find either of your parents appearing in your dreams as an authority figure: when someone you know materializes in a dream, it is usually as themselves. Generally, they do not come to bring you a message from

CARDINAL
DICTATOR

your subconscious, but merely project themselves as characters in your dreams. The appearance, however, of a solemn **CARDINAL** or an austere **DICTATOR** may symbolize a part of your own personality that your unconscious is bringing to your attention. So an authority figure in your dream may be telling you something that you already know.

TRAFFIC
COP
TICKET
COLLECTOR
CAPTAIN
148
AMBASSADOR
LANDLORD
PROPHET

Authority figures may appear in your dreams in many different identities. The character may, for example, be a **TRAFFIC COP**, a **TICKET COLLECTOR**, a **CAPTAIN**, an **AMBASSADOR**, a **LANDLORD**, or a **PROPHET**. You should take note of the message, since it will be significant, not only to a current problem, but also to the general course of your life.

·ESTABLISHMENT·

THE TERM "THE ESTABLISHMENT" is a pejorative description of the institutions and forces that represent authority, legitimacy, tradition, and the status quo.

Dreams about "The Establishment" or an establishment figure, have something in common with dreams of an authority figure (*see opposite*). However, while an authority figure in a dream may instruct you to be anarchic or disobedient, an establishment figure is more likely to remind you of certain disadvantages that may flow from a departure from conventionally "correct" behavior.

LAWYER
ARMY OFFICER
POLICEMAN
164

A dream about a **LAWYER**, an **ARMY OFFICER**, or a **POLICEMAN**, may have an echo of establishment behavior rather than representing authority. If you are particularly conscious of the "respectable" behavior or appearance of someone in your dream who seems overtly or by example to be commenting on your own untidiness, there may be a suggestion not just that you should improve your appearance, but that you should pay attention to certain aspects of your behavior in waking life that may upset others. Even if you believe that your behavior reflects your true feelings or decisions, it will be worth considering whether you are not weakening your case by appearing to intentionally flout received opinion.

·DISCIPLINE·

MANY PEOPLE HAVE DIFFICULTY in maintaining a disciplined attitude in their lives. Therefore, their lives may not be lived to the full extent that could result from a rational approach to daily routines.

ACROBAT
72
BALLET DANCER
BALANCE
72
TEAM
DRILL
115
LINE

The appearance in a dream of someone who can only succeed as the result of practice, may be a reminder that we should apply ourselves to certain tasks in waking life. An undisciplined **ACROBAT** or **BALLET DANCER** in a dream may lose **BALANCE** and fall over. This may refer to your emotional balance in waking life. A dream of watching an army **TEAM** at **DRILL** may be critical of your careless approach to a problem. Was the drill impeccable? If not, consider how you are failing to apply yourself to an area of your life that is currently out of control. A **LINE** is an example of orderly behavior, so a dream of this kind implies that your waking life is well balanced.

Some dreams will suggest that rather than a pattern in your life being disturbed, or not properly worked out, what you need in your waking life is

BRIDLED HORSE
CONTRACT
GLUE

restraint. This may be the suggestion if you dream of a **BRIDLED HORSE** – the animal side of your nature needs to be reined in. Similarly, a **CONTRACT** – while it may offer you money – also contains clauses insisting that you deliver something on time and as ordered. Could such a dream be a reminder that an emotional relationship has two sides? A dream featuring **GLUE** may be suggesting that the discipline in your waking life has gone too far. The context and mood of your dream should help with the analysis.

THE WORLD OF NATURE

FANTASY & FABLE

ARTS & SCIENCES

THE HUMAN BODY

BUILDINGS & INTERIORS

EVERYDAY THINGS

HUMAN EMOTIONS

HUMAN ACTIVITIES

HUMAN CONDITIONS

RITUALS & RELIGION

THE DREAM THESAURUS

THE WORLD
OF NATURE

FANTASY &
FABLE

ARTS &
SCIENCES

THE HUMAN
BODY

BUILDINGS &
INTERIORS

EVERYDAY
THINGS

HUMAN
EMOTIONS

HUMAN
ACTIVITIES

HUMAN
CONDITIONS

RITUALS &
RELIGION

THE DREAM
THESAURUS

SALUTE

A **SALUTE** may certainly be considered a sign of discipline, but was your dream salute genuine or ironic? Were you saluting an idea, a project, or a situation in your waking life? Alternatively, were you perhaps giving yourself approval for remaining loyal to a particular opinion and not being swayed by others?

**TRAFFIC
LIGHTS
ROAD SIGNS**

TRAFFIC LIGHTS, along with other **ROAD SIGNS**, are instructions that should be obeyed not only for your own good, but also for the general good of the community. A dream in which you are ignoring such directions may be hinting that in some area of your waking life you are behaving foolishly.

—◆— JUSTICE —◆—

EVEN THOSE WHO HAVE consciously decided that their main duty is to themselves and their families, and that they should not unduly concern themselves with fairness or lack of prejudice in life, are sometimes reminded in dreams – as if by their better selves – that justice should be served.

**COURTROOM
DOCK
JUDGE**
125, 162
**MAGISTRATE
JURY
MONARCH
POLICE
OFFICER**
163

In a dream of being in a **COURTROOM**, you may have been in the **DOCK**. On the other hand, you may have been the **JUDGE**, the **MAGISTRATE**, or part of the **JURY**. You may even have been a **MONARCH** dispensing justice, or a **POLICE OFFICER** attempting to ensure that it is carried out. A dream in which justice is the theme is almost certainly about a moral quandary in your waking life. The fact that you are on the side of the law rather than being tried or reproved by it, may suggest that someone in waking life is relying on your sense of justice to make a fair decision. This may be a simple family decision or something considerably more important. The nature of the decision you must make should be obvious after examining the other clues in the dream.

JUDGE
125, 162
**PROSECUTOR
DEFENDANT
WEIGHING**

In order to interpret a dream of justice, you should consider the behavior of the authority figure (*see page 162*) in the dream. Did you unquestioningly accept the judgment? Or was there vacillation and even injustice? If you were the **JUDGE** in the dream, perhaps in waking life you need to overcome prejudice of some kind, or marshal some available evidence more convincingly. If you were a **PROSECUTOR** in your dream, were you also the **DEFENDANT**, and is your conscience busily at work? Dreams of **WEIGHING**

SCALES

something, particularly on **SCALES**, certainly suggest that you need to consider both sides of a question in waking life. Alternatively, it may be an indication that you have done so, but for some reason (should the scales be heavily overbalanced on the wrong side) you have not given full weight to one side of the argument.

DREAM ANALYSIS

"I was on a bus on my way to work when someone took me by the arm, hurried me onto a parade ground, and told me I had to command a large number of soldiers in ceremonial dress. I knew that the President was due to inspect them in half an hour. I knew how the parade ground should look, but I had no idea how to give the men their orders. I shouted 'You lot over there, go around the back!' But they all laughed and the band began to play a funeral march. I could hear cheering crowds, and knew the President was almost there, and then I woke up in a cold sweat."

George is a stage manager who was working on a musical that involved many scene changes. He was increasingly worried about whether these would work smoothly, and conscious that he had not been giving enough time to the tricky problem of how to get the actors in one scene off-stage before setting the next scene. The President in the dream represented the director of the musical. This was in some ways a classic anxiety dream, but there was also a strong suggestion that he should try to "get his act together" and organize his work more efficiently.

—◆— IMAGE —◆—

ALTHOUGH WE MAY NOT ALL be particularly image-conscious, most of us need to conform to certain standards of appearance, usually those set by our own generation. Whether we are a follower of rock music or classical music, almost all of us have a norm to which we adhere — or from which we must make a conscious effort to break away. Our dreams can suggest or obstruct changes in our image.

HAIR
92, 146
BALDNESS
92

Dreams in which your **HAIR** is prominent are often making some kind of statement about your physical and psychological well-being, and may symbolize virility and the life force. If you dreamed that you were brushing your luxuriant hair your dream may have been saying that you are doing well in your life, and looking good. If in your dream your hair was falling out, or you were actually **BALD**, perhaps your self-esteem is low because someone in your life is sapping your self-confidence. If you were trying on a **WIG** in a dream, there may be a suggestion that you are being pretentious in waking life. A dream of a hair **TRANSPLANT** may contain a similar meaning. Alternatively, such a dream may signal a need to recapture your youth. Young boys frequently have a fear of the **BARBER**, and if this is carried into an adult man's dream there may be an implication of fear of psychological castration. The identity of the barber in the dream will be crucial. **BEARDS** are often a symbol of masculinity and virility, but your dream may be questioning you about what you are trying to hide behind your beard. Are you trying to conceal a weak chin (an emotional weakness), or are you aiming to look more masculine than you actually feel?

WIG
TRANSPLANT
BARBER
150
BEARD
92

TEETH
92, 95

Some of the most common dreams we have are about our **TEETH** — they are either falling out, have fallen out, or are so unsightly that we feel compelled to keep our mouths closed. Most people have experienced such a dream at one time or another. Sometimes the dream may be suggesting that you have spoken out of place, and that you do need to keep your mouth shut, but more often it shows that you are self-conscious about your appearance (your teeth are, after all, crucial to the way others see you). There may be a hint that you are not looking your best.

COSMETICS
BODY PAINT

We apply cosmetics for many reasons: to enhance our appearances, to disguise blemishes, or perhaps to attract other people. When our dreams use this symbol they may be commenting on inhibitions that we are reluctant to face. If you were applying **COSMETICS** in a dream, are you trying to hide something in your waking life? You may, of course, be trying to hide something from yourself. Your dream may have focused on one particular feature — your eyes, for instance. If so, what are you trying not to see or understand in waking life? What aspect of your life, your attitudes, or your character should you be examining? You may not be facing up to reality. In your dream you may have been painting yourself all over with some specific cosmetic or **BODY PAINT**. A more intimate act than merely dressing in different clothes (*see page 84*), this may relate to your most intimate emotions and feelings. The color you were using (*see page 75*) may be significant.

SUNTAN

We often feel that our image and well-being is considerably enhanced when we exhibit a **SUNTAN**. However, if you were sunbathing in your dream, while you could be feeling optimistic, positive, and assertive in waking life, your dream may

THE WORLD OF NATURE

FANTASY & FABLE

ARTS & SCIENCES

THE HUMAN BODY

BUILDINGS & INTERIORS

EVERYDAY THINGS

HUMAN EMOTIONS

HUMAN ACTIVITIES

HUMAN CONDITIONS

RITUALS & RELIGION

THE DREAM THESAURUS

THE WORLD
OF NATURE

FANTASY &
FABLE

ARTS &
SCIENCES

THE HUMAN
BODY

BUILDINGS &
INTERIORS

EVERYDAY
THINGS

HUMAN
EMOTIONS

HUMAN
ACTIVITIES

HUMAN
CONDITIONS

RITUALS &
RELIGION

THE DREAM
THESAURUS

be giving you a warning. You should consider whether you are at risk of getting "burned" in waking life, perhaps by overelaborating your image.

TATTOO

Decorating your body with a **TATTOO** in a dream has a similar meaning to using body paint (*see page 165*). The important difference is that tattoos are permanent; you are decidedly making a commitment of some sort. What sort of tattoo was it? If it was simply decorative, the implication may be that you need to pay considerable attention to your image, and make a permanent improvement. However, if the tattoo was of a name, a motto, or a recognizable symbol, the reference may not be to image at all, but to your desire to make permanent a memory or an important fact in waking life. You may dream that you are having a tattoo removed, so you should face up to the fact that whatever or whoever you are trying to expunge from your life, you are in for a long and arduous operation. If you were aware of the needle, your dream may also have sexual overtones.

**MASK
DRAG
FANCY DRESS
TRANS-
VESTISM**

Most people enjoy dressing up, and disguising themselves in **FANCY DRESS**, or going to a party wearing a **MASK** or "**DRAG.**" However, dreams of such episodes may be saying something of far greater importance than we assume. As is the case with cosmetics (*see page 165*), in such dreams we are changing our appearance, and in waking life we may be attempting to disguise some aspect of our personality. A dream of **TRANSVESTISM** — of consciously adopting clothing of the opposite sex — may be commenting on the balance between the masculine and feminine sides of your personality. Such dreams are unlikely to suggest homosexuality.

**INVISIBILITY
MODESTY
INFERIORITY**

Wanting to be **INVISIBLE**, or achieving that state in a dream, may indicate that you are afraid of, or embarrassed about, some area of your waking life. The context of the dream should provide you with further clues. The dream may be commenting on your self-confidence, or lack of it. A dream of **MODESTY** may simply suggest the desirability of dressing — or even behaving — less ostentatiously than usual. If you felt markedly **INFERIOR** to others in the dream, you could ask your dreams (*see page 33*) to show you how to increase your self-confidence. Perhaps it could be through a dramatic change of image.

MIRROR A dream in which you were looking at yourself in a **MIRROR** may simply reflect a concern with your image. On the other hand, we see ourselves in reverse in a looking glass, so there may be a suggestion that you should try to see yourself as others see you. Was the dream mirror cracked or dirty, so that you could not see yourself clearly? If so, the dream may be suggesting that there is an element of self-deception in your waking life. If, however, you were startled by the clarity of the glass in the dream, and perhaps saw some blemishes that you had not previously noticed, the implication may be that you are making appropriate changes in your waking life.

FASHION MANNEQUIN Dreams in which **FASHION** appears as a general theme may be relating to your attitude toward the present time. If you felt dowdy, are you and your opinions rather out-of-date? If in your dream you were admiring models on a runway, what about them did you find attractive? If you want to be a model then your dream may be of wish-fulfillment (*see page 150*). You may have dreamed that you were looking at a **MANNEQUIN** in the window of a boutique or department store. Was your dream suggesting that you are doll-like – pretty but without character? In other words, was that dream mannequin you?

—◆— ACHIEVEMENT —◆—

OUR DREAMS DO NOT ALWAYS rebuke us; sometimes they congratulate us, recognizing an achievement that our waking selves may for some reason not acknowledge. When this happens, we should be strengthened in our course of action.

DEGREE DIPLOMA GRADUATING *177* **MEDAL GOAL PARENTS PARTNER** *90* You may dream that you are being recognized by authority: you may be receiving a **DEGREE** or **DIPLOMA**, **GRADUATING** from school or college, receiving a **MEDAL** at an investiture, or scoring a **GOAL** for your favorite team. In waking life, our personal achievements sometimes seem to mean more to other people than to ourselves, and so in our dreams we may seem to be allowing ourselves too much credit. In such a case, you are probably unaware of the size of your accomplishment in waking life. Also, if in your dream you are watched by admiring **PARENTS** or **PARTNER**, you should recognize that by your achievement you have increased their admiration and regard for you.

RACE *134* **PRIZE** The kind of dream achievement that results in your winning a **RACE** or being given a **PRIZE** suggests that your feat in waking life has been based on physical rather than mental accomplishments. You may have succeeded (or are on your way to success) in a new exercise regime, or in giving up smoking.

FAME A dream of **FAME** may be wish-fulfillment (*see page 150*), a reflection of some public act, or may reflect the fact that more people recognize your waking behavior (for good or ill) than you realize.

HARVEST A dream of a **HARVEST** contains the suggestion that every act has its result: what you sow, you shall reap. Did you reap your dream harvest successfully or did rain spoil the crop?

HALO Dreaming of a **HALO** may suggest that you have a good opinion of yourself – but is it justified? Or you may have seen a halo around the head of someone you admire: if so, your dream may be summing up your feelings about them.

THE WORLD OF NATURE

FANTASY & FABLE

ARTS & SCIENCES

THE HUMAN BODY

BUILDINGS & INTERIORS

EVERYDAY THINGS

HUMAN EMOTIONS

HUMAN ACTIVITIES

HUMAN CONDITIONS

RITUALS & RELIGION

THE DREAM THESAURUS

◆ CHANGE ◆

HUMANS OFTEN FIND CHANGE difficult to cope with; we find it
unsettling, we often fail to see every possibility in view, and we are
too easily swayed by emotion or by the need of the moment.
However, dreams are always ready to tell us the truth, and if we are
prepared to listen to them, to give good advice. Indeed, this is one
area of life in which they can be most useful.

**FAREWELL
EMIGRATION**

A dream of death (*see page 86*) is almost
always symbolic of a coming change,
either practical or psychological, and can
be among the most positive of symbols in
the dream dictionary. A dream in which
you are taking leave of someone is similar
to a dream of death. You must decide
from what, in waking life, you are taking
your leave. A dream of a **FAREWELL** to a
friend or a partner does not necessarily
mean that you are going to leave them;
you may be saying good-bye to something
they represent. In the same way, leaving a
house or a locality may mean that you are
bidding farewell to your past, or some
element of it. There should be a symbol
somewhere in the dream that will give
you a clue to the dream's meaning. A
dream that you are **EMIGRATING** is likely
to be particularly powerful. The place in
which you grew up or lived for some
time is probably meaningful to you, and
the change in your waking life is likely
to be a radical one.

ALCHEMY

ALCHEMY is not simply about changing
base metal into gold, so if this symbol
appears in your dreams, consider what in
your life needs enhancing. What unlikely
element could reveal you as a more
worthwhile and valuable member of the
community? However, in the tradition of
alchemy, there is an equally strong legacy
of psychological change: of turning a
human being from base matter into
angelic gold. Your dream may be driving
you toward the conclusion that you need
to change for the better.

**DISGUISE
KALEID-
OSCOPE**
68

If you dream of putting on a **DISGUISE**,
there may be an indication that you have
something to hide in waking life, but
there may equally be a
reference to change. What
sort of disguise were you
wearing? For example,
were you masquerading
as a clown, a monster, or
simply as another person?
What was the main
characteristic of the person or
creature you were disguised as? Do you
want to become more like them in your
waking life? A dream that features a
KALEIDOSCOPE is an obvious hint that your
life needs more color and change.

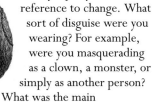

REVOLUTION

Revolution is a radical and violent image.
If you dreamed that you were caught up
in a **REVOLUTION**, consider what in your
waking life needs brutal change. It may
be a personal trait that you need to
dispose of with the utmost speed and
brutality. On the other hand, the
reference may be to a situation in your
domestic or working life that needs
transfiguring in some way. You should
also remember that revolutions are
fueled and motivated by anger; your
dream may be encouraging you to give
vent to some pent-up anger.

THE WORLD
OF NATURE

FANTASY &
FABLE

ARTS &
SCIENCES

THE HUMAN
BODY

BUILDINGS &
INTERIORS

EVERYDAY
THINGS

HUMAN
EMOTIONS

HUMAN
ACTIVITIES

HUMAN
CONDITIONS

RITUALS &
RELIGION

THE DREAM
THESAURUS

TEMPTATION

THERE WAS A PERIOD IN the early development of Christianity when dreams were believed to be messages from the Devil, who used them to tempt devout men and women into sin. There are many records of saints being tempted by erotic dreams.

PROSTITUTE
151
GIGOLO
151
FISHING
152

Nowadays, it is understood that our dreams are "sent" by no one. They are messages from ourselves to ourselves, and dreams in which we are tempted to carry out actions that we regard as immoral in our waking lives remind us of unconscious desires that we have repressed. A dream in which you are visiting a **PROSTITUTE** or **GIGOLO** may be a simple expression of sexual starvation, or of a desire for sexual variety. A dream in which you are **FISHING**, with an irresistible bait on your line may suggest that you want to attract someone, or that there is some temptation that you find almost irresistible. You may be repressing your waking urges and longings for admirable reasons, but you should recognize your emotions. You should also give them free rein, at least to the

extent of considering whether your waking repressions are leading you into psychological difficulties.

DREAM ANALYSIS

"I was playing billiards, even though it is a game I know nothing about. My opponent was beating me, but I knew that I could win if I could get the pale blue ball into the pocket. When my opponent was not looking, I picked up the pale blue ball to put it into the pocket. However, I immediately felt ashamed and dropped the ball, pretending that I had knocked it off the table."

The dreamer was in love with his friend's girlfriend (the day before the dream he had seen her in a pale blue dress). The dreamer believed that he could "put her in his pocket" if he exercised his charm, but the dream was telling him that the temptation was unworthy, and that he should resist it.

RESTRICTION

OUR FRUSTRATION AT THE restrictions that life puts upon us – whether practically or psychologically – often spills over into our dreams. However, dreams are usually constructive and may contain a hint of some way in which we can overcome, or alleviate, our frustration.

PRISON
124

Dreams in which our physical movement is restricted need not refer to any physical restriction in waking life. In fact, those people whose freedom is impeded usually dream of liberty, although the circumstances of their confinement may lead to nightmares (*see page 154*). Dreams of **PRISON** may refer to psychological constraints. Do you feel "tied down" within a claustrophobic personal relationship, or to a responsibility that weighs too heavily upon you? Note carefully the circumstances of your imprisonment, and in particular whether

LOCK
153
ROPE

it was alleviated in any way – by a view from the cell window, or the kindness of a warden (who does this represent in your waking life?). Because one is usually "sent" to prison, the implication is that someone is directly responsible for the restriction in your waking life that prompted the dream. The same is true of dreams in which you are **LOCKED** up or tied with a **ROPE**, and it will be important to

THE WORLD OF NATURE

FANTASY & FABLE

ARTS & SCIENCES

THE HUMAN BODY

BUILDINGS & INTERIORS

EVERYDAY THINGS

HUMAN EMOTIONS

HUMAN ACTIVITIES

HUMAN CONDITIONS

RITUALS & RELIGION
THE DREAM THESAURUS

THE WORLD OF NATURE

FANTASY & FABLE

ARTS & SCIENCES

THE HUMAN BODY

BUILDINGS & INTERIORS

EVERYDAY THINGS

HUMAN EMOTIONS

HUMAN ACTIVITIES

HUMAN CONDITIONS

RITUALS & RELIGION

THE DREAM THESAURUS

discover the motivation behind your imprisonment (remembering that you may be your own judge or jailer).

**PIT
TRAP
NET**

If you dream of falling into a **PIT**, there may be a reference to an accident in waking life that has restricted your movement or thought. The circumstances of the dream should reveal the meaning of the symbol, remembering that a pit is underground (*see Earth, page 48*). If you fall into a dream **TRAP**, however, the implication is different. Although someone has set the trap to catch you, there is a suggestion that the situation is partly your own fault. The dream may be criticizing your recent actions. A dream in which you are caught like a bird in a **NET** is associated with erotic misbehavior (the symbol is connected with feminine power).

A dream of physical restriction based on illness may refer to a waking difficulty, but an asthmatic person will be more

ASTHMA

likely to dream of breathing freely than of their illness. A healthy person dreaming of **ASTHMA** may be the subject of a comment on some form of physical restriction in their waking life (*see also Illness, page 95*).

HORSE
42, 144
REINS
HARNESS

The horse has traditionally been a symbol of life itself, as well as of many other forces, including wisdom, thought, and reason. (The early Christians also saw it as the symbol of lust.) A **HORSE** in your dream will probably represent you or some aspect of your personality. If you dream that the horse was in a **HARNESS** or on **REINS**, the reference may be to some constraint in waking life (either self-imposed or imposed by someone else) that is preventing you from a full expression of an important part of your personality or psyche. Did the horse want to go in any particular direction? Was it carrying a rider? Was the animal distressed, or patient and phlegmatic? The dream will certainly be reflecting your own attitude toward the problem that it presents in symbolic form, but it may also be suggesting ways of overcoming it.

—◆— PUNISHMENT —◆—

IN THE COURSE OF TELLING us things that we do not want to know, dreams also inflict the punishment that we subconsciously know we deserve. Sometimes dreams will inflict such punishment for deeds not yet committed, or which we have carried out thoughtlessly.

GALLOWS
125
CRIMINAL
124
MOB
175

Dreamers are occasionally rebuked for thoughts and deeds of which their better selves disapprove. The dream symbols often seem disproportionate: for example, if you have thoughtlessly spoken ill of a friend, you may find yourself on the **GALLOWS** in a dream, the implication being that you have murdered your friend's reputation. Dreams of punishment can also reflect our belief that someone else deserves castigation. A dream symbol can represent anyone or anything, and the **CRIMINAL** may be yourself or someone else. Even a **MOB**, in a dream, can be a reflection of your own

LYNCHING
125
GALLOWS
125
CANE
GUILLOTINE
125
BIRCH
51

personality, but it can also symbolize public opinion. If you dream that you are being **LYNCHED**, consider whether you are behaving antisocially in waking life. You could be the instrument of punishment: the **GALLOWS**, **CANE**, **GUILLOTINE**, or **BIRCH**; you should consider who is being chastised, and why.

BIRCH
51
CANE

The infliction of physical pain, for example being beaten by a **BIRCH** or a **CANE**, may not be a punishment at all. If this occurs in a dream, and is enjoyable, it may be a reflection of a tendency toward masochism in the dreamer.

HELL
88

Images of **HELL** probably appear less frequently in 20th-century dreams than in the dreams of people who lived in more puritanical ages. In fact, dreams have been recorded in our own time in which Hell has appeared as a pleasant place. However, it is still a frightening symbol in many dreams, and will generally reflect our own idea of the ultimate punishment. If you dream that you are condemned to Hell, or suffering the torments of the damned, there must be a reference to a serious misdemeanor of which you are (consciously or unconsciously) aware,

and the force with which you are rebuking or warning yourself in the dream is considerable.

LESSON
SCHOOL
89, 174

If you dream that you are back in **SCHOOL** learning a **LESSON**, or being forced to stay after school because you have not learned it properly, there may be a suggestion that you are not absorbing some instruction in waking life.

DREAM ANALYSIS

"I was at Washington Square in New York, and realized that a public hanging was taking place. Curious and horrified, I pushed my way to the front of the crowd. Looking up at the gallows, I saw a body swinging at the end of a rope, and realized that it was me. A man next to me said 'Let's go and cut him down — he may still be alive.' The crowd suddenly vanished, and we got a ladder and cut down the body. The man said 'It's too late — he's been hanging too long,' but I opened my eyes and winked at myself."

Jonathan thought at first that the dream must be suggesting that he should be punished, but he could not imagine why. After some time, he recognized the man in the dream: it was someone to whom he owed money. Jonathan realized that the dream was simply a rebuke for delaying to repay the money. The wink at himself was a tacit recognition of the fact that he was consciously not repaying his debt, even though he had the money to do so,

—◆—LOSS—◆—

IMAGES OF LOSS IN DREAMS frequently appear after the death of a loved one. However, such images may appear when what we have lost is not a person, but something less tangible – love or respect for someone, perhaps, or even our own self-respect.

AMPUTATION

A dream that some part of our body has been **AMPUTATED** is not uncommon, and leaves us predominantly with a feeling of loss. When examined, these dreams almost always symbolize the loss of a particular physical attribute. If you dream that you have no legs, the allusion may be to a lack of mobility – for example an unfulfilled wish to travel, or the necessity to cancel a planned journey. If in waking life you have recently lost a

VIRGINITY

colleague, or a friend upon whom you relied, you may dream of losing your right hand. In a man, dream of castration (*see page 97*) will almost certainly relate to a loss of sexual virility. The loss of **VIRGINITY** may not be a sexual image, but a reflection of the loss of childhood innocence. What have you learned recently in your waking life that may have damaged a previous naive belief or conception and disillusioned you?

THE WORLD OF NATURE

FANTASY & FABLE

ARTS & SCIENCES

THE HUMAN BODY

BUILDINGS & INTERIORS

EVERYDAY THINGS

HUMAN EMOTIONS

HUMAN ACTIVITIES

HUMAN CONDITIONS

RITUALS & RELIGION

THE DREAM THESAURUS

ASHES

A dream that something has been lost in a fire (*see page 45*) – particularly if it has been purposefully burned on a bonfire – would seem to suggest the dying of some impulse or energy. Was the symbol in your dream reduced to ASHES? If so, there may be an allusion in waking life to the loss of some ideal or the rejection of an ambition. Your dream may be warning you that you are overworking: you may be "burning up" too much emotional or physical energy.

**FRIEND
APPARITION**

A dream of the loss of a FRIEND or companion may reflect the loss of a particular characteristic you admire in them. The nature of your farewell will reflect the degree of your loss; whether it is serious, or unpleasant, but without any real significance. The appearance in a dream of a person you have lost is often consoling, and rarely frightening. Such an APPARITION can underline your loss, but you may wake feeling comforted.

**MAZE
LABYRINTH**

A MAZE or LABYRINTH is often the symbol of difficulty or confusion in various areas of life. If you find yourself lost and confused in a dream maze, there may be a suggestion that the possibilities set before you in waking life are complex and difficult, and merit careful thought before a decision is made. Consider any possible hints in your dream. If you finally decided to try a particular way out, what led to the decision? What symbols presented themselves to you?

◆ DIFFICULTY ◆

ONE OF THE MAIN PURPOSES of our dreams is to represent the difficulties of our waking lives so that we can better understand them. These difficulties are usually represented by individual symbols that we can understand, but symbols may also appear without obvious connotations.

**BOG
MOUNTAIN**
58, 144
CLIFF
58
ICE
130
SNOW
46, 160
**MAZE
LABYRINTH**

Dreams in which you are struggling through a BOG, tackling the difficult ascent of a MOUNTAIN or CLIFF, fighting your way through ICE or SNOW, or trying to find the way out of a MAZE or LABYRINTH (*see above*) may apply to a number of waking difficulties. These dreams usually present themselves when all of your attempts to see your way out of a particular problem have been exhausted. Such a dream may simply be a mirror image of your real difficulties, translated from the mental or emotional sphere to the physical one. It will be worthwhile informing your dreams that you need some more information. Just before going to sleep, ask your dreams to show you how to find your way out of the bog or up the mountain. Your dreams will often respond with a clue. You may not be confronted in dreams again with the quagmire or peak but instead be shown a symbol that will suggest a way to a solution to your waking problem.

THESAURUS
CROSSWORD
133
MATHEMATICS
LANGUAGE
138

Dreaming of more cerebral puzzles may imply that in our waking lives our approach to our problems is too lofty or intellectual. Such dreams may be suggesting that we allow our emotions to play a larger part in decision making. If you are involved in a difficult personal relationship, for instance, sitting down to consider the matter calmly is one thing, and ignoring the passions that put you in your quandary is quite another. A dream of searching through a **THESAURUS** for a synonym for "love," or being unable to work out a **CROSSWORD** clue that clearly refers to your partner, is probably telling you to tear up the thesaurus or the crossword, and listen to your emotions. If in your dream you were puzzled by a **MATHEMATICS** equation or baffled by a phrase in a **LANGUAGE** you did not understand, you are probably in waking life equally confounded by a type of behavior or an emotional outburst. How you reacted in the dream may give you a hint about a new approach to a problem.

DECK CHAIR
INDIGESTION
HEDGEHOG

The disguises adopted by dream symbols are legion, and every idea and object that appears in a dream should be examined from every possible angle. If you are trying to set up a **DECK CHAIR** and failing, what simple problem in waking life is proving intractable? A dream of **INDIGESTION** is extremely unlikely to follow a heavy meal, but may follow an unappealing argument that you had to "swallow." If in your dream you were trying to pick up a **HEDGEHOG** with your bare hands, what prickly customer are you engaged with in your waking life?

—◆— LONELINESS —◆—

DREAMS ABOUT BEING LONELY often offer a solution to a solitary waking life. Moreover, symbols of loneliness may refer not to a friendless life, but to our "going out on a limb" – separating ourselves from friends and colleagues in some important non-social context.

CROWD
175, 177
ASTRONAUT
GARDEN
52, 54
CHILD
89

To dream that you are alone in a **CROWD** may imply that you are too isolated from the feelings of those around you, while being alone in a landscape (*see page 58*) may suggest that you prefer to make decisions by yourself. The dream may remind you, if you were sad at being alone, that this is not always a good thing. A dream of being an **ASTRONAUT** on a spacewalk may be a disturbing image, and may refer to your deepest feelings of yourself as being "all alone." If you dreamed that you were alone in a **GARDEN**, your withdrawn state may seem more tolerable, but the context of the dream may suggest otherwise. Finding yourself once more a **CHILD**, alone in the dark, is a potent symbol of simple loneliness: the implication is that you must learn to rely on others, and to seek out those who can help you.

——— DREAM ANALYSIS ———

"I was a child again, and had been given a quarter to spend on candy. On the way to the candy store, I lost the coin, and was searching through my clothes. However, the pockets were full of holes, and I knew that the coin had dropped through one of them. I thought that if only I had better clothes I would not have lost the coin, and when I got to the store the man said, 'Why didn't you keep your money in your hand?' But he gave me some candy anyway."

James was a young man starting out in a new job. He was conscious that he had to look stylish, but he did not have the money to buy the new clothes that he felt he needed. The fact that in the dream he had lost his pocket money because of the state of his clothing, reflected his anxiety about appearing respectable enough to warrant the salary paid to him at work. The dream pointed out that he could be trusted with his responsible new position, even if he made a few basic errors at first.

THE WORLD OF NATURE

FANTASY & FABLE

ARTS & SCIENCES

THE HUMAN BODY

BUILDINGS & INTERIORS

EVERYDAY THINGS

HUMAN EMOTIONS

HUMAN ACTIVITIES

HUMAN CONDITIONS

RITUALS & RELIGION

THE DREAM THESAURUS

—◆— GATHERINGS —◆—

IN ALL LARGE GATHERINGS of people there is a strong emotional charge, of either unanimity or diversity, of good feeling, or of stress and tension. When we are part of a gathering or observing one, in a dream, we should begin our interpretation by considering the basic atmosphere and emotion of the occasion. Remember, too, that a crowd of people in a dream can represent a crowd of problems.

CLUB

Being a member of a **CLUB** gives us a sense of security; here we meet like-minded people with a common cause, and similar objectives and opinions. What was going on in your dream will probably reflect on your present feelings. If the dream was pleasant and you were enjoying yourself, in waking life it would appear that you are currently in a secure position with your family and friends. However, if you were thrown out of the club, and felt shame, your dream may be stirring up some kind of guilt feelings over a waking action. The tribal instinct is present in most of us, but particularly

TRIBE

so when we are young — we hate to be different from our particular gang or set of friends. As an adult, if your dream had any **TRIBAL** overtones, you should decide whether you are not expressing your own individuality in waking life, or whether you are looking for greater support or protection from your peer group.

SCHOOL
89, 171
TEACHER
88, 89

When we are taken back to our **SCHOOL** days in dreams, we are finding out how the past affects the present. Perhaps you can make a connection between the dream and a recent event or action, and relate the **TEACHER** — an authority figure

COLLEGE
UNIVERSITY
LECTURE
TUTOR

(see page 162) – to someone in your present waking life. At **COLLEGE** or **UNIVERSITY**, there is greater freedom of expression than at school. You may have dreamed that you were at a **LECTURE**, and were trying to attract the attention of the **TUTOR**. Who does the tutor represent in your waking life, and why were you so eager to be noticed? Alternatively, does the tutor symbolize some part of your intelligence that is not being sufficiently honored by you? Your dream may be suggesting that you are in need of greater intellectual stimulation and challenge, and that you need to expand your horizons in some way in waking life.

COMMUNE
COMMUNITY

In a similar way to a club (see opposite), a commune or community is generally a gathering of like-minded people. But working and living in a commune usually involves an element of sacrifice: we are paid little for a lot of hard work. In your dream **COMMUNE** or **COMMUNITY** were you a willing worker, or did you feel as if you were being exploited? In waking life, are you being taken advantage of at work? Alternatively, did you work well in the dream, knowing that everyone was pulling their weight for the common cause? If so, you may feel that you need to do more work for the general good of the community.

CONFERENCE
CONVENTION
AUDIENCE
81

When our dreams send us to a **CONFERENCE** or a **CONVENTION** they may be suggesting that we should listen to other people's opinions and experiences, and perhaps become more flexible in our own. In your dream you may have been speaking at such a gathering. If so, your analysis will largely depend on whether you were being listened to with great interest and attention, having to shout to be heard, or were sent off the platform with shouts of disapproval. These should not be difficult symbols for you to interpret, since your dream is making an obvious statement about your present attitude toward life, and warning you how other people are reacting to it. Perhaps the most negative symbol would be if you were speaking and saw that half of the **AUDIENCE** was

RECEPTION
GUEST
102

asleep. If you were the host or hostess at a dream **RECEPTION**, and receiving **GUESTS**, your dreams may be suggesting that you are being particularly open-minded in waking life. If some of your guests were being difficult, they may represent some waking problems currently surrounding you (see Crowd, below).

CONGREG-
ATION

Being part of a **CONGREGATION** in a dream may signify your assent to some general moral statement. It will certainly be connected with your moral attitude, or perhaps your conception of your present spiritual state. Your mood, attitude, and reaction to the service is essential in the interpretation of such a dream.

CROWD
173, 177
MOB
170

Dreams in which a **CROWD** or **MOB** of people is jostling us can be extremely frightening, and it is only if we can push our way through and out of them that we can feel relatively at ease. It is nearly always the case that a dream crowd will represent problems surrounding you in waking life. The denser and more claustrophobic the crowd, the greater and more demanding the problems. The dream will be positive if you hold control

---

DREAM ANALYSIS

"I was in an unruly crowd celebrating Easter in Greece. There was a tremendous crush, and people began setting off firecrackers. I've always been terrified of fireworks, and became hysterical because I could not escape the crowd. A man standing next to me said, 'Don't worry, they can't harm you,' and handed me one. I thought it would explode, but it simply spluttered. Then roots began to grow out of it, and it turned into a beautiful orchid."

The dreamer was a teacher who was having problems with the schedule that she had to draw up assigning other teachers to various classes. She was being harried by her colleagues, all eager for their needs to be satisfied. She was afraid that sooner or later there would be an explosive argument. The dream was assuring her that if she grasped the situation firmly and dealt with it in her own way, the result would be satisfactory. The dreamer also bred orchids as a hobby, and she knew that they were long-lasting plants. The appearance of the orchid may have been an assurance to her that the work she was doing would be to her long-enduring credit.

THE WORLD OF NATURE

FANTASY & FABLE

ARTS & SCIENCES

THE HUMAN BODY

BUILDINGS & INTERIORS

EVERYDAY THINGS

HUMAN EMOTIONS

HUMAN ACTIVITIES

HUMAN CONDITIONS

RITUALS & RELIGION

THE DREAM THESAURUS

THE WORLD
OF NATURE

FANTASY &
FABLE

ARTS &
SCIENCES

THE HUMAN
BODY

BUILDINGS &
INTERIORS

EVERYDAY
THINGS

HUMAN
EMOTIONS

HUMAN
ACTIVITIES

HUMAN
CONDITIONS

RITUALS &
RELIGION

THE DREAM
THESAURUS

GANG

over your dream crowd. If you were nervous of being trampled, there may be a suggestion that you need a great deal of help. This may be the case if you are working too hard to hold down a job and keep your family together, or if your problems are more personally oriented, and causing you to be depressed and confused. Being chased by an unruly **GANG** may also relate to problems of one kind or another, but that gang may also be similar to a monster (*see page 154*) who must be faced. Consider who or what the gang represents – it is probably someone known to you.

**RALLY
POLITICAL
PARTY**

When analyzing a dream of attending a **RALLY**, you must decide whether you were supporting the cause or **POLITICAL PARTY** concerned, or were antagonistic toward it. In either case, there is possibly some anger in your waking life that needs expression or examination.

Although very different, a regiment and an orchestra do have certain things in common. They must conform to a very strict discipline (*see page 163*), and they must work together – one to produce

REGIMENT
141
ORCHESTRA
70

music, the other to protect, defend, and fight. To be part of either a **REGIMENT** or an **ORCHESTRA** in your dream, may signify the need for discipline or communal action with your friends or colleagues in waking life – perhaps you must all play in tune or march in step. If you were playing in the orchestra or marching with the troop, the group of people may represent those with whom you are working in waking life. How well was the orchestra playing, and was the troop marching purposefully?

REUNION

A dream of a **REUNION** has echoes of nostalgia, so have you recently been preoccupied with the past, or does some past experience have advice to offer on a present waking situation? On the other hand, was your dream suggesting that you are dwelling too much on the past, rather than looking to the future?

—◆— CELEBRATIONS —◆—

DREAMS OF CELEBRATIONS seem most likely to reflect a waking feeling of satisfaction about something we have accomplished. Our attitude toward what is going on in the dream, how we react to it, and how we actually feel, should uncover the deeper meaning of the message.

**CHRISTMAS
CARNIVAL**
179

A dream of some disappointment at **CHRISTMAS** may be warning you to lower your expectations, or may simply be trying to prepare you for this or some other demanding time. The religious side of the festival should also be considered. Was your dream prompting you to pay greater attention to your spiritual beliefs? For many people, a carnival also involves months of preparation, so there are some parallels with Christmas. If you were participating in a dream **CARNIVAL**, you should consider how you were dressed (*see Image, page 165*). On the other hand,

perhaps the carnival was just passing by. Are you perhaps missing out on what waking life has to offer?

**FESTIVAL
FETE**

If your dream **FESTIVAL** was celebrating something specific, this will probably be the key symbol. If you are personally involved in the festival, are your dreams praising you for recent efforts, and encouraging you to have greater self-confidence in what you are doing? At village fetes there is often rivalry and competition, so perhaps you should relate this to your dream **FETE**.

FLAG
INVESTITURE

The raising or lowering of a flag has national and territorial overtones. If in your dream you were flying your own **FLAG**, there may be a suggestion that you should show others what you can do, and become more confident in your own actions and capabilities. Is your personal "territory" being invaded; do you lack privacy, or are you claiming your rights in some way? To be at or participating in an **INVESTITURE** in a dream may also signify increased self-confidence in waking life. Alternatively, your dream may be saying something about a recent important decision – perhaps concerning your personal prestige – which meant a considerable investment of time and money. To dream of general rejoicing is almost certainly a positive symbol, and if you were not joining in, your dream may have been suggesting that you should be more positive in your outlook.

—◆— CEREMONIES —◆—

WHEN ANY KIND OF CEREMONY appears in our dreams we usually wake feeling elated, since it may be that our dreams are praising us for recent progress – either at work or in our personal life. If this is not our reaction, we should consider whether our dreams are saying, "This is what you could be like."

WEDDING
131
BRIDE
BRIDEGROOM
151
BRIDESMAID

If you are unmarried, and you enjoyed your **WEDDING** dream, it was most likely a dream of wish-fulfillment (*see page 150*). Your dream may be advising you not to try so hard to find the right partner. This may particularly be so if you were the **BRIDE** or **BRIDEGROOM**. If you were wearing white, (*see Colors, page 75*), there may be a comment on your attitude toward sex in this dream. If you were the **BRIDESMAID**, what was your attitude toward the bride? You should also consider your wedding dream in the context of commitment: in waking life, are you about to be "married" to a new job or a bigger mortgage?

GRADUATION
167
GRADUATE

If you dream of a **GRADUATION** ceremony, or if you were a **GRADUATE**, your dreams are almost certainly praising you for past efforts in waking life. They may also be encouraging you to concentrate on the future, and if you are uncertain what your next move should be, ask your dreams for more help (*see page 33*).

CROWD
173, 175
PROCESSION

If you dreamed that you were in a **CROWD** waiting for a **PROCESSION** to pass by, who or what was in the procession? The meaning of that symbol – what it could represent in waking life – may relate to something or someone you admire, or to what they represent and to which you aspire. If you were in the procession and crowds were cheering you, are you besieged with good ideas in waking life, all clamoring for your attention?

THE WORLD OF NATURE

FANTASY & FABLE

ARTS & SCIENCES

THE HUMAN BODY

BUILDINGS & INTERIORS

EVERYDAY THINGS

HUMAN EMOTIONS

HUMAN ACTIVITIES

HUMAN CONDITIONS

RITUALS & RELIGION

THE DREAM THESAURUS

ENTERTAINMENT

WHEN WE HAVE DREAMS in which entertainment is the main theme, they may be advising us that we are not getting as much pleasure out of our waking lives as we should. If we are participating in the entertainment, there may be a suggestion in the dream that we make more of an effort to enjoy life and allow ourselves time to have fun.

CIRCUS

Your reaction to your dream **CIRCUS** is probably important to your analysis. You may think the circus in your dream is marvelous, and be full of admiration for the dedicated and clever performers, or you may recoil at the way noble animals are used to entertain. What was going on in the ring must be individually examined (*see The Mandala, page 68*). Is the free, wandering lifestyle of the performers relevant? Were you performing in the circus? In which case, are you taking dangerous or daring risks in your waking life? Did you fall from a **TRAPEZE** or **TIGHTROPE** and wake up feeling anxious? If so, the dream

TRAPEZE
72
TIGHTROPE
CLOWN

may contain warnings. If you were a circus **CLOWN** in your dream, are you laughing at or mocking someone in waking life, or is someone laughing at you? Or are you pretending to be happy and smiling when in reality you are feeling very unhappy?

COMEDIAN
CONJURER
62

A similar interpretation might be relevant if a **COMEDIAN** appeared in your dream. A dream of a **CONJURER** may be drawing your attention to some kind of deception (*see page 152*). Is someone in your waking life behaving deceptively toward you. Alternatively, are you the guilty one?

FAIR

Your dream **FAIR** may be representing different possibilities that are facing you in waking life. Think of the sideshows and merry-go-rounds, and what, if

FIREWORKS

anything, frightened or excited you. Fireworks entertain and give us momentary wonder, but they are highly transitory and can be frightening. Your dream of **FIREWORKS** may have sexual overtones: there may be a comment about orgasm, or the fact that you are nervous about sexual commitment.

PERFORMING
81
WRESTLING
134
TOY

If you were watching people **PERFORMING** in your dream, you should consider the possibility that the dream was showing you your present position. Could you identify with any of the performers? If you were taking part, in waking life are you putting on some kind of an act and not being true to yourself, perhaps to impress other people? A dream that you were at a **WRESTLING** match may signify that in waking life you are "wrestling" with some problem. What was the result of the match? A dream **TOY** may symbolize yourself: is someone playing with your feelings in waking life?

RITUAL

MOST OF US NEED A CERTAIN amount of ritual in our lives; it marks times of change and progression to higher levels, and gives us a sense of security. This is particularly so when it is performed with like-minded fellow beings. However, if, in our dreams, we are not allowed to participate, we may be harboring feelings of guilt and shame because we have broken important rules.

CORONATION Of all rituals, a **CORONATION** is probably the most impressive. If you were being crowned in your dream, you may have considerable cause to feel proud of your success and achievements. However, wearing a crown carries a great deal of responsibility and an equally great amount to live up to. Your dream may carry a warning: after your moment of glory, can you cope with what lies ahead?

RELIGIOUS PROCESSION **RELIGIOUS PROCESSIONS** are intended to increase our faith by stimulating our imagination. Perhaps you were playing the part of

one of the main characters. If so, do you aspire to be like them in waking life? A great deal depends on your attitude toward your faith — whatever your religion or cultural background. If you are troubled by your dream, or if you cannot reach any definite conclusions about it, you may need to seek professional help — particularly if the dream recurs.

CARNIVAL *176*

CARNIVALS can also have religious significance — they often take place before Lent, for instance. If this theme colors your dream, you may be living too hedonistic a lifestyle in the knowledge that you will have to make sacrifices later.

THE HUMAN BODY

BUILDINGS & INTERIORS

EVERYDAY THINGS

HUMAN EMOTIONS

HUMAN ACTIVITIES

HUMAN CONDITIONS

RITUALS & RELIGION

THE DREAM THESAURUS

SOYER

—✦— RELIGION —✦—

RELIGION IS MANY THINGS to many people: the spectrum is so vast that the subject must present difficulties to dream analysts attempting to suggest which symbols in dreams touch on this area of life. Some symbols are obvious, but the subject of religion is so pervasive and widespread that other references in dreams may be heavily disguised.

THE WORLD OF NATURE

FANTASY & FABLE

ARTS & SCIENCES

THE HUMAN BODY

BUILDINGS & INTERIORS

EVERYDAY THINGS

HUMAN EMOTIONS

HUMAN ACTIVITIES

HUMAN CONDITIONS

RITUALS & RELIGION

THE DREAM THESAURUS

In relatively modern times, it has still been possible to believe that dreams are sent by God. Bishop Thomas Ken (1637–1710) argued that since God was omnipresent it was impossible to believe that He was not present in dreams; and that if He was, it was surely in order to send messages to His people. Although no dreams by Christ are recorded in the *New Testament*, both Mahomet and Buddha dreamed, and the *Koran* was revealed in a dream. However, dreams that contain a strong religious factor do not only occur to those who practice a faith. In fact, Jung said that the majority of his patients who brought him dreams relying on religious symbolism had lost their faith, and the dreams were predominately alluding to personal feelings of regret and loss. It is impossible to include here references to the symbols of all religions, but most of the symbols mentioned below can be easily "translated" into faiths other than Christianity. You should always keep in mind, however, the context in which this type of symbol appears in the religious books or canons of a particular faith. A dream of visiting a religious place may be

CHURCH *100*
CATHEDRAL
CHAPEL *100*
CRYPT

commenting on the lack of a spiritual element in your life. If the **CHURCH** in your dream was quiet, peaceful, and calming, the implication may be that you need to seek out a space in which your spiritual self can expand and breathe. There is a difference of tone between a **CATHEDRAL** and a **CHAPEL**, but this may be a reference to the nature of your spiritual aspirations. In the same way, if you dreamed that you were in a **CRYPT**, there may be a suggestion that your spiritual self is too deeply buried beneath your material ambition. If the religious building you visited in your dream was in ruins, a note of regret may permeate the dream, and you should consider what area of your spiritual being is in ruins.

PULPIT *125*
ALTAR

If in your dream a message was delivered from the **PULPIT** or **ALTAR**, it is coming from the highest authority (*see page 162*). This may not be religious authority, but may be coming from the loftiest part of your own inner resources. You should note the manner in which the message was delivered, since it will certainly be important to the interpretation.

POPE
BISHOP
CURATE

A message communicated from an officer of a church is a message from an authority figure (*see page 162*), and will usually be important. There will be very rare exceptions, for example a rationalist who is disparaging about the clergy would be unlikely to see them in dreams as figures of authority. On the other hand, if their statements appear to have weight, and you take them seriously in your dream, their message will be an earnest one. Whether the figure is of the **POPE**, a **BISHOP**, or a **CURATE**, does not

CHRIST
60
HOLY VIRGIN

have a great deal of significance: the message given will still be a serious one, although it may have greater force if expressed by the former rather than by the latter. Some figures, such as **CHRIST** or the **HOLY VIRGIN**, will be important if they appear in a dream, since they have great significance in the religious sphere.

BAPTISM

A dream of **BAPTISM** hints strongly at a new life of some kind for the dreamer. In your dream, were you baptized under a new name, and what significance could that name carry? If you were attending the baptism of a baby or small child, think about that symbol in relation to your waking life. The infant may represent an idea or project that you are beginning work on, for which you are seeking approval and support. Such a dream will be giving your waking venture a name, and you may be on course for such approval.

BLASPHEMY
00

If **BLASPHEMY** occurs in your dream, the form it takes will be important, since it may reflect irreverence of some sort in waking life. Blasphemy is a form of insult, rather than of constructive criticism, so are your objections to something in waking life merely taking the form of violent protest rather than practical argument or action?

BLESSING

A dream of being **BLESSED** signifies approval (by yourself or by someone else) of some attitude or action. The more fervent the blessing and the more authoritative the figure who blesses you, the more satisfied you may feel about your waking decision or behavior.

EUCHARIST
COMMUNION

The **EUCHARIST** or **COMMUNION** are other forms of blessing – of forgiveness and renewal. The religious symbolism of the bread and wine suggests that such a dream may refer to the basic elements of your life, about which you may need reassurance. Your attitude in the dream will be vital to your interpretation. Did you feel renewed and blessed, or did you approach the dream communion table tentatively and in fear of refusal?

CROSS
60
CRUCIFIX
60
CRUCIFIXION

A relatively simple dream in which the **CROSS** or a **CRUCIFIX** (or indeed the unadorned symbol of any religious faith) is the predominant symbol, is likely to be a plain affirmation or condemnation – particularly if you are devoutly religious. Such a symbol is unlikely to appear in the dream of an agnostic, but if it does, it may be an indication of the stirring of a need for some kind of faith in your waking life. A dream that you are being **CRUCIFIED** may be a reflection on an area of your life, or some specific problem, in which you are metaphorically being crucified, or perhaps making some disproportionate sacrifice.

CRUSADE

Who or what was your dream **CRUSADE** against? It is important to discover the nature of the enemy, and why you are fighting against it. Such a dream would seem to suggest that you need to fight (for or against) some antagonist in waking life. You should think carefully about the separate elements of the dream, and the direction in which they may be pointing you.

RESURREC-TION

A dream of the **RESURRECTION** is clearly a dream of hope, for example recovery from an illness, the "rebirth" of an idea or ambition, or the renewal of a romantic, platonic, or professional relationship.

DREAM ANALYSIS

"I was walking through a bare landscape when it began to rain. There were no trees to take shelter under, but I saw a church in the distance and ran toward it. The door was open, but when I entered I found that the building was a roofless ruin, and the rain was pelting down. I walked up the nave, but where the altar should have been there was a gap. Although I could hear a choir singing in the distance, I could not discover its location."

Originally intending to study for the priesthood, Bill had lost his faith while at college. The dream reflected the aridity of his spiritual life, and the fact that he now believed he had nowhere to look for shelter from his problems.

The dream was suggesting that he had a gap at the center of his life. The distant sound of a choir suggested that traces of his original conviction still existed, although at that time he did not know how to recover it.

THE WORLD OF NATURE

FANTASY & FABLE

ARTS & SCIENCES

THE HUMAN BODY

BUILDINGS & INTERIORS

EVERYDAY THINGS

HUMAN EMOTIONS

HUMAN ACTIVITIES

HUMAN CONDITIONS

RITUALS & RELIGION

THE DREAM THESAURUS

THE WEDDING DREAM

"I was about to get married, and was walking down the aisle. However, I was dressed entirely in black, with heavy black shoes and a black veil, and was carrying a bouquet of dead, black roses. I did not want to get married, and seemed neither to know nor care who the bridegroom was.

Suddenly, the aisle of the large and crowded church began to slope, so that I began to walk faster and faster towards the altar, despite my efforts to hang back. Reluctant and full of dread, I tried to keep away from the altar, which I now saw was piled high with dirty washing and a huge mound of earthy potatoes. I knew that I would have to do the washing and peel the potatoes.

The slope of the aisle now became even steeper, and all the people in the church began to chant 'Go, go, go!' As I approached the altar I dropped my bouquet, which then burst into hundreds of different things: saucepans, a shovel, socks, pieces of paper, and all kinds of garbage. The crowd shouted at me to clear up the mess so that they could all go home, and people started to poke me with long, skinny fingers. I tried to pick everything up, but it was difficult — the garbage was suddenly blowing around and away from me. Then I caught a glimpse of a colorful butterfly; I reached out for it, but it flew up into the sky."

BUTTERFLY FLIES
UP INTO SKY

BOUQUET BURSTS
INTO HUNDREDS
OF THINGS

LAURA
WEARS
BLACK
WEDDING
DRESS

BOUQUET
OF DEAD,
BLACK
ROSES

LAURA RUNS AS
AISLE BECOMES
STEEP

INTERPRETATION

Laura had for a long time been living a fulfilled life as an artist, but had been able to sell only a few paintings. Money became scarce, and when her boyfriend lost his job they slipped deeper into debt. At the time of the dream she was being forced into taking a dull job in a factory. She knew that she would hate the job, but it was essential that she earned some money.

The wedding represented for Laura a reluctant commitment to her new job, and the dead roses were a symbol of her faded hopes. She was extremely depressed at the time, and the prominence of black was symbolic of this. The veil over her face seemed to be hiding her shame; and perhaps also symbolized her aversion to what was ahead of her in her waking life. The unsympathetic crowd represented her problems, and the garbage and her inability to gather it up symbolized her reaction to the work she would be doing in the factory. The altar was a symbol of sacrifice, and the piles of washing and potatoes represented drudgery. The potatoes also represented the sustenance that she would receive as a result of her dull, laborious work. The one positive element in the dream was the colorful butterfly. It was a ray of hope (although she was unable to catch it), and she drew a parallel between the bright colors of the creature and her painting. It is possible that when her financial situation improved she would, in a future dream, catch the butterfly. While the dream was clearly summing up her present situation and her deep depression and reluctance, there was also a message of hope.

Laura was "dragging her feet" due to the weight of her shoes – an indication of reluctance. The aisle of the church started to slope downwards, showing the increasingly serious financial situation. The exploding bouquet represented her anger, but she tried to counter this by attempting to accept the situation, even if it meant sacrificing her real work. She had visited the factory and knew that she would be working under considerable pressure to keep up with the production lines. This is signified by the jeering crowd.

THE DREAM THESAURUS

THE WORLD OF NATURE

FANTASY & FABLE

ARTS & SCIENCES

THE HUMAN BODY

BUILDINGS & INTERIORS

EVERYDAY THINGS

HUMAN EMOTIONS

HUMAN ACTIVITIES

HUMAN CONDITIONS

RITUALS & RELIGION

THE DREAM THESAURUS

THE IMAGES INCLUDED in the following section are among those likely to appear from time to time in your dreams. Each image is related to one or more of the main dream themes in the preceding section. In the Dream Thesaurus, the themes are listed indented below each entry in small capitals, and are followed by the relevant page number. The words in italics are pointers to follow if the suggested theme or themes do not seem to apply.

ABANDONMENT – main dream image
■ LONELINESS 173 – relevant dream theme and page number
desertion, neglect – pointers (other ideas to try)

To give an example of the way the Dream Thesaurus works, if you were in some way "abandoned" in your dream, or if that word seems otherwise appropriate (you may have been left alone in an unfamiliar landscape, or the dream may have been of a kitten or puppy you or someone else abandoned) a likely main theme of the dream will be loneliness. However, your dream may alternatively point to desertion or neglect. The entries that are underlined are the main dream themes in the preceding section.

If you find it difficult to relate the words suggested here to your dream, it may be worth trying a simple "word association" test: think of the main image in your dream, and say the word that first comes into your mind. This may well suggest a connection that you have so far overlooked.

It is impossible to provide a comprehensive list of possible subjects, since we can literally dream of anything. If the principle subject of your dream does not appear in the Dream Thesaurus, consult the nearest suggestion. For example, if you dream that you are dancing a tango, look for the entry "dancing". It is also worth remembering that the word you first think of when recollecting your dream will be an important clue. Wish-fulfillment is another aspect that should be considered, since dreams often reflect a conscious or unconscious desire to achieve something in your waking life.

A

ABANDONMENT
■ LONELINESS 173
desertion, neglect

ABBEY
■ BUILDINGS 100
■ RELIGION 180

ABDUCTION
■ WISH-FULFILLMENT 150
kidnap, seize, sex

ABORTION
■ BIRTH 86
■ CHANGE 168
finality

ABROAD
■ ESCAPISM 136
■ INSECURITY 121
■ LANDSCAPE 58
■ TRAVEL 134

ABSENCE
■ LONELINESS 173
scarcity

ABSTINENCE
■ DISCIPLINE 163
■ FOOD AND DRINK 106

ABUSE
■ ANGER 123
■ HOSTILITY 122
addiction, corruption, drugs, maltreatment

ABYSS
■ NIGHTMARE 154
confusion

ACCELERATOR
■ VEHICLES 116
energy, progress, speed

ACCESSARY
■ CRIME 140
sharing

ACCESSORY
■ CLOTHING 84
detail

ACCIDENT 160
■ DANGER 158
■ GAMBLING 139
chance, shock

ACCOUNTANT
■ CALCULATION 77
■ DISCIPLINE 163

ACE
■ AMBITION 151
■ GAMBLING 137
■ GAMES 132

ACHE
■ HEALTH 93

ACHIEVEMENT 167

ACID
■ FOOD AND DRINK 106
drugs

ACOLYTE
■ RELIGION 180
■ THE SUPERNATURAL 60
assistant, inferior

ACORN
■ TREES 50
nature, new start, small beginnings

ACQUITTAL
■ CRIME 140
innocence

ACROBAT
■ DISCIPLINE 163
■ FEAR 120
■ INSECURITY 121
■ SKILL 72
balance

ACTOR
■ OCCUPATIONS 148
■ THEATER 81

ACTIVITIES 144

ADDICT
■ ESCAPISM 136

ADMISSION
■ MONEY 110
acceptance

ADOLESCENCE
■ WISH-FULFILLMENT 150
puberty

ADOLESCENT
■ CHANGE 168
■ YOUTH 89
puberty

ADOPTION
■ LOVE 126
choice

ADULTERY
■ GUILT 124
betrayal, corruption, debasement

ADVENTURE 136
■ AMBITION 151
■ DANGER 158
excitement, risk

ADVERTISEMENT
■ AMBITION 151
■ THEATER 81
■ WISH-FULFILLMENT 150

ACHE
■ HEALTH 93

AEROBATICS
■ DECEPTION 152
■ FLYING 147
■ SKILL 72

AEROBICS
■ MOVEMENT 148

AFFAIR
■ EROTIC DREAMS 96

AGGRESSION
■ HOSTILITY 122
■ WAR 140
forcefulness, invasion, quarrel, threat, violence

AGITATION
■ FEAR 120
tension, unrest, worry

AIR 48

AIRPLANE
■ DISASTER 160
■ FLYING 147
■ TRAVEL 134

AIRPORT
■ TRAVEL 134

ALARM
■ DANGER 158

ALBATROSS
■ WINGED CREATURES 43

ALCHEMY
■ CHANGE 168

ALCOHOL
■ ESCAPISM 136
■ FOOD AND DRINK 106
irresponsibility

ALIMONY
■ GUILT 124
betrayal, mistakes, sex

ALLAH
■ RELIGION 180
■ THE SUPERNATURAL 60

ALLERGY
■ FEAR 120
■ GUILT 124

ALLEY
■ LANDSCAPE 58

ALLOWANCE
■ MONEY 110
freedom of expression

ALMS
■ MONEY 110
charity

ALTAR
■ CEREMONIES 177
■ RELIGION 180

AMBASSADOR
- AUTHORITY 162
- COMMUNICATION 137
diplomacy, tact

AMBER
- JEWELRY 114

AMBITION 151

AMBULANCE
- DANGER 158
- FEAR 120
- WARNING 159
assistance, caring

AMBUSH
- ANGER 123
- HOSTILITY 122
- WAR 140
forcefulness, invasion, secrecy, threat, violence

AMETHYST
- JEWELRY 114

AMMONIA
- WEAPONS 118
poison, urine

AMMUNITION
- HOSTILITY 122
- WAR 140
- WEAPONS 118
threat, violence

AMPUTATION
- LOSS 171

ANATOMY
- THE BODY 91
analysis, construction, decomposition, research

ANCHOR
- INSECURITY 121
- SECURITY 153
- WATER 46

ANESTHETIC
- ILLNESS 95
- LOSS 171
indifference, suppression

ANGEL
- RELIGION 180
- THE SUPERNATURAL 60
beauty

ANGER 123

ANGLING
- AMBITION 151
- DECEPTION 152
- WATER 46
hope

ANIMALS
- ACTIVITIES 144
- FEAR 120
- LOVE 126
- NIGHTMARES 154

ANKLE
- INSECURITY 121
- THE BODY 91

ANNEX
- BUILDINGS 100

ANNOUNCER
- AUTHORITY 162
truth

ANNUITY
- MONEY 110

ANOREXIA
- EMOTION 130
- FOOD AND DRINK 106
self-sacrifice

ANT
- MAMMALS AND REPTILES 42
- SWIMMERS AND CRAWLERS 44

ANTARCTIC *see* **ARCTIC**

ANTEROOM
- BUILDINGS 100
expectation, frustration

ANTHILL
- CONTAINERS 108
- DANGER 158
- SWIMMERS AND CRAWLERS 44
activity

ANTIDOTE
- ILLNESS 95
reassurance, recovery

ANTIFREEZE
- EMOTION 130
- VEHICLES 116

ANTIQUE
- BUILDINGS 100
age, furniture, tradition

ANTLERS
- MAMMALS AND REPTILES 42
antagonism, phallus

ANVIL
- CHANGE 168
- HOSTILITY 122
- WAR 140
quarrel, threat, violence

APARTMENT
- BUILDINGS 100

APE
- MAMMALS AND REPTILES 42

APHRODISIAC
- WISH-FULFILLMENT 150

APHRODITE
- MYTHOLOGY 64

APOLOGY
- INSECURITY 121

APPARITION
- INSECURITY 121
- LOSS 171

APPETITE
- FOOD AND DRINK 106
emotional needs

APPLAUSE
- ENTERTAINMENT 178
- THEATER 81
reassurance, self-confidence

APPLE
- FOOD AND DRINK 106
- FRUIT 54
desire, sin

APRICOT
- FOOD AND DRINK 106
- FRUIT 54

APRON
- CLOTHING 84
dependency, embarrassment, modesty

AQUARIUM
- CONTAINERS 108
- SWIMMERS AND CRAWLERS 44
- WATER 46

AQUARIUS
- THE ZODIAC 69

ARCH
- BUILDINGS 100
protection, support

ARCHER
- ACTIVITIES 144
- SKILL 72

ARCHBISHOP
- AUTHORITY 162
- RELIGION 180

ARCTIC
- LANDSCAPE 58
- WEATHER 49
emotional coldness

ARGUMENT
- ANGER 123
- HOSTILITY 122

ARIES
- THE ZODIAC 69

ARK
- WATER 46
animals

ARM
- THE BODY 91
strength, violence

ARMCHAIR
- HOME 102
furniture, relaxation

ARMOR
- HOSTILITY 122
- SECURITY 153
- WAR 140
self-defense, violence

ARMY
- HOSTILITY 122
- WAR 140

ARMY OFFICER
- ESTABLISHMENT 163

ARREST
- AUTHORITY 162
- GUILT 124
catch the attention, delay, stop

ARROW
- LOVE 126
- GAMES 132
- SKILL 72
- WEAPONS 118
decisiveness, sex, speed

ARTIST
- OCCUPATIONS 148

ARSENIC
- RELIGION 180
- WEAPONS 118
poison

ASH
- TREES 50

ASHES
- DIRT 119
- LOSS 171
disappointment, dust, penitence, rejection

ASS
- MAMMALS AND REPTILES 42

ASSASSINATION
- ANGER 123
- HOSTILITY 122
violence

ASSAULT
- ANGER 123
- HOSTILITY 122
violence

ASTHMA
- ILLNESS 95
- RESTRICTION 169
health

ASTROLOGER
- INSECURITY 121

ASTROLOGY
- AMBITION 151
- PRECOGNITION AND PREDICTION 62
- THE ZODIAC 69
- WISH-FULFILLMENT 150

ASTRONAUT
- ESCAPISM 136
- FLYING 147
- LONELINESS 173
- TRAVEL 134

ASTRONOMY
- AMBITION 151
- RELIGION 180

ATHLETICS
- AMBITION 151
- SPORTS 134
- THE BODY 91

ATLAS
- LANDSCAPE 58
- TRAVEL 134

ATTACK
- DANGER 158
- FEAR 120
- NIGHTMARE 154
- WEAPONS 118

ATTIC
- BUILDINGS 100
clutter

AUCTION
- AMBITION 151
- INSECURITY 121
- MONEY 110
competition

AUDIENCE
- COMMUNICATION 137
- INSECURITY 121
- THEATER 81
self-expression

AUDITION
- THEATER 81
examination

AUNT
- THE FAMILY 90

AUTHORITY 162

AVALANCHE
- DANGER 158
- DISASTER 160
- INSECURITY 121
- LANDSCAPE 58
overwork

AVENUE
- LANDSCAPE 58

AX
- HOSTILITY 122
- PUNISHMENT 170
- WEAPONS 118

AXLE
- VEHICLES 116
breakdown

B

BABOON
- MAMMALS AND REPTILES 42

BABY
- BIRTH 86
- CHILDHOOD 88
pregnancy, responsibility

BABY-SITTER
- CHILDHOOD 88

BACK, BACKBONE
- THE BODY 91
assistance, firmness, nostalgia, strength

THE WORLD OF NATURE

FANTASY & FABLE

ARTS & SCIENCES

THE HUMAN BODY

BUILDINGS & INTERIORS

EVERYDAY THINGS

HUMAN EMOTIONS

HUMAN ACTIVITIES

HUMAN CONDITIONS

RITUALS & RELIGION

THE DREAM THESAURUS

THE WORLD OF NATURE

FANTASY & FABLE

ARTS & SCIENCES

THE HUMAN BODY

BUILDINGS & INTERIORS

EVERYDAY THINGS

HUMAN EMOTIONS

HUMAN ACTIVITIES

HUMAN CONDITIONS

RITUALS & RELIGION

THE DREAM THESAURUS

BACKSEAT DRIVER
- Vehicles 116

BADGE
- Clothing 84
- *label*

BAG
- Containers 108

BAGGAGE
- Containers 108
- *burdens, problems*

BAGPIPES
- Music 70

BAILIFF
- Guilt 124
- Loss 171

BAKE, BAKER
- Fire 45
- Food and Drink 106
- Occupations 148

BALANCE
- Discipline 163
- Emotion 130
- Fear 120
- Insecurity 121
- Skill 72
- *comparison, fairness, scales*

BALCONY
- Buildings 100

BALDNESS
- Image 165
- The Body 91

BALLS
- Games 132
- *courage, energy, masculinity, sex*

BALLET
- Movement 148

BALLET DANCER
- Discipline 163
- Skill 72

BALLOON
- Flying 147

BALLROOM
- Buildings 100
- Movement 148

BANANA
- Fruit 54
- *phallic symbol*

BAND
- Music 70

BANK
- Buildings 100
- Insecurity 121
- Landscape 58
- Money 110
- Security 153

BANKNOTES
- Wish-fulfillment 150

BANKRUPTCY
- Insecurity 121
- Money 110
- Security 153
- *lack of confidence*

BANNER
- Image 165
- *leadership*

BANQUET
- Food and Drink 106

BAPTISM
- Change 168
- Religion 180
- Water 46
- *a new start*

BAR
- Food and Drink 106
- Justice 164

BARBECUE
- Fire 45
- Food and Drink 106

BARBER
- Image 165
- Occupations 148
- The Body 91
- *hair*

BARGE
- Vehicles 116
- Water 46

BARMAID
- Food and Drink 106
- *succubus*

BARMAN/BARTENDER
- Food and Drink 106
- *incubus*

BARN
- Buildings 100

BAROMETER
- Calculation 77
- *emotional state*

BARRACKS
- Buildings 100
- Discipline 163
- *army*

BARREL
- Containers 108
- *secrecy, storage*

BASEBALL
- Games 132

BASIL
- Other Plants 52

BASIN
- Containers 108

BASKET
- Containers 108

BAT
- Winged Creatures 43
- *blind*

BATH
- Cleansing 146
- Containers 108
- Guilt 124
- Water 46
- *cleanliness, remorse*

BATTLE
- Anger 123
- War 140
- *independence, violence*

BAY
- Trees 50

BAYONET
- Hostility 122
- Weapons 118

BAZAAR
- Activities 144
- *economy, searching*

BEACH
- Landscape 58
- Love 126
- Wish-fulfillment 150
- *rejection (to beach a ship), rescue*

BEACON
- Fire 45
- Warning 159

BEAK
- Mammals and Reptiles 42
- Winged Creatures 43

BEAM
- Buildings 100
- *strength*

BEANS
- Vegetables 55

BEAR
- Mammals and Reptiles 42

BEARD
- Image 165
- The Body 91

BEATING
- Guilt 124

BEAUTICIAN
- Occupations 148

BEAUTY
- Image 165
- Wish-fulfillment 150

BEAVER
- Mammals and Reptiles 42

BED
- Home 102
- *furniture, sex*

BEDROOM
- Rooms 103

BEECH
- Trees 50

BEEHIVE
- Activities 144
- Containers 108
- *sweetness*

BEER
- Food and Drink 106

BEGGAR
- Guilt 124
- Money 110
- *demand, request, subjugation*

BELL
- Celebration 176
- Love 126
- Music 70
- Religion 180
- Warning 159
- *winning*

BELT
- Clothing 84

BENCH
- Rooms 103
- *furniture*

BEREAVEMENT
- Death 86
- Guilt 124
- Loss 171
- *regret*

BET
- Gambling 139
- *conviction*

BICYCLE
- Vehicles 116
- *freedom, effort*

BIGAMY
- Guilt 124
- *sex*

BIKINI
- Clothing 84

BILL
- Money 110
- *payment, penalty*

BILLIARDS
- Games 132
- Skill 72

BIN
- Containers 108
- Refuse 119
- *rejection*

BINGO
- Gambling 139
- *ideas, realization, understanding*

BIRCH
- Guilt 124
- Hostility 122
- Punishment 170
- Trees 50
- *conscience, pain, violence*

BIRCHING
- Punishment 170

BIRD
- Trees 50
- Winged Creatures 43
- *freedom*

BIRD'S NEST
- Buildings 100
- Home 102
- Security 153
- *fecundity*

BIRTH 86

BISHOP
- Authority 162
- Religion 178

BITE, BITING
- Food and Drink 106

BLACK
- Colors 75

BLACKBOARD
- Childhood 88
- *learning, memory*

BLACKMAIL
- Guilt 124

BLANKET
- Security 153
- *cover-up, indiscriminate*

BLASPHEMY
- Religion 180

BLAZE
- Fire 45
- *row*

BLESSING
- Authority 162
- Religion 180
- *cry for attention*

BLINDNESS
- Emotion 130
- Health 93
- The Body 91
- *obduracy*

BLISTER
- Illness 95
- The Body 91
- *sarcasm*

BLOOD, BLEEDING
- Illness 95
- The Body 91
- *emotional wounding*

BLOSSOMING
- Flowers 53
- *development*

BLOW
- Anger 123
- *violence*

BLUE
- Colors 75
- *depression, regret, sorrow*

BOAR
- MAMMALS AND REPTILES 42

BOAT
- THE BODY 91
- VEHICLES 116
- WATER 46

BODY, THE 91

BODY PAINT
- IMAGE 165

BOG
- DIFFICULTY 172
- RESTRICTION 169
puzzle

BOMB
- HOSTILITY 122
- WEAPONS 118
violence

BONDAGE
- RESTRICTION 169
restraint, sex, slavery, work

BOND, JAMES
- MYTHOLOGY 64

BONE
- THE BODY 91

BONFIRE
- FIRE 45
- REFUSE 119
destruction, rejection

BOOK
- COMMUNICATION 137
- RECORDING 74
knowledge

BOOKING OFFICE
- TRAVEL 134
delay, planning

BOOKKEEPER
- CALCULATION 77
- NUMBERS 80
detail, knowledge

BOOKMAKER
- GAMBLING 139
conviction

BOOKSELLER
- COMMUNICATION 137
knowledge

BOOT
- CLOTHING 84

BORDER
- LANDSCAPE 58
- TRAVEL 134
tension

BOREDOM
- EMOTION 130

BOSOM
- LOVE 126
- THE BODY 91
- THE FAMILY 90
embrace, friend, intimacy

BOTTLE
- CONTAINERS 108

BOULDER
- LANDSCAPE 58
- RESTRICTION 169
- SECURITY 153
- TRAVEL 134
tension

BOUNDARY
- LANDSCAPE 58

BOUQUET
- FLOWERS 53
acclamation, praise

BOWL
- CONTAINERS 108

BOWLER/PITCHER
- GAMES 132

BOWLING
- GAMES 132

BOX
- CONTAINERS 108
secrecy

BOXING
- SPORTS 134

BOX OFFICE
- THEATER 81
delay, long-term planning, popularity, success

BOY
- CHILDHOOD 88

BRACELET
- JEWELRY 114

BRAIN
- THE BODY 91
imagination, intelligence, knowledge

BRAKE
- VEHICLES 116
caution, delay

BRAMBLE
- OTHER PLANTS 52
thorns

BRANCHES
- TREES 50

BRANDY
- FOOD AND DRINK 106

BRASS
- DECEPTION 152
- MONEY 110

BRAZIER
- FIRE 45

BREAD
- FOOD AND DRINK 106
livelihood

BREAKFAST
- FOOD AND DRINK 106
hospitality, preparation

BREAST
- LOVE 126
- THE BODY 91
- THE FAMILY 90
children, embrace, intimacy, protection

BREATHING
- THE BODY 91
freedom

BREEZE
- WEATHER 49
liveliness, quarrel

BRIDE, BRIDEGROOM, BRIDESMAID
- CEREMONIES 177
- WISH-FULFILLMENT 150
expectancy, innocence, new start

BRIDGE
- BUILDINGS 100
- GAMES 132
closing a gap, means to an end, overcoming

BRIDLE
- DISCIPLINE 163

BRIDLED HORSE
- DISCIPLINE 163

BROOCH
- JEWELRY 114

BROOM
- OTHER PLANTS 52
- UTENSILS 109

BROTHEL
- EROTIC DREAMS 96
- WISH-FULFILLMENT 150
sex

BROTHER
- LOVE 126
- THE FAMILY 90
compassion, friendship

BRUISE
- EMOTION 130
- ILLNESS 95
damage, ego, offense

BRUSH
- LANDSCAPE 58
cleaning out, new start, secrecy

BUBBLE
- EMOTION 130
effervescence, insignificance

BUCKET
- CONTAINERS 108

BUCKLE
- CLOTHING 84
fastening

BUD
- FLOWERS 53
new start, small beginnings

BUDDHA
- RELIGION 180
- THE SUPERNATURAL 60

BUDGERIGAR
- WINGED CREATURES 43

BUFFALO
- MAMMALS AND REPTILES 42

BUILDINGS 100

BULB
- OTHER PLANTS 52
nature, planning

BULL
- MAMMALS AND REPTILES 42

BULLDOZER
- TOOLS 115
destruction, obduracy

BULLET
- WEAPONS 118

BUN
- FOOD AND DRINK 106

BUNGALOW
- BUILDINGS 100

BUNGEE JUMPING
- ADVENTURE 136

BUOY
- WATER 46

BURGLAR
- CRIME 140

BURROW
- BUILDINGS 100
- SECURITY 153
hiding, protection, secrecy

BURROWING
- EARTH 48

BUS
- INSECURITY 121
- VEHICLES 116
crowds

BUTCHER
- OCCUPATIONS 148
brutality, lack of mercy

BUTLER
- OCCUPATIONS 148
- SERVICE 141
sycophancy

BUTTER
- FOOD AND DRINK 106

BUTTERCUP
- FLOWERS 53

BUTTERFLY
- SWIMMERS AND CRAWLERS 44
beauty, effervescence

BUTTOCKS
- THE BODY 91

BUTTON
- CLOTHING 84

C

CABARET
- ENTERTAINMENT 178
- THEATER 81
disguise, showing off

CABIN
- BUILDINGS 100
- TRAVEL 134
- WATER 49
claustrophobia, voyages

CABINET
- AUTHORITY 162
- CONTAINERS 108

CABLE
- COMMUNICATION 137
knitting, television

CAFE
- BUILDINGS 100
- FOOD AND DRINK 106

CALCULATOR
- CALCULATION 77
- NUMBERS 80
detail, planning, self-reliance

CALCULATION 77

CALENDAR
- TIME 80
appointments, nostalgia, timetable

CALF
- MAMMALS AND REPTILES 42
- YOUTH 89
inexperience, puberty

CAMEL
- MAMMALS AND REPTILES 42
determination, endurance

CAMELLIA
- FLOWERS 53
nostalgia, regret, sentimentality, sorrow

CAMEO
- PICTURES 76
nostalgia, observation, record

CAMERAMAN
- OCCUPATIONS 148

CAMOUFLAGE
- CLOTHING 84
- SECURITY 153
disguise, hiding, secrecy

THE WORLD OF NATURE

FANTASY & FABLE

ARTS & SCIENCES

THE HUMAN BODY

BUILDINGS & INTERIORS

EVERYDAY THINGS

HUMAN EMOTIONS

HUMAN ACTIVITIES

HUMAN CONDITIONS

RITUALS & RELIGION

THE DREAM THESAURUS

THE WORLD OF NATURE

FANTASY & FABLE

ARTS & SCIENCES

THE HUMAN BODY

BUILDINGS & INTERIORS

EVERYDAY THINGS

HUMAN EMOTIONS

HUMAN ACTIVITIES

HUMAN CONDITIONS

RITUALS & RELIGION

THE DREAM THESAURUS

CAMP
- BUILDINGS 100
- DISCIPLINE 163
- LANDSCAPE 58
holidays, homosexuality

CAMPAIGN
- DISCIPLINE 163
appeal, determination, objectives, will

CAMPER
- BUILDINGS 100
- VEHICLES 116
freedom, independence

CAN
- CONTAINERS 108

CANAL
- TRAVEL 134
- WATER 46

CANCER
- HEALTH 93
- THE ZODIAC 69
corruption, malignancy

CANDLE
- FIRE 45
light, sex

CANE
- GUILT 124
- HOSTILITY 122
- PUNISHMENT 170
pain, sugar, violence

CANNIBALISM
- LOVE 126

CANNABIS
- ESCAPISM 136
- WISH-FULFILLMENT 150
fantasy, rejection

CANNON
- WAR 140
- WEAPONS 118
violence

CANOE
- WATER 46
- VEHICLES 116

CANOPY
- BUILDINGS 100
protection

CANTEEN
- BUILDINGS 100
- FOOD AND DRINK 106
colleagues

CAP
- CLOTHING 84
- THE BODY 91
contraception, secrecy

CAPE
- CLOTHING 84
- LANDSCAPE 58
disguise, secrecy

CAPRICORN
- THE ZODIAC 69

CAPTAIN
- AUTHORITY 162
- OCCUPATIONS 148
- RESTRICTION 169

CAR
- DISASTER 160
- TRAVEL 134
- VEHICLES 116

CAR TRUNK
- CONTAINERS 108

CARDS
- COMMUNICATION 137
- GAMBLING 139
trickery

CARDINAL
- AUTHORITY 162
- RELIGION 180

CARETAKER
- OCCUPATIONS 148
responsibility

CARNIVAL
- CELEBRATION 176
- RITUAL 179

CARPENTER
- CREATIVITY 73
- OCCUPATIONS 148
repair

CARRIAGE
- VEHICLES 116

CARROT
- VEGETABLES 55
encouragement, sight

CART
- VEHICLES 116

CARTOON
- PICTURES 76
belittlement, cruelty

CARTRIDGE
- WAR 140
- WEAPONS 118
violence

CASH
- MONEY 110

CASHIER
- MONEY 110
- OCCUPATIONS 148

CASINO
- BUILDINGS 100
- GAMBLING 139
risk-taking

CASSEROLE
- FOOD AND DRINK 106

CASSETTE
- MUSIC 70
- RECORDING 74
repetition

CASTLE
- BUILDINGS 100
protection, self-sufficiency

CASTRATION 97

CASUALTY
- ACCIDENT 160
- THE BODY 91
caring, injury

CAT
- MAMMALS AND REPTILES 42

CATALOGUE
- RECORDING 74
order, taking stock, valuables

CAT-CALL
- THEATER 81
abuse, sexual attraction

CATERING
- FOOD AND DRINK 106
- SERVICE 141

CATERPILLAR
- SWIMMERS AND CRAWLERS 44

CATHEDRAL
- BUILDINGS 100
- RELIGION 180
- RITUAL 179

CAULDRON
- CONTAINERS 108
magic, witchcraft

CAVE
- BUILDINGS 100

CAVIAR
- FOOD AND DRINK 106
individuality, rarity

CELEBRATION 176

CELLAR
- BUILDINGS 100

CELLO
- MUSIC 70

CEMENT
- BUILDINGS 100
friendship, rigidity, togetherness

CEMETERY
- DEATH 86

CENTAUR
- MYTHOLOGY 64
- THE SUPERNATURAL 60
duality

CEREAL
- FOOD AND DRINK 106

CEREMONIES 177

CERTIFICATE
- ACHIEVEMENT 167
- AUTHORITY 162
accomplishment, completion, examination, praise

CHAIN
- AUTHORITY 162
- GUILT 124
- RESTRICTION 169
compliance

CHAIR
- AUTHORITY 162
- HOME 102

CHAIRPERSON
- AUTHORITY 162
- DISCIPLINE 163
power, supervision

CHALK
- CHILDHOOD 88

CHAMBER
- EARTH 48

CHAMBERMAID
- SERVICE 141

CHAMPAGNE
- CELEBRATIONS 176
- FOOD AND DRINK 106

CHANGE 168

CHAPEL
- BUILDINGS 100
- RELIGION 180
nonconformity

CHAPLAIN
- RELIGION 180
- SERVICE 141

CHARIOT
- VEHICLES 116
triumph, victory

CHASM
- DIFFICULTY 173
- LANDSCAPE 58
difference, separation

CHAUFFEUR
- SERVICE 141
- VEHICLES 116

CHEAT
- DECEPTION 152
- GUILT 124
deprivation, fraud

CHECK
- MONEY 110

CHEEK
- THE BODY 91
confidence, impertinence

CHEESE
- FOOD AND DRINK 106

CHERUB
- CHILDHOOD 88
- RELIGION 180
- THE SUPERNATURAL 60
goodness, innocence

CHESS
- GAMES 132
duplicity, intelligence

CHEWING
- FOOD AND DRINK 106

CHESTNUT
- FOOD AND DRINK 106

CHICKEN
- FEAR 120
- WINGED CREATURES 43
cowardice, innocence

CHIEF
- AUTHORITY 162
importance, leadership

CHIFFON
- CLOTHING 84

CHILD, CHILDREN
- CHILDHOOD 88
- LONELINESS 173
- WISH-FULFILLMENT 150
- YOUTH 89
innocence, nostalgia

CHILDBIRTH
- BIRTH 86
freshness, new start

CHILDHOOD 88

CHIMNEY
- BUILDINGS 100
smoke

CHIMPANZEE
- MAMMALS AND REPTILES 42
intelligence, trickery

CHIN
- THE BODY 91
strength

CHOCOLATE
- FOOD AND DRINK 106
sweetness, teeth

CHOIR
- MUSIC 70
- RELIGION 180

CHOIRBOY
- RELIGION 180
- WISH-FULFILLMENT 150
innocence

CHRIST
- RELIGION 180
- THE SUPERNATURAL 60

CHRISTMAS
- CELEBRATION 177
- THE FAMILY 90
nostalgia

CHURCH
- AUTHORITY 162
- BUILDINGS 100
- RELIGION 180

CIGAR
- ESCAPISM 136

CIGARETTE
- ESCAPISM 136
- HEALTH 93

CINEMA
- ESCAPISM 136
- PICTURES 76

CIRCLE
- THE MANDALA 68
confidence, restraint

CIRCUS
- ENTERTAINMENT 178
rings

CITY
- AUTHORITY 162
- BUILDINGS 100
- LANDSCAPE 58
- MONEY 110
confusion, crowds, stress

CLAIRVOYANT
- PRECOGNITION AND PREDICTION 62
the future

CLEANLINESS
- CLEANSING 146
- HEALTH 93

CLEANSING 146

CLEMATIS
- FLOWERS 53
social climbing

CLIFF
- DIFFICULTY 172
- LANDSCAPE 58
obstruction

CLIMBING
- ACTIVITIES 144
- AMBITION 151
- DANGER 158

CLOAKROOM
- BUILDINGS 100
- ROOMS 103

CLOCK
- TIME 80
punctuality, speed

CLOCKWORK
- DISCIPLINE 163
ease, regularity

CLOGS
- CLOTHING 84
frustration

CLOTH
- CLOTHING 84

CLOTHING 84

CLOUD
- WEATHER 49
bad mood

CLOWN
- ESCAPISM 136
- ENTERTAINMENT 178
foolishness, sorrow

CLUB
- GATHERINGS 174
- RITUAL 179
acceptance, escape, organization, status

COACH
- VEHICLES 116

COAL
- DIRT 119
- FIRE 45

COAST
- LANDSCAPE 58

COAST GUARD
- WARNING 159

COAT
- CLOTHING 84
cover-up

COBRA *see* SNAKE

COCKEREL
- WINGED CREATURES 43
male sexuality

COCKROACH
- SWIMMERS AND CRAWLERS 44
greed, insects, sycophancy

COCKTAIL
- FOOD AND DRINK 106
sociability

COCOA
- FOOD AND DRINK 106
relaxation, rest

COCONUT
- FOOD AND DRINK 106

CODE
- DECEPTION 152
secrecy

COFFEE
- FOOD AND DRINK 106
stimulation

COFFIN
- DEATH 86

COIN
- MONEY 110

COLD
- ILLNESS 95
- WEATHER 49

COLLAR
- CLOTHING 84

COLLEGE
- GATHERINGS 174
learning

COLORS 75

COLT
- MAMMALS AND REPTILES 42
- YOUTH 89

COLUMN
- BUILDINGS 100

COMB
- IMAGE 165
thoroughness

COMEDIAN
- ENTERTAINMENT 178
- ESCAPISM 136
foolishness, playfulness

COMIC
- CHILDHOOD 88
childishness, foolishness

COMMISSIONAIRE/ DOORMAN
- SERVICE 141
beginnings

COMMITTEE
- AUTHORITY 162

COMMON
- LANDSCAPE 58
sharing

COMMUNE
- GATHERINGS 174

COMMUNICATION 137

COMMUNION
- RELIGION 180

COMMUNITY
- GATHERINGS 174

COMPASS
- LANDSCAPE 58
- RESTRICTION 169
guidance

COMPETITION
- GAMES 132
opposition

COMPUTER, COMPUTING
- CALCULATION 77
- DIFFICULTY 172
order, resolution

CONCERT
- CREATIVITY 73
- GATHERINGS 174
- MUSIC 70
agreement

CONDOM
- EROTIC DREAMS 96
- RESTRICTION 169
prevention, safety, sex

CONDUCTOR
- AUTHORITY 162
- MUSIC 70

CONFERENCE
- GATHERINGS 174
discussion, thoughtfulness

CONFESSION
- GUILT 124
- RELIGION 180
secrecy

CONFETTI
- MARRIAGE 146
- WISH-FULFILLMENT 150
spontaneity, variety

CONGREGATION
- GATHERINGS 174
- RELIGION 180
conformity

CONJURER
- DECEPTION 152
- ENTERTAINMENT 178
- THE SUPERNATURAL 60
deception, trickery

CONSERVATORY
- BUILDINGS 100
frankness, openness, warmth

CONTAINERS 108

CONTEST
- GAMES 132
opposition

CONTRACT
- DISCIPLINE 163
agreement, commitment

CONVENTION
- GATHERINGS 174
discussion, thoughtfulness

COOK
- OCCUPATIONS 148

COOKER/STOVE
- ENERGY 73
- FIRE 45

COOKING
- ENERGY 73
- FIRE 45

CORAL
- JEWELRY 114

CORD
- AUTHORITY 162
- BIRTH 86
- GUILT 124
- RESTRICTION 169
possessiveness

CORKSCREW
- TOOLS 115
determination, deviousness

CORN
- CREATIVITY 73
consequence (harvest)

CORONATION
- AUTHORITY 162
- CEREMONIES 177
- RITUAL 179

CORRESPONDENCE
- COMMUNICATION 137

CORSET
- CLOTHING 84
- RESTRICTION 169

COSMETICS
- IMAGE 165
enhancement, imitation, pretense, superficiality

COSTUME
- CLOTHING 84
fun, pretense

COT/CRIB
- CHILDHOOD 88
- WISH-FULFILLMENT 150
peace, relaxation

COUGH
- THE BODY 91
revelation

COUNCIL, COUNSELOR
- AUTHORITY 162
- OCCUPATIONS 148

COUNTING
- CALCULATION 77
- NUMBERS 80
reaching conclusions

COUNTRY
- LANDSCAPE 58

COURTROOM
- AUTHORITY 162
- JUSTICE 163
- RITUAL 179
romance

COURTYARD
- BUILDINGS 100
enclosure

COUSIN
- THE FAMILY 90

COW
- MAMMALS AND REPTILES 42
domesticity, fecundity

COWARDICE
- EMOTION 130
- FEAR 120
reluctance, shame

CRAB
- MYTHOLOGY 64
- SWIMMERS AND CRAWLERS 44
- THE ZODIAC 69
sideways movement

CRADLE
- CHILDHOOD 88
- WISH-FULFILLMENT 150
peace, relaxation

CRATER
- FIRE 45
- LANDSCAPE 58
threat

CREAM
- FOOD AND DRINK 106
profit

CREATIVITY 73

THE WORLD OF NATURE

FANTASY & FABLE

ARTS & SCIENCES

THE HUMAN BODY

BUILDINGS & INTERIORS

EVERYDAY THINGS

HUMAN EMOTIONS

HUMAN ACTIVITIES

HUMAN CONDITIONS

RITUALS & RELIGION

THE DREAM THESAURUS

THE WORLD OF NATURE

FANTASY & FABLE

ARTS & SCIENCES

THE HUMAN BODY

BUILDINGS & INTERIORS

EVERYDAY THINGS

HUMAN EMOTIONS

HUMAN ACTIVITIES

HUMAN CONDITIONS

RITUALS & RELIGION

THE DREAM THESAURUS

CRECHE
- CHILDHOOD 88
- WISH-FULFILLMENT 150

CREW
- AUTHORITY 162

team

CRICKET
- GAMES 132

CRIME 140

CRIMINAL
- CRIME 140
- GUILT 124
- PUNISHMENT 170

CRIMSON
- COLORS 75

embarrassment, passion

CRIPPLE
- HEALTH 93
- RESTRICTION 169

antagonism, threat

CROCHET
- ACTIVITIES 144
- CREATIVITY 73

CROCODILE
- MAMMALS AND REPTILES 42

CROISSANT
- FOOD AND DRINK 106

beginnings

CROP
- CREATIVITY 73

diminishment

CROSS
- GUILT 124
- RELIGION 180
- THE SUPERNATURAL 60

disapproval, mixture

CROSSWORD
- DIFFICULTY 172
- GAMES 132

puzzle

CROW
- WINGED CREATURES 43

CROWD
- CEREMONIES 176
- GATHERINGS 174
- LONELINESS 173

lack of discipline

CROWN
- AUTHORITY 162
- JEWELRY 114
- RITUAL 179

CRUCIFIX
- GUILT 124
- PUNISHMENT 170
- RELIGION 180
- THE SUPERNATURAL 60

CRUCIFIXION
- RELIGION 180

CRUISE
- WATER 46

ease, sexuality

CRUMPET
- FOOD AND DRINK 106

CRUSADE
- RELIGION 180

campaigning

CRUST
- FOOD AND DRINK 106

charity, endurance, rejection

CRUTCH

prop, reliance, support

CRYING
- EMOTION 130

appeal, despair, helplessness, need, nostalgia, sorrow

CRYPT
- BUILDINGS 100
- RELIGION 180

CRYSTAL
- JEWELRY 114

clarity, transparency

CRYSTAL BALL
- JEWELRY 114

CUB
- YOUTH 89

CUBE
- CALCULATION 77

reliability

CUBICLE
- ROOMS 103

privacy

CUCKOLD
- EMOTION 130
- MARRIAGE 146
- WISH-FULFILLMENT 150

adultery

CUCKOO
- WINGED CREATURES 43

foolishness, predatoriness, rejection

CUCUMBER
- FOOD AND DRINK 106

CUFF
- CLOTHING 84

CUP
- CONTAINERS 108

CURATE
- AUTHORITY 162
- RELIGION 180

CURE
- THE BODY 91

CURRENCY
- MONEY 110

CURRY
- FIRE 45
- FOOD AND DRINK 106

spice

CURSE
- GUILT 124
- NIGHTMARE 154
- PUNISHMENT 170

blame, guilt, impatience, nightmare

CURTAIN
- HOME 102

concealment, decoration

CURTSY
- ACTIVITIES 144
- AUTHORITY 162

acknowledgment, admiration, subjugation

CUSHION
- HOME 102

comfort

CUSTARD
- FOOD AND DRINK 106

CUSTOMER
- SERVICE 141

CUT FLOWERS
- FLOWERS 53

CUTLERY
- IMAGE 165
- TOOLS 115

care, social manners

CYCLING
- SPORTS 134

CYMBAL
- MUSIC 70

joy, triumph

CYPRESS
- TREES 50

D

DAGGER
- WEAPONS 118

rivalry

DAIRY
- BUILDINGS 100
- FOOD AND DRINK 106

DANCER
- ACTIVITIES 144
- MOVEMENT 148
- OCCUPATIONS 148
- THEATER 81

DANCING
- ACTIVITIES 144
- MOVEMENT 148

DANCING SHOES
- ACTIVITIES 144

DANGER 158

DARKROOM
- PICTURES 76

DARTS
- DIFFICULTY 172
- GAMES 132

accuracy, quickness

DAUGHTER
- THE FAMILY 90

DAWN
- BIRTH 86
- EMOTION 130

beginnings, hope

DEAD FLOWERS
- FLOWERS 53

DEADLY NIGHTSHADE
- OTHER PLANTS 52

DEAF
- EMOTION 130

ignorance

DEATH 86

DEATH WARRANT
- DEATH 86
- WARNING 159

apprehension, threat

DEBATE
- GATHERINGS 174

argument, problem

DEBRIS
- REFUSE 119

clutter, problems, waste

DEBT
- EMOTION 130
- GUILT 124
- MONEY 110

DEBT COLLECTOR
- GUILT 124

DECEPTION 152

DECK CHAIR
- DIFFICULTY 172
- INSECURITY 121

furniture, relaxation

DEFEAT
- WARNING 159

depression, threat

DEFENDANT
- JUSTICE 164

DEFENSE
- EMOTION 130
- WARNING 159

violence

DEFORMITY
- HEALTH 93
- RESTRICTION 169
- THE BODY 91

DEGREE
- ACHIEVEMENT 167
- AMBITION 151
- AUTHORITY 162

DELEGATE
- AUTHORITY 162

colleagues, hesitation, reluctance, trust

DEMOLITION
- BUILDINGS 100
- CHANGE 168
- EMOTION 130

criticism, betrayal, restructuring

DEMON
- GUILT 124
- PUNISHMENT 170
- RELIGION 180
- TEMPTATION 169

incubus, succubus

DENTIST
- ILLNESS 95
- IMAGE 165
- OCCUPATIONS 148

speech

DEPUTATION
- GATHERINGS 174

argument, ideas, pleading, responsibility

DEPUTY
- SERVICE 141

DESERT
- LANDSCAPE 58

betrayal, cowardice, desertion, irresponsibility

DESERT ISLAND
- LANDSCAPE 58

DESK
- WORKPLACES 116

furniture, work

DESSERT
- FOOD AND DRINK 106

sweetness

DESTROY, DESTRUCTION
- FLOWERS 53
- HOSTILITY 122
- WAR 140
- WARNING 159
- WATER 46

DETECTIVE
- GUILT 124
- OCCUPATIONS 148
- SERVICE 141

curiosity, intrusion, questioning

DEVIL
- GUILT 124
- PUNISHMENT 170
- RELIGION 180
- TEMPTATION 169
- THE SUPERNATURAL 60

incubus, succubus

THE WORLD OF NATURE

FANTASY & FABLE

ARTS & SCIENCES

THE HUMAN BODY

BUILDINGS & INTERIORS

EVERYDAY THINGS

HUMAN EMOTIONS

HUMAN ACTIVITIES

HUMAN CONDITIONS

RITUALS & RELIGION

THE DREAM THESAURUS

THE WORLD OF NATURE

FANTASY & FABLE

ARTS & SCIENCES

THE HUMAN BODY

BUILDINGS & INTERIORS

EVERYDAY THINGS

HUMAN EMOTIONS

HUMAN ACTIVITIES

HUMAN CONDITIONS

RITUALS & RELIGION

THE DREAM THESAURUS

ENEMY
- HOSTILITY 122
- WAR 140

ENERGY 73

ENGAGEMENT
- LOVE 126
- MARRIAGE 146
- WISH-FULFILLMENT 150

commitment, obligation

ENGINE
- TOOLS 115
- VEHICLES 116

driving force, motivation

ENGINEER
- OCCUPATIONS 148

ENTERTAINMENT 178

ENTRAILS
- EMOTION 130

courage

ENTRANCE
- BUILDINGS 100
- THEATER 81

beginnings, understanding

ENVELOPE
- COMMUNICATION 137
- CONTAINERS 108
- DECEPTION 152

EPITAPH
- IMAGE 165

EQUATION
- CALCULATION 77
- NUMBERS 80

equality

ERECTION
- BUILDINGS 100

sex

EROTIC DREAMS 96

ESCALATOR
- AMBITION 151

machinery

ESCAPE
- EMOTION 130
- NIGHTMARE 154

ESCAPING
- WARNING 136

ESCAPISM 136

ESTABLISHMENT 163

EUCHARIST
- RELIGION 180

EUTHANASIA
- DEATH 86

kindness, mercy

EVICTION
- ANGER 123
- CHANGE 168

endings

EVIL
- NIGHTMARE 154

EXAMINATION
- AMBITION 151
- AUTHORITY 162
- IMAGE 165
- INSECURITY 121

evaluation, testing

EXCAVATING
- ACTIVITIES 144

curiosity, discovery

EXCREMENT
- DIRT 119

rejection

EXCURSION
- CHANGE 168
- TRAVEL 134

pleasure

EXECUTION
- DEATH 86
- HOSTILITY 122

endings, self-criticism

EXERCISE
- ACTIVITIES 144
- DISCIPLINE 163
- ENERGY 73

willpower

EXHIBITION
- EMOTION 130
- IMAGE 165

extravagance, self-publicity, voyeurism

EXILE
- CHANGE 168
- EMOTION 130

rejection

EXPEDITION
- LANDSCAPE 58

determination, exploration

EXPERT
- AUTHORITY 162

EXPLORER
- LANDSCAPE 58

analysis, challenge, determination

EXPLOSION
- DANGER 158
- EMOTION 130

EXPOSURE
- INSECURITY 121
- NUDITY 96

frankness, openness

EXTERMINATION
- CHANGE 168
- DEATH 86

self-criticism, violence

EXTRAVAGANCE
- MONEY 110

EYE
- THE BODY 91

observation, point of view

F

FABRIC
- CLOTHING 84

lifestyle, structure

FACADE
- BUILDING 100
- DECEPTION 152

pretense

FACE
- IMAGE 165
- THE BODY 91

appearance, surface

FACSIMILE
- COMMUNICATION 137

immediacy, speed

FACTORY
- BUILDING 100
- DISCIPLINE 163
- WORKPLACES 116

productiveness, work

FAIR
- ENTERTAINMENT 178
- ESCAPISM 136
- GAMBLING 137

blondes, buying and selling

FAIRY
- THE SUPERNATURAL 60

luck

FAIRYTALE
- MYTHOLOGY 64

FAKE
- DECEPTION 152

counterfeit

FALLING
- FLYING 147

FAME
- ACHIEVEMENT 167
- IMAGE 165

FAMILY, THE 90

FAMINE
- DISASTER 160

FAN
- AIR 48

coolness, comfort, machinery

FANCY DRESS
- IMAGE 165

pretense

FANFARE
- MUSIC 70

FANTASY
- SURREALIST DREAMS 82

FAREWELL
- CHANGE 168

FARMER
- EARTH 48
- LANDSCAPE 58
- OCCUPATIONS 148

nature, productivity

FARMHOUSE
- BUILDINGS 100
- LANDSCAPE 58

FASHION
- CLOTHING 84
- IMAGE 165

self-respect, up-to-date

FAT
- THE BODY 91
- IMAGE 165

comfort, wealth

FATE
- THE SUPERNATURAL 60

destiny, foreboding, fortune-telling, future, threat

FATHER
- AUTHORITY 162
- THE FAMILY 90

FAX *see* FACSIMILE

FEAR 120

FEAST
- CELEBRATIONS 176
- FOOD AND DRINK 106

FEATHERS
- ESCAPISM 136
- WINGED CREATURES 43

lightness, superficiality

FECES
- DIRT 119
- THE BODY 91

FEE
- MONEY 110

FEEDING
- FLOWERS 53
- FOOD AND DRINK 106

FENCE
- CRIME 140
- LANDSCAPE 58
- RESTRICTION 169
- SECURITY 153

FERN
- OTHER PLANTS 52

delicacy

FERRY
- COMMUNICATION 137
- WATER 46

transport

FERTILIZER
- DIRT 119

encouragement, growth, pregnancy, richness

FESTIVAL
- CELEBRATIONS 176

FETE
- CELEBRATIONS 176

FEUD
- ANGER 123
- THE FAMILY 90

FEVER
- ILLNESS 95

agitation, excitement, heat, illogicality

FIANCE
- LOVE 126
- MARRIAGE 144
- WISH-FULFILLMENT 150

commitment, obligation

FIELD
- LANDSCAPE 58

FIEND
- THE SUPERNATURAL 60

evil

FIG
- FOOD AND DRINK 106
- FRUIT 54

shame, shyness

FIGHT
- ANGER 123
- HOSTILITY 122
- WAR 140

determination, dislike, opposition, violence

FIGURE
- NIGHTMARE 154
- THE SHADOW 97

FILE
- DISCIPLINE 163

knowledge, memory, organization

FILM
- PICTURES 76
- RECORDING 74
- THEATER 81

FINE
- GUILT 124
- PUNISHMENT 170

quality

FINGER
- THE BODY 91

accuse

FIRE 45

FIREFIGHTER
- OCCUPATIONS 148

bravery, passion

FIREPLACE
- FIRE 45
- HOME 102

domesticity

FIREWORKS
- DANGER 158
- ENTERTAINMENT 178

brilliance, display, surprise

THE WORLD OF NATURE

FANTASY & FABLE

ARTS & SCIENCES

THE HUMAN BODY

BUILDINGS & INTERIORS

EVERYDAY THINGS

HUMAN EMOTIONS

HUMAN ACTIVITIES

HUMAN CONDITIONS

RITUALS & RELIGION

THE DREAM THESAURUS

THE WORLD OF NATURE

FANTASY & FABLE

ARTS & SCIENCES

THE HUMAN BODY

BUILDINGS & INTERIORS

EVERYDAY THINGS

HUMAN EMOTIONS

HUMAN ACTIVITIES

HUMAN CONDITIONS

RITUALS & RELIGION

THE DREAM THESAURUS

GIN
- FOOD AND DRINK 106
liveliness, spice

GINGER
- FOOD AND DRINK 106

GIRDER
- BUILDINGS 100
burden, support

GIVING BIRTH
- BIRTH 86

GLACIER
- WATER 46
- WEATHER 49
cold

GLASS
- CONTAINERS 108
drinking

GLASSES
- IMAGE 165
clarity, spectacles, visibility

GLIDER
- FLYING 147
ease, freedom, lack of effort

GLOBE
- THE MANDALA 68
comprehensiveness

GLOVES
- CLOTHING 84
lack of dexterity, protection

GLUE
- DISCIPLINE 163
mending situations, obstruction, tenacity

GLUTTONY
- FOOD AND DRINK 106
excess

GNAT
- SWIMMERS AND CRAWLERS 44
insignificance, irritation

GOAL
- ACHIEVEMENT 167
- GAMES 132
aim, defense, objective

GOAT
- MAMMALS AND REPTILES 42

GOD, GODDESS
- AUTHORITY 162
- RELIGION 180

GODFATHER
- AUTHORITY 162
- FEAR 120
- THE FAMILY 90
domination, protection

GOLD
- ACHIEVEMENT 167
- JEWELRY 114
- MONEY 110
self-esteem, standards, value

GOLF
- GAMES 132

GONDOLA
- VEHICLES 116
romance

GOOSE
- WINGED CREATURES 43

GOOSEBERRY
- FOOD AND DRINK 106
intrusion

GORGE
- LANDSCAPE 58
greed, sickness

GRADUATE, GRADUATION
- ACHIEVEMENT 167
- AUTHORITY 162
- CEREMONIES 177
knowledge

GRANDPARENT
- AUTHORITY 162
- THE FAMILY 90

GRANDCHILD
- THE FAMILY 90
dependence

GRANDSTAND
- BUILDINGS 100
observation, overview

GRANITE
- LANDSCAPE 58
image (granite-faced), nature, obduracy, stubbornness

GRASS
- OTHER PLANTS 52
nature

GRAVE
- DEATH 86
dignity, silence

GRAVESTONE
- COMMUNICATION 137
- DEATH 86
truth

GRAVITY
- FLYING 147
seriousness

GREASEPAINT
- IMAGE 165
- THEATER 81

GREEN
- COLORS 75

GREENHOUSE
- BUILDINGS 100
care, growth, moisture, protection, warmth

GREETING
- COMMUNICATION 137
- WISH-FULFILLMENT 150

GRENADE
- WEAPONS 118
antagonism, outrage, surprise

GRIEF
- EMOTION 130
- GUILT 124
regret

GRILL
- FIRE 45
antagonism

GRIT
- DIRT 119
courage, discomfort, endurance, irritation

GROCER
- FOOD AND DRINK 106
- OCCUPATIONS 148
shopping

GROUND ELDER
- OTHER PLANTS 52

GRUB
- FLOWERS 53
insects

GUARD
- SECURITY 153
protection, supervision, watchfulness

GUARDIAN
- AUTHORITY 162
defense

GUERRILLA
- WAR 140

GUEST
- GATHERINGS 175
- HOME 102
invitation

GUIDE
- AUTHORITY 162
- OCCUPATIONS 148
knowledge

GUILLOTINE
- GUILT 124
- PUNISHMENT 170
sharpness

GUILT 124

GUITAR
- MUSIC 170
sex

GUN
- WEAPONS 118
beginnings (starting gun), deterrent, violence

GUNPOWDER
- WEAPONS 118
antagonism, outrage, surprise

GUTTER
- REFUSE 119
drain

GYM
- ACTIVITIES 144

GYPSY
- OCCUPATIONS 148
freedom

H

HACKSAW
- TOOLS 115
force, separation

HAGGIS
- FOOD AND DRINK 106
Scotland

HAIL
- WEATHER 49
cold, ice

HAIR
- CLEANSING 146
- IMAGE 165
- THE BODY 91

HAIRDRESSER
- OCCUPATIONS 148
beauty, vanity

HALL
- BUILDINGS 100

HALLUCINATION
- ESCAPISM 136
- INSECURITY 121
delusion, mistake

HALO
- ACHIEVEMENT 167
- RELIGION 180
goodness, perfection

HALTER
- AUTHORITY 162
leading/being led

HAM
- FOOD AND DRINK 106

HAMMER
- ANGER 123
- TOOLS 115
force, violence, work

HAMMOCK
- ESCAPISM 136
- INSECURITY 121
relaxation

HAND
- MARRIAGE 146
- SKILL 72
- THE BODY 91
dexterity, writing

HANDBAG
- CONTAINERS 108

HANDICAP
- RESTRICTION 169
- THE BODY 91

HANDKERCHIEF
- CLEANSING 146

HANDLE
- EMOTION 130
- SKILL 72
- TOOLS 115
assistance, safety, touch, utensils

HANDSHAKE
- COMMUNICATION 137
acknowledgment, agreement, friendship, greeting

HANGING
- GUILT 124
- PUNISHMENT 170
deterrent

HANGOVER
- FOOD AND DRINK 106
- GUILT 124
- ILLNESS 95
- PUNISHMENT 170
regret

HARBOR
- ACHIEVEMENT 167
- AMBITION 151
- WATER 46
safety

HAREM
- WISH-FULFILLMENT 150
possessiveness, protection, sex

HARNESS
- AUTHORITY 162
- RESTRICTION 169
leading/being led

HARVEST
- ACHIEVEMENT 167
conclusions, nature, reap, results

HAT
- CLOTHING 84

HATCHET
- TOOLS 115
violence

HAWK
- WINGED CREATURES 43
sharp-eyed

HAY
- OTHER PLANTS 52

HEAD
- THE BODY 91
leadership, thought

HEADLIGHTS
- VEHICLES 116

HEADLINE
- COMMUNICATION 137
- PRECOGNITION AND PREDICTION 62
newspapers

HEADMASTER, HEADMISTRESS
- AUTHORITY 162
- DISCIPLINE 163
school

HEALTH 93

HEART
- EMOTION 130
- LOVE 126
- THE BODY 91
commitment

HEARTH
- FIRE 45
- HOME 102
domesticity

HEAT
- EMOTION 130
- FIRE 45
passion

HEAVEN
- ACHIEVEMENT 167
- DEATH 86
- ESCAPISM 136
- RELIGION 180
approval, happiness, pleasure

HEDGE
- LANDSCAPE 58
- RESTRICTION 169
division, obstruction

HEDGEHOG
- DIFFICULTY 172
- MAMMALS AND REPTILES 42
prickliness

HEEL
- THE BODY 91
progress, support

HELICOPTER
- FLYING 147
control, dexterity

HELL
- DEATH 86
- GUILT 124
- PUNISHMENT 170
disapproval

HELMET
- CLOTHING 84
- WAR 140
protection

HEM
- CLOTHING 84

HEMORRHAGE
- ILLNESS 95
- THE BODY 91

HERD
- MAMMALS AND REPTILES 42
conformity

HERMES
- MYTHOLOGY 64
messenger

HERO, HEROINE
- ADVENTURE 136
- IMAGE 165
- MYTHOLOGY 64
admiration, courage, emulation, endurance

HIDING
- DECEPTION 152
- GUILT 124
- IMAGE 165
- INSECURITY 121

HIGHWAY
- LANDSCAPE 58
- TRAVEL 134
direction, purpose

HILL
- LANDSCAPE 58
- ACTIVITIES 144
climbing

HIVE
- ACTIVITIES 144
- BUILDINGS 100
crowds, storage, sweetness

HOLE
- DANGER 158
- LOSS 171
awkwardness, dilemma, excavation

HOLIDAY
- EMOTION 130
- TRAVEL 134
- WISH-FULFILLMENT 150
relaxation, tension

HOLY VIRGIN
- RELIGION 180

HOME 102

HONEYMOON
- MARRIAGE 146
- WISH-FULFILLMENT 150
happiness

HONEYSUCKLE
- FLOWERS 53
- OTHER PLANTS 52

HOOD
- CLOTHING 84
- DECEPTION 152
cover-up, menace, mystery, secrecy

HOOK
- TOOLS 115
suspension

HOOP
- THE MANDALA 68
play, wholeness

HORIZON
- LANDSCAPE 58
boundary, hope

HOROSCOPE
- IMAGE 165
the future

HORSE
- ACTIVITIES 144
- MAMMALS AND REPTILES 42
- TEMPTATION 169

HORSE RACE
- GAMBLING 139
intelligence, reliability, speed

HOSE
- DIRT 119
- WATER 46
ejaculation

HOSPITAL
- ILLNESS 95
caring, healing, protection, mending

HOSTILITY 122

HOTEL
- BUILDINGS 100
- GATHERINGS 174
gregariousness

HOUSE
- BUILDINGS 100
- DISASTER 160
- HOME 102

HOUSEWORK
- OCCUPATIONS 148
boredom, pride, routine

HUMILIATION
- IMAGE 165
faults, shortcomings

HUNGER
- EMOTION 130
- FOOD AND DRINK 106
deprivation, need

HUNTING
- ACTIVITIES 144
- GAMES 132
cruelty, discovery, pursuit, ruthlessness, searching

HURDLE
- LANDSCAPE 58

HURRICANE
- ENERGY 73
- WEATHER 49
enthusiasm, destruction, violence

HUSBAND
- MARRIAGE 146
- THE FAMILY 90

HUT
- BUILDINGS 100
isolation, poverty

HYGIENE
- CLEANSING 146
- HEALTH 93
protection

HYMN
- RELIGION 180
- RITUAL 179

I

ICE
- DIFFICULTY 172
- EMOTION 130
- WATER 46
- WEATHER 49
collective unconscious

ICE CREAM
- FOOD AND DRINK 106
ice

ICING
- FOOD AND DRINK 106
enjoyment (icing on the cake)

ICON
- AUTHORITY 162
- RELIGION 182

IDOL
- RELIGION 180
adulation, falsehood

IGNITION
- VEHICLES 116
beginnings

ILLNESS 95

IMAGE 165

IMPOTENCE
- INSECURITY 121
frustration, sex, weakness

INCENSE
- RELIGION 180
- RITUAL 179
praise

INCEST
- NIGHTMARE 154
- THE FAMILY 90
sex

INCUBUS
- THE SUPERNATURAL 60
succubus

INCUBUS ATTACK
- NIGHTMARES 154
- THE SUPERNATURAL 60

INDECENCY
- INSECURITY 121
exposure, impropriety, sex

INDIGESTION
- DIFFICULTY 172
- THE BODY 91
awkwardness, complexity

INDISCRETION
- IMAGE 165

INDUSTRY
- ACTIVITIES 144
enthusiasm, routine, work

INFANT
- CHILDHOOD 88
- WISH-FULFILLMENT 150

INFANTRY
- ACTIVITIES 144
effort, slow progress

INFECTION
- ILLNESS 95
bad feeling or opinion

INFERIORITY
- IMAGE 165

INFIDELITY
- MARRIAGE 146
betrayal

INGRATITUDE
- EMOTION 130

INHERITANCE
- MONEY 110
- THE FAMILY 90
characteristics

INHIBITION
- IMAGE 165
resistance, restraint, sex

INJECTION
- ILLNESS 95
prevention, sex

INJURY
- EMOTION 130
- THE BODY 91
hurt feelings, violence

INK
- COMMUNICATION 137
mistakes (ink blots)

INOCULATION
- ILLNESS 95
prevention, sex

INQUEST
- JUSTICE 164
detail, discussion, inquiry

INSANITY
- ESCAPISM 136
- FEAR 120
foolishness, irrationality

INSECT
- SWIMMERS AND CRAWLERS 44
contempt, insignificance

INSECURITY 121

INSPECTION
- AUTHORITY 162
inquiry, supervision

INSTRUCTION
- AUTHORITY 162
- IMAGE 165
education, knowledge

INSTRUMENT
- MUSIC 70
legality, measurement

THE WORLD OF NATURE

FANTASY & FABLE

ARTS & SCIENCES

THE HUMAN BODY

BUILDINGS & INTERIORS

EVERYDAY THINGS

HUMAN EMOTIONS

HUMAN ACTIVITIES

HUMAN CONDITIONS

RITUALS & RELIGION

THE DREAM THESAURUS

THE WORLD OF NATURE

FANTASY & FABLE

ARTS & SCIENCES

THE HUMAN BODY

BUILDINGS & INTERIORS

EVERYDAY THINGS

HUMAN EMOTIONS

HUMAN ACTIVITIES

HUMAN CONDITIONS

RITUALS & RELIGION

THE DREAM THESAURUS

INTERCOURSE
- COMMUNICATION 137
commerce, friendship, sex

INTERFERENCE
- COMMUNICATION 137
- HOSTILITY 122
assault (sexual), hindrance, obstruction

INTERPRETER
- COMMUNICATION 137
- TRAVEL 134
explanation, understanding

INTERVIEW
- COMMUNICATION 137
consultation, inquiry, examination

INTRODUCTION
- COMMUNICATION 137
explanation, meeting, presentation

INTRUDER
- CRIME 140
- FEAR 120
- HOSTILITY 122
invasion

INVASION
- HOSTILITY 122
- WAR 140
interloper (invasion of privacy)

INVENTION, INVENTOR
- CREATIVITY 73
falsehood

INVESTMENT
- MONEY 110
commitment, profit

INVESTIGATION
- COMMUNICATION 137
consultation, inquiry, examination, system

INVESTITURE
- ACHIEVEMENT 167
- CELEBRATIONS 176
honor

INVISIBILITY
- IMAGE 165
concealment, insignificance

INVITATION
- CREATIVITY 73
attraction, social life

INVOICE
- MONEY 110
obligation

ISLAND
- LANDSCAPE 58
- TRAVEL 134
- WATER 46
detachment, isolation

ISOLATION
- EMOTION 130
- LONELINESS 172
remoteness, uniqueness

ISVARA
- THE SUPERNATURAL 60

IVORY
- IMAGE 165

IVY
- OTHER PLANTS 52
climbing, clinging, nature, poison

J

JACKAL
- MAMMALS AND REPTILES 42

JACKET
- CLOTHING 84
protection, support

JACUZZI
- WATER 46
- WISH-FULFILLMENT 150
relaxation, sexuality

JADE
- JEWELRY 114
worn-out

JAIL see PRISON

JAM
- FOOD AND DRINK 106
sweetness

JAR
- CONTAINERS 108
blow, discord, shock

JAUNDICE
- ILLNESS 95
cowardice

JAW
- THE BODY 91
disapproval, talkativeness

JELLY
- FOOD AND DRINK 106
weakness

JESTER
- EMOTION 130
foolishness, lack of seriousness, laughter

JET
- FIRE 45
- WATER 46

JETTY
- BUILDINGS 100

JEWELRY 114

JIG
- MOVEMENT 148
happiness, liveliness

JIGSAW
- DIFFICULTY 173
attention, organization, problem, puzzlement

JOB
- DISCIPLINE 163
- OCCUPATIONS 148
routine

JOCKEY
- OCCUPATIONS 148
horse

JOGGING
- ACTIVITIES 144
- HEALTH 93
- MOVEMENT 148
determination, steadiness

JOINT
- ESCAPISM 136
- THE BODY 91
marijuana, sharing

JOURNALIST
- COMMUNICATION 137
information, intrusion

JUDGE
- AUTHORITY 162
- GUILT 124
- JUSTICE 164
- PUNISHMENT 170
consideration, judgment, opinion

JUDO
- SPORTS 134
defense

JUG
- CONTAINERS 108

JUGGLING
- OCCUPATIONS 148
- SKILL 72
dexterity, misrepresentation

JUICE
- FOOD AND DRINK 106
essence, spirit

JUKEBOX
- MUSIC 70
old-fashioned

JUMPING
- MOVEMENT 148
- SPORTS 134
advancement, concluding, excitement, overcoming

JUNGLE
- FEAR 120
- LANDSCAPE 58
confusion, nature, problems, struggle, tangle, uncouthness, wildness

JUNK
- REFUSE 119
cheapness, risk, rubbish, uselessness

JUPITER
- MYTHOLOGY 64

JURY
- AUTHORITY 162
- ESTABLISHMENT 163
- GUILT 124
- JUSTICE 164
- PUNISHMENT 170
judgment, public opinion

JUSTICE 164

K

KALEIDOSCOPE
- CHANGE 168
- COLORS 75
- THE MANDALA 68
interest, pattern, repetition, variation

KANGAROO
- MAMMALS AND REPTILES 42

KARAOKE
- MUSIC 70
dependence, exhibitionism

KARATE
- SPORTS 134
attack, defense

KEEPING FIT
- HEALTH 93

KENNEL
- HOME 102
- MAMMALS AND REPTILES 42
detention, protection

KERB/CURB
- LANDSCAPE 58
- RESTRICTION 169

KEY
- BUILDINGS 100

KEYHOLE
- BUILDINGS 100

KICKING
- MOVEMENT 148
dislike, stimulation, violence

KID
- MAMMALS AND REPTILES 42
- YOUTH 89

KIDNEY
- FOOD AND DRINK 106
- THE BODY 91

KILLING
- DEATH 86
defeat, deprivation, violence

KING
- AUTHORITY 162
- JEWELRY 114
- JUSTICE 164
reward, snobbery

KISS
- LOVE 126
acknowledgment, admiration, comfort, farewell, friendship, sex

KITCHEN
- ROOMS 103

KITE
- FLYING 147
- SPORTS 134

KITTEN
- MAMMALS AND REPTILES 42
inexperience, prettiness, skittishness

KNEE
- THE BODY 91
submission

KNIFE
- ANGER 123
- TOOLS 115
- WEAPONS 118
violence

KNITTING
- ACTIVITIES 144
- OCCUPATION 148
complication, connection (knit together), repetition, satisfaction

KNOCKING
- ACTIVITIES 144
- COMMUNICATION 137
attention, criticism

KNOT
- GAMES 132
puzzle, tangle, union

KNUCKLE
- THE BODY 91

L

LABEL
- IMAGE 165
category, class, self-knowledge

LABOR
- BIRTH 86

LABORATORY
- CREATIVITY 73
- ROOMS 103
discovery, experiment

LABYRINTH
- BUILDINGS 100
- DIFFICULTY 172
- LOSS 171
confusion

LACE
- CLOTHING 84
complexity, delicacy

LADDER
- AMBITION 151
- TOOLS 115

advancement, aspiration, demotion, promotion

LADY
- IMAGE 165

refinement, social status, superiority

LAGOON
- WATER 46
- WISH-FULFILLMENT 150

LAKE
- WATER 46

LAMB
- CHILDHOOD 88
- FOOD AND DRINK 106
- MAMMALS AND REPTILES 42
- RELIGION 180

innocence

LAMENESS
- THE BODY 91

disability

LAMP
- ROOMS 103

LANDLORD
- AUTHORITY 162

oppression

LANDSCAPE 58

LANGUAGE
- COMMUNICATION 137
- DIFFICULTY 172

knowledge

LATCH
- DIFFICULTY 172
- RESTRICTION 169
- SECURITY 153

prevention

LAUGHTER
- EMOTION 130

mockery

LAUNDRY
- CLEANSING 146
- CLOTHING 84
- GUILT 124

LAVATORY
- HEALTH 93
- REFUSE 119
- THE BODY 91
- WATER 46

LAW
- AUTHORITY 162
- GUILT 124
- JUSTICE 164

LAWYER
- ESTABLISHMENT 163

LAWN
- LANDSCAPE 58

nature, play, recreation

LEAD
- EMOTION 130

heaviness, weight

LEAFLET
- COMMUNICATION 137

argument, information

LEAK
- DANGER 158
- WARNING 159
- WATER 46

disclosure, urination, waste

LEAPING
- ADVENTURE 136
- MOVEMENT 148

daring, drama, force, speed

LEATHER
- CLOTHING 84

endurance, sex, toughness

LEAVES
- TREES 50

beginnings, hope, nature, shelter

LECTURE
- AUTHORITY 162
- GATHERINGS 174

information, instruction, knowledge, reprimand

LEFTOVERS
- FOOD AND DRINK 106

LEG
- THE BODY 91

support, uprightness

LEGACY
- THE FAMILY 90
- MONEY 110
- WISH-FULFILLMENT 150

tradition

LEGEND
- ADVENTURE 136
- MYTHOLOGY 64

LEISURE
- ACTIVITIES 144
- WISH-FULFILLMENT 150

overwork, unemployment

LEMON
- FOOD AND DRINK 106

bitterness, refreshment, regret

LEO
- THE ZODIAC 69

lion

LEOTARD
- ENERGY 73
- SPORTS 134

diet, exercise

LESSON
- PUNISHMENT 170

encouragement, experience, instruction, knowledge, warning

LETTER
- COMMUNICATION 137

LEVER
- TOOLS 115

LEVITATION
- FLYING 147
- THE SUPERNATURAL 60

LIBEL
- ANGER 123

attack, misrepresentation

LIBRA
- THE ZODIAC 69

LIBRARY
- RECORDING 74

knowledge

LICENSE
- AUTHORITY 162

LICKING
- FOOD AND DRINK 106

beating, sex

LIE
- DECEPTION 152

LIFEBOAT
- INSECURITY 121

LIFT/ELEVATOR
- AMBITION 151

machinery, progress

LIGHT
- FIRE 45

LIGHTHOUSE
- BUILDINGS 100
- WARNING 159

hope, light

LIGHTNING
- DANGER 158
- WEATHER 49
- WARNING 159

illumination, nature, speed

LILY
- FLOWERS 53

LIMOUSINE
- VEHICLES 116

LINE
- DISCIPLINE 163

LINGERIE
- CLOTHING 84

sex

LION
- MAMMALS AND REPTILES 42

courage, masculinity, pride, strength

LIPS
- THE BODY 91

LIQUID
- WATER 46

LITTER
- GUILT 124
- REFUSE 119

carelessness, untidiness

LOAD
- EMOTION 130

burden, grief, oppression, responsibility, work

LOAF
- FOOD AND DRINK 106

LOCK
- RESTRICTION 169
- SECURITY 153

LOG
- TREES 50

nature, roughness

LONELINESS 173

LORRY
- VEHICLES 116

LOSS 171

LOTTERY
- GAMBLING 139

chance, risk

LOUNGE
- ROOMS 103

leisure, idleness

LOUSE
- SWIMMERS AND CRAWLERS 44

contempt, parasite, unpleasantness

LOVE 126

LOVEMAKING
- LOVE 126
- WISH-FULFILLMENT 150

LOVER
- LOVE 126

sex

LUCK
- THE SUPERNATURAL 60

LUGGAGE
- CONTAINERS 108

belongings, burdens, responsibilities

LUNACY
- ILLNESS 95

eccentricity, foolishness

LUXURY
- EMOTION 130
- THE BODY 91
- WISH-FULFILLMENT 150

comfort, desire, expense

LYNCHING
- GUILT 124
- PUNISHMENT 170

violence

M

MACHINE GUN
- DEATH 86
- WEAPONS 118

injury, violence

MACHINERY
- TOOLS 115

MADNESS
- EMOTION 130

irrationality, violence

MAGAZINE
- COMMUNICATION 137

information, learning, variety

MAGIC
- DECEPTION 152
- THE SUPERNATURAL 60

malevolence, mystery, surprise, wonder

MAGISTRATE
- AUTHORITY 162
- GUILT 124
- JUSTICE 164
- PUNISHMENT 170

courtroom

MAGPIE
- WINGED CREATURES 43

collecting, petty thieving

MAIL see **LETTERS**

MAKEUP
- DECEPTION 152
- IMAGE 165
- THEATER 81

enhancement, temperament

MAMMALS AND REPTILES 42

MANAGER
- AUTHORITY 162

administration, control, promotion

MANDALA, THE 68

MANDRAKE
- FOOD AND DRINK 106

MANICURE
- IMAGE 165

beauty, enhancement, neatness

MANNEQUIN
- IMAGE 165

model

MANSION
- BUILDINGS 100
- WISH-FULFILLMENT 150

grandeur

THE WORLD OF NATURE

FANTASY & FABLE

ARTS & SCIENCES

THE HUMAN BODY

BUILDINGS & INTERIORS

EVERYDAY THINGS

HUMAN EMOTIONS

HUMAN ACTIVITIES

HUMAN CONDITIONS

RITUALS & RELIGION

THE DREAM THESAURUS

THE WORLD OF NATURE

FANTASY & FABLE

ARTS & SCIENCES

THE HUMAN BODY

BUILDINGS & INTERIORS

EVERYDAY THINGS

HUMAN EMOTIONS

HUMAN ACTIVITIES

HUMAN CONDITIONS

RITUALS & RELIGION

THE DREAM THESAURUS

MANTELPIECE
- ROOMS 103
display

MANURE
- CREATIVITY 703
- DIRT 119
fertilization

MAP
- LANDSCAPE 58
- TRAVEL 134
direction, knowledge, representation, way ahead

MARBLES
- GAMES 132
- SKILL 72
competition

MARIJUANA
- ESCAPISM 136

MARKET
- ACTIVITIES 144
- GATHERINGS 174
- MONEY 110
buying and selling

MARRIAGE 146

MARS
- AMBITION 151
- MYTHOLOGY 64

MARTYR
- IMAGE 165
pain, persecution, principle

MASCARA
- IMAGE 165
seduction

MASK
- DECEPTION 152
- IMAGE 165
- THEATER 81
disguise

MASSACRE
- DEATH 86
indiscrimination, violence

MASSAGE
- THE BODY 91
comfort, cure, luxury, sex

MATCH
- FIRE 45
- GAMES 132
opposition

MATHEMATICS
- CALCULATION 77
- DIFFICULTY 173
complexity, manipulation

MATRON
- AUTHORITY 162
- DISCIPLINE 163
care

MAZE
- DIFFICULTY 173
- LOSS 171
bewilderment, confusion, obscurity

MEASUREMENT
- CALCULATION 77

MEDAL
- ACHIEVEMENT 167

MEDICINE
- ILLNESS 95
- PUNISHMENT 170

MEDIUM
- THE SUPERNATURAL 60

MEETING
- COMMUNICATION 137
- GATHERINGS 174
assembling, joining

MELON
- FRUIT 54

MENAGERIE
- MAMMALS AND REPTILES 42
- WINGED CREATURES 43
wildness confined

MENOPAUSE
- THE BODY 91

MENSTRUATION
- THE BODY 91
woman

MENU
- FOOD AND DRINK 106
expense, planning, price

MERCURY
- AMBITION 151
- MYTHOLOGY 64

MERMAID
- DANGER 158
- WATER 46
- WISH-FULFILLMENT 150
frustration, sex

MESS
- DIRT 119
confusion, laxity, muddle

MESSAGE
- COMMUNICATION 137

MESSENGER
- MYTHOLOGY 64
Mercury

METER
- CALCULATION 77
- TIME 80

MICROPHONE
- COMMUNICATION 137

MICROSCOPE
- TOOLS 115

MIDWIFE
- CREATIVITY 73
- WISH-FULFILLMENT 150
realization of ideas

MILESTONE
- ACHIEVEMENT 167
- AMBITION 151
- CHANGE 168
- IMAGE 165
- TIME 80

MILK
- FOOD AND DRINK 106
nourishment

MINE
- WORKPLACES 116

MINEFIELD
- LANDSCAPE 58
need for care, unseen danger

MINER
- CREATIVITY 73
- OCCUPATIONS 148
exploration

MINING
- JEWELRY 114

MINK
- CLOTHING 84
lack of compassion, luxury, snobbery

MINOTAUR
- THE SUPERNATURAL 60

MIRACLE
- RELIGION 180
- THE SUPERNATURAL 60
- WISH-FULFILLMENT 150
remarkable developments, unexpected

MIRROR
- IMAGE 165

MISCARRIAGE
- CHANGE 168
- ILLNESS 95
failure, incompletion, worry

MISER
- MONEY 110
misery

MISPRINT
- ACTIVITIES 144
mistake

MISSILE
- WEAPONS 118

MISSIONARY
- OCCUPATIONS 148
- RELIGION 180
persuasion, sex (missionary position)

MIST
- WEATHER 49
confusion, obscurity

MOB
- GATHERINGS 174
- PUNISHMENT 170
disorder, lack of thought, threat

MODEL
- BUILDINGS 100
- IMAGE 165
- WISH-FULFILLMENT 150
display, fashion, presentation

MODESTY
- IMAGE 165
humility, moderation, restraint

MOLE
- MAMMALS AND REPTILES 42
concealment, excavation, spying

MONARCH
- JUSTICE 164

MONASTERY
- BUILDINGS 100
- RELIGION 180
chastity, retirement, seclusion, silence

MONEY 110

MONK
- RELIGION 180
chastity, silence, thoughtfulness, wisdom

MONKEY
- MAMMALS AND REPTILES 42
chatter, gossip, mimicry, mischief

MONROE, MARILYN
- MYTHOLOGY 64

MONSTER
- NIGHTMARE 154

MONUMENT
- BUILDINGS 100
reminder

MOON
- TIME 80
chastity, female cycle, nature

MORSE CODE
- COMMUNICATION 137

MORTGAGE
- HOME 102
- MONEY 110
commitment, debt, responsibility

MORTUARY
- DEATH 86

MOSAIC
- IMAGE 165
detail, symmetry

MOSQUITO
- SWIMMERS AND CRAWLERS 44
blood, infection, irritation, shock

MOSS
- OTHER PLANTS 52
nature

MOTH
- SWIMMERS AND CRAWLERS 44
age, damage, destruction

MOTHER
- THE FAMILY 90
care, older woman, platonic love

MOTORCYCLE
- ACTIVITIES 144
- VEHICLES 116
speed

MOUNTAIN
- ACTIVITIES 144
- AMBITION 151
- DIFFICULTY 172
- LANDSCAPE 58
problem

MOUSE
- DIRT 119
- MAMMALS AND REPTILES 42
greed, nimbleness, smallness

MOUSETRAP
- TEMPTATION 169
- WEAPONS 118
bait, dangerous, shock

MOUTH
- THE BODY 91
impudence, ranting, sexuality

MOVEMENT 148

MUD
- EARTH 48

MUG
- CONTAINERS 108

MULE
- MAMMALS AND REPTILES 42
obstinacy, servitude, stupidity

MURDER
- ANGER 123
violence

MUSCLE
- THE BODY 91
- WISH-FULFILLMENT 150
force, intimidation, power

MUSEUM
- BUILDINGS 100
age, culture, knowledge, old-fashioned

MUSHROOM
- FOOD AND DRINK 106
expansion, sudden development

MUSIC 70

MUSSEL
- FOOD AND DRINK 106
- SECURITY 153
closeness

MUSTACHE
- THE BODY 91
male, maturity

MUSTARD
- FOOD AND DRINK 106
attack, strength, vigor

MUTINY
- ACTIVITIES 144
protest, resistance

MUTTON
- FOOD AND DRINK 106
age, experience, toughness

MYTHICAL CREATURE
- MYTHOLOGY 64
- THE SUPERNATURAL 60
animals

MYTHOLOGY 64

N

NAGGING
- COMMUNICATION 137
- WARNING 159
boredom

NAIL
- TOOLS 115

NAKED *see* **NUDITY**

NAME
- IMAGE 165
personality

NAPKIN
- CLEANSING 146
behavior, politeness

NATURISM *see* **NUDITY**

NAVIGATION
- TRAVEL 134
direction, planning, ships

NAVY
- OCCUPATIONS 148
ships

NECK
- THE BODY 91

NECKLACE
- JEWELRY 114
restriction

NECROPHILIA
- DEATH 86

NECTAR
- FOOD AND DRINK 106
approval, sweetness

NEEDLE
- CREATIVITY 73
- NUDITY 96
- TOOLS 115
- UTENSILS 109
repair, sharpness

NEEDLEWORK
- CREATIVITY 73
application, complexity, fineness

NEGATIVE
- PICTURES 76

NEGLIGEE
- CLOTHING 84
- WISH-FULFILLMENT 150
revelation, sex

NEIGHBOR
- HOME 102
friendliness, disapproval, nearness

NEPHEW
- THE FAMILY 90

NEST
- BUILDINGS 100
- HOME 102
comfort

NET
- RESTRICTION 169
limitation, profit

NETTLES
- ACCIDENT 160
- OTHER PLANTS 52
- PUNISHMENT 170
irritation

NEWSPAPER
- COMMUNICATION 137
events

NEWS
- COMMUNICATION 137
tidings

NIGHTCLUB
- ENTERTAINMENT 178
- WISH-FULFILLMENT 150

NIGHTGOWN
- CLOTHING 84
sex

NIGHTINGALE
- WINGED CREATURES 43

NIGHTMARES 154

NINE
- NUMBERS 80

NOSE
- THE BODY 91
curiosity

NOTEBOOK
- RECORDING 74
knowledge, memory

NOTICE
- COMMUNICATION 137
- WARNING 159
announcement, intention, notification, observation

NOVEL
- ENTERTAINMENT 178
- TIME 80
identification, narrative

NUDITY 96

NUMBERS 80

NUN
- RELIGION 180
chastity, silence, uncommunicativeness

NURSE
- ILLNESS 95
attention, care, fostering, strictness

NURSERY
- CHILDHOOD 88
comfort, nurture, play

NUTS
- FOOD AND DRINK 106
nature

O

OAK
- TREES 50

OATH
- DISCIPLINE 163
- RITUAL 179
commitment

OBELISK
- BUILDINGS 100
sex

OBITUARY
- DEATH 86
- IMAGE 165
memory

OCCUPATIONS 148

OCEAN
- WATER 46
vastness

OCTOPUS
- SWIMMERS AND CRAWLERS 44
influence, interference

OFFAL
- FOOD AND DRINK 106
- REFUSE 119

OFFICE
- AUTHORITY 162
- ROOMS 103
- WORKPLACES 116
colleagues, organization

OFFICER
- AUTHORITY 162
- ESTABLISHMENT 163
information, instructions

OINTMENT
- ILLNESS 95
- IMAGE 165
- THE BODY 91
calm, healing, illness, image

OLIVE
- FOOD AND DRINK 106
nourishment, peace

OMELETTE
- FOOD AND DRINK 106
confusion (breaking eggs), muddle, threat

ONE
- NUMBERS 80

ONION
- VEGETABLES 55
complications, tears

OPAL
- JEWELRY 114
mystery

OPERA
- MUSIC 70
- THEATER 81
artificiality, complications, drama, overstatement

OPIUM
- ESCAPISM 136
sleep

OPTICIAN
- GUILT 124
- IMAGE 165
- OCCUPATIONS 148
self-examination

ORANGE
- COLORS 75
- FOOD AND DRINK 106
refreshment

ORCHARD
- LANDSCAPE 58
fruitfulness, sin (apples)

ORCHESTRA
- GATHERINGS 174
- MUSIC 70
agreement/disagreement, background

ORCHID
- FLOWERS 53
- IMAGE 165
beauty, fantasy, rarity

ORDERS
- AUTHORITY 162
conformity, guidance, harmony, instruction, reward, tidiness

ORGAN
- MUSIC 70
phallus

ORGY
- WISH-FULFILLMENT 150
sex

ORPHAN
- EMOTION 130
- LONELINESS 172
bereavement, deprivation

OSTRICH
- WINGED CREATURES 43
speed

OTHER PLANTS 52

OUTDOORS
- ADVENTURE 136
- LANDSCAPE 58
exercise, freedom

OUTHOUSE
- BUILDINGS 100
distancing

OUTING
- ACTIVITIES 144
- ADVENTURE 136
company, exercise, freedom, relaxation

OVEN
- FIRE 45
argument, heat

OVERALLS
- CLOTHING 84
cover-up, protection

OVERDOSE
- EMOTION 130
- ESCAPISM 136
depression, excess

OVERDRAFT
- MONEY 110
emotional overspending, rashness

OVERFLOW
- WATER 46
abundance, waste

OVERSPENDING
- WARNING 159
extravagance

OVERTAKING
- AMBITION 151
- ENERGY 73
- VEHICLES 116
showing off

OVERTIME
- ENERGY 73
finance, generosity, overwork

OVERTURE
- MUSIC 70
preparation

OWL
- WINGED CREATURES 43
observation, wakefulness

THE WORLD OF NATURE

FANTASY & FABLE

ARTS & SCIENCES

THE HUMAN BODY

BUILDINGS & INTERIORS

EVERYDAY THINGS

HUMAN EMOTIONS

HUMAN ACTIVITIES

HUMAN CONDITIONS

RITUALS & RELIGION

THE DREAM THESAURUS

OWNERSHIP
- EMOTION 130
possessiveness, pride

OX
- MAMMALS AND REPTILES 42
clumsiness, power, tenacity

OXYGEN
- AIR 48
- ENERGY 73
- HEALTH 93
life force, refreshment

OYSTER
- FOOD AND DRINK 106
chance, potency, wealth

P

PACKAGE
- COMMUNICATION 137
- CONTAINERS 108
gift, surprise

PADDLE
- WATER 46
progress

PADLOCK
- RESTRICTION 169

PAINTING
- IMAGE 165
- PICTURES 76
- RECORDING 74

PAJAMAS
- CLOTHING 84

PALACE
- AUTHORITY 162
- BUILDINGS 100
grandeur

PALM-TREE
- TRAVEL 134
- TREES 150

PALMIST
- PREDICTION AND PRECOGNITION 62
analysis, self-knowledge

PANIC
- FEAR 120
- NIGHTMARES 154

PANTOMIME
- THEATER 81
- YOUTH 89
fantasy, unreality

PANTS
- CLOTHING 84

PANTRY
- FOOD AND DRINK 106
- ROOMS 103
dearth, plenty

PAPER
- COMMUNICATION 137
knowledge

PAPERWEIGHT
- RESTRICTION 169

PARACHUTE
- ADVENTURE 136
- ESCAPISM 136
- FLYING 147
- SECURITY 153

PARAKEET
- WINGED CREATURES 43
imitation

PARALYSIS
- ILLNESS 95
- THE BODY 91
- NIGHTMARE 154
powerlessness

PARCEL
- COMMUNICATION 137
- CONTAINERS 108
gift, surprise

PARENTS
- THE FAMILY 90

PARK
- LANDSCAPE 58
- VEHICLES 116
relaxation, sanctuary

PARKING METER
- GUILT 124
- RESTRICTION 169
payment, penalty

PARLOR
- ROOMS 103
friends, relaxation

PAROLE
- RESTRICTION 169
honor

PARROT
- WINGED CREATURES 43
gossip, imitation, lack of understanding

PARTING
- EMOTION 130
choice, division, separation

PARTNER
- ACHIEVEMENT 167
- THE FAMILY 90
business, sharing

PASSAGE
- BUILDINGS 100
- MOVEMENT 148
access, confinement

PASSENGER
- ESCAPISM 136
- TRAVEL 134
indolence

PASSION
- EMOTION 130

PASSPORT
- AUTHORITY 162
- TRAVEL 134
- WISH-FULFILLMENT 150

PASTOR
- AUTHORITY 162
- RELIGION 180
counsel

PATH
- COMMUNICATION 137
- DISCIPLINE 163
- LANDSCAPE 58
- MOVEMENT 148
duty

PATIENT
- ILLNESS 95
criticism, patience

PATTERN
- DISCIPLINE 163
- SECURITY 153
- SKILL 72
- THE MANDALA 68
behavior, conformity

PAWNBROKER
- EMOTION 130
- LOSS 171
- MONEY 110
- SECURITY 153
interest

PAY
- MONEY 110
- SECURITY 153
debt, profit, reward, work

PEACH
- FOOD AND DRINK 106
- FRUIT 54
- WISH-FULFILLMENT 150

PEACOCK
- IMAGE 165
- WINGED CREATURES 43
display, pride

PEAR
- FOOD AND DRINK 106
- FRUIT 54

PEARL
- IMAGE 165
- JEWELRY 114
rarity, richness, value

PEAS
- VEGETABLES 55

PEEL
- NUDITY 96
revelation

PEN, PENCIL
- COMMUNICATION 137
- RECORDING 74
information, knowledge

PENDULUM
- CALCULATION 77
machinery, regularity

PENSION
- SECURITY 153
age, retirement

PENTHOUSE
- AMBITION 151
- BUILDINGS 100
display, luxury

PEPPER
- CHANGE 168
- FOOD AND DRINK 106
liveliness, spice

PERFORMING
- DECEPTION 152
- ENTERTAINMENT 178
- THEATER 81
completion, dissimulation

PERFUME
- DECEPTION 152
- IMAGE 165
dissimulation, enhancement

PERSPIRATION
- EMOTION 130
- GUILT 124
worry

PERVERSION
- EROTIC DREAMS 96

PET
- EMOTION 130
- MAMMALS AND REPTILES 42
affection, pampering

PETITION
- AUTHORITY 162
- INSECURITY 121
approval

PETROL/GAS
- ENERGY 73

PHALLUS
- EROTIC DREAMS 96
sex

PHOTOGRAPH
- IMAGE 165
- PICTURES 76
- RECORDING 74
knowledge, memory

PHOTOGRAPHER
- OCCUPATIONS 148

PIANO, PIANIST
- MUSIC 70

PICK
- TOOLS 115
demolition, excavation

PICNIC
- FOOD AND DRINK 106
- LANDSCAPE 58
casualness, ease, enjoyment

PICTURES 76

PIE
- CONTAINERS 108
- FOOD AND DRINK 106

PIG
- MAMMALS AND REPTILES 42
bad behavior, indulgence

PILL
- ILLNESS 95

PILLAR
- BUILDINGS 100
decoration, support

PILLOW
- ESCAPISM 136
relaxation

PILOT
- TRAVEL 134
guidance, safety

PIN
- JEWELRY 114
- UTENSILS 109
injury, reminder, safety

PINCH
- ACTIVITIES 144
antagonism, distress

PINEAPPLE
- FRUIT 54

PINUP
- PICTURES 76
- WISH-FULFILLMENT 150
sex

PIP
- CREATIVITY 73
- FOOD AND DRINK 106

PIPE
- FIRE 45
- WATER 46

PIRATE
- ADVENTURE 136
- WISH-FULFILLMENT 150
illegality, plunder, violence

PISCES
- THE ZODIAC 69

PIT
- DEATH 86
- EARTH 48
- LANDSCAPE 58
- RESTRICTION 169
excavation, obscurity

PLACARD
- AUTHORITY 162
- COMMUNICATION 137
pride, publicity, self-advertisement

PLAGUE
- DANGER 158
- ILLNESS 95
threat, infestation

PLAN
- PICTURES 76
information, knowledge, preparation, project

PLANET
- MYTHOLOGY 64
- THE SUPERNATURAL 60

distance, remoteness

PLANTS *see* OTHER PLANTS

PLASTER
- IMAGE 165

concealment

PLATE
- FOOD AND DRINK 106
- UTENSILS 109

PLATFORM
- COMMUNICATION 137
- TRAVEL 134

delay, politics, procrastination

PLATINUM
- JEWELRY 114

riches, scarcity, value

PLAY
- GAMBLING 139
- GAMES 132
- THEATER 81

pretense, relaxation, sex

PLAYGROUND
- GAMES 132
- LANDSCAPE 58

relaxation, openness, scope

PLOTTING
- DECEPTION 152

intrigue, narrative, secrecy

PLOUGH
- CREATIVITY 73
- TOOLS 115

force, preparation, sex

PLUMBER
- OCCUPATIONS 148
- WATER 46

POACHER
- CRIME 140
- GUILT 124

unfairness

POCKET
- CONTAINERS 108
- SECURITY 153

POISON
- WEAPONS 118

POKER
- GAMBLING 139

chance

POKING
- FIRE 45

violence

POLICE OFFICER
- AUTHORITY 162
- FEAR 120
- GUILT 124
- JUSTICE 164

protection

POLISH
- IMAGE 165

presentation, smoothness

POLITICAL PARTY
- GATHERINGS 174

POLLUTION
- DIRT 119
- GUILT 124

POLYGAMY
- GUILT 124
- MARRIAGE 146
- WISH-FULFILLMENT 150

POOL
- WATER 46

POPE
- AUTHORITY 162
- GUILT 124
- RELIGION 180

morality

PORNOGRAPHY
- EROTIC DREAMS 96

PORTER
- SERVICE 141

assistance, burden

POSTMAN, POSTWOMAN
- COMMUNICATION 137
- OCCUPATIONS 148

punctuality, variety

POT
- CONTAINERS 108
- UTENSILS 109

POTTER
- CREATIVITY 73
- OCCUPATIONS 148

relaxation

PREACHER
- GUILT 124

counsel, exhortation, explanation, morality

PRECIPICE
- DANGER 158
- FEAR 120
- LANDSCAPE 58

obstruction

PRECOGNITION AND PREDICTION 62

PREGNANCY
- BIRTH 86
- CHANGE 168
- CREATIVITY 73
- WISH-FULFILLMENT 150

beginnings, new ideas

PRESCRIPTION
- COMMUNICATION 137
- ILLNESS 95

advice

PRIEST
- AUTHORITY 162
- RELIGION 180

PRINCE
- AUTHORITY 162
- WISH-FULFILLMENT 150

PRISON
- GUILT 124
- JUSTICE 164
- PUNISHMENT 170
- RESTRICTION 169

PRIZE
- ACHIEVEMENT 167
- AMBITION 151

congratulation, merit

PROCESSION
- CEREMONIES 177
- RELIGION 180
- RITUAL 179

merit, order

PROFESSOR
- OCCUPATIONS 148

knowledge

PROMENADE
- LANDSCAPE 58

relaxation, showing off

PROMPTER
- GUILT 124
- THEATER 81

forgetfulness

PROPERTY
- BUILDINGS 100
- MONEY 110

ownership, possessions

PROPHET
- AUTHORITY 162
- PREDICTION AND PRECOGNITION 62

PROSECUTOR
- GUILT 124
- JUSTICE 164
- PUNISHMENT 170

PROSTITUTE
- TEMPTATION 169
- WISH-FULFILLMENT 150

debasement, misuse, sex

PSYCHIATRIST
- EMOTION 130
- INSECURITY 121

imbalance

PSYCHOLOGIST
- INSECURITY 121

PUBLICITY
- IMAGE 165

exploitation, notoriety

PUDDING
- FOOD AND DRINK 106
- IMAGE 165

diet

PUDDLE
- DIRT 119
- EMOTION 130

confusion, mistake

PULPIT
- AUTHORITY 162
- GUILT 124
- RELIGION 180

morality, preaching

PUMP
- TOOLS 115

inflation, self-importance

PUNCH
- WARNING 159

antagonism, violence

PUNCTURE
- VEHICLES 116

let-down

PUNISHMENT 170

PUPPY
- LOVE 126
- MAMMALS AND REPTILES 42

helplessness, innocence

PURPLE
- COLORS 75

royalty

PURSE
- CONTAINERS 106
- EMOTION 130
- MONEY 110

PURSUIT 147

QUARREL
- ANGER 123
- HOSTILITY 122

antagonism, complaint

QUARRY
- CREATIVITY 73
- LANDSCAPE 58

explosives, knowledge

QUAY
- LANDSCAPE 58
- WATER 46

QUEEN
- AUTHORITY 162
- JEWELRY 114
- MYTHOLOGY 64

effeminacy, fertility

QUILT
- HOME 102
- SECURITY 153

domesticity, comfort

QUIZ
- SKILL 72

curiosity, examination, knowledge, observation, oddity, questioning, television

RABBIT
- MAMMALS AND REPTILES 42

fecundity, speed

RACE
- ACHIEVEMENT 167
- AMBITION 151
- COLORS 75
- SPORTS 134

competition, prejudice

RACING
- GAMBLING 139
- SPORTS 134

competing

RADAR
- GUILT 124

detection, exposure

RADIO
- COMMUNICATION 137

RAFFLE
- GAMBLING 139

RAGE
- EMOTION 130
- INSECURITY 121

passion, vehemence

RAILWAY STATION
- TRAVEL 134

transport

RAIN
- WATER 46
- WEATHER 49

depression, growth, refreshment, sorrow

RAIN FOREST
- LANDSCAPE 58

RALLY
- GATHERINGS 174

appeal, enthusiasm, support

RAM
- MAMMALS AND REPTILES 42

RAPE
- ANGER 123
- HOSTILITY 122

sex, violation, violence

RASH
- ILLNESS 95

impulsive

RAT
- MAMMALS AND REPTILES 42

betrayal, criticism, desertion

RAZOR
- IMAGE 165
- UTENSILS 109

censorship, division

R

THE WORLD OF NATURE

FANTASY & FABLE

ARTS & SCIENCES

THE HUMAN BODY

BUILDINGS & INTERIORS

EVERYDAY THINGS

HUMAN EMOTIONS

HUMAN ACTIVITIES

HUMAN CONDITIONS

RITUALS & RELIGION

THE DREAM THESAURUS

THE WORLD OF NATURE

FANTASY & FABLE

ARTS & SCIENCES

THE HUMAN BODY

BUILDINGS & INTERIORS

EVERYDAY THINGS

HUMAN EMOTIONS

HUMAN ACTIVITIES

HUMAN CONDITIONS

RITUALS & RELIGION

THE DREAM THESAURUS

READING *see* **BOOK**

REBELLION
- ANGER 123
- HOSTILITY 122
disapproval, opposition

RECEIPT
- MONEY 100
knowledge, learning, profit

RECEPTION
- GATHERINGS 174
acceptance, colleagues, friends

RECIPE
- DISCIPLINE 163
- FOOD AND DRINK 106
discipline, knowledge, organization

RECITAL
- MUSIC 70
formality, narrative, performance

RECORDING 74

RED
- COLORS 75
heat

REFEREE
- AUTHORITY 162
- DISCIPLINE 163
- GAMES 132
- GUILT 124
- PUNISHMENT 170
disputation, order

REFLECTION
- IMAGE 165
criticism, reversal, self-approval, self-criticism

REFRIGERATOR
- EMOTION 130
coolness, distancing

REFUSE 119

REGIMENT
- DISCIPLINE 163
- GATHERINGS 174
- WAR 140
compulsion, comradeship, order

REGISTER
- RECORDING 74
knowledge, presence, understanding

REHEARSAL
- THEATER 81
preparation, unreadiness

REINS
- RESTRICTION 169
- SECURITY 153
direction, guidance

REJECTION
- EMOTION 130
- LOSS 171
refusal, repulsion

REJOICING
- CELEBRATION 176
acceptance, pleasure

RELATIVES
- THE FAMILY 90

RELIGION 180

RELIGIOUS PROCESSION
- RITUAL 179

RENT
- HOME 102
- MONEY 110
borrowing, contract

REPAIR
- ACTIVITIES 144
restoration, unsoundness

REPORT
- COMMUNICATION 137
congratulation, criticism, summary

RESCUE
- ACTIVITIES 144
- DANGER 158
- WARNING 159
help

RESTRICTION 169

RESURRECTION
- CHANGE 168
- RELIGION 180
- WISH-FULFILLMENT 150
new beginnings, rebirth

RETIREMENT
- ACTIVITIES 144
- WISH-FULFILLMENT 150
age, boredom, withdrawal, work

RETREAT
- ACTIVITIES 144
withdrawal

REUNION
- GATHERINGS 174
friendship, memory, nostalgia

REVENGE
- GUILT 124
- INSECURITY 121
antagonism

REVOLUTION
- CHANGE 168
turnaround

REVOLVER
- WEAPONS 118
aggression

REWARD
- MONEY 110
acknowledgment

RHEUMATISM
- ILLNESS 95
inflexibility, pain

RIBBON
- CELEBRATION 176
- CLOTHING 84
recognition, remembrance

RICE
- FOOD AND DRINK 106
fecundity

RIDING
- ACTIVITIES 144
pleasure, recreation, speed, urgency

RIFLE
- WEAPONS 118

RIGGING
ships

RING
- JEWELRY 114
- MARRIAGE 146
possession

RINGS
- TREES 50

RITUAL 179

RIVAL
- DANGER 158
jealousy

RIVER
- LANDSCAPE 58
- WATER 46

ROAD
- LANDSCAPE 58
aim, direction, progression

ROAD SIGNS
- DISCIPLINE 163

ROCK
- LANDSCAPE 58
intransigence

ROCKET
- COMMUNICATION 137
display, distress, sex

ROOF
- BUILDINGS 100
protection

ROOMS 103

ROOSTER
- WINGED CREATURES 43

ROOT VEGETABLES
- EARTH 48
- VEGETABLES 55

ROOTS
- ACHIEVEMENT 167
- ESTABLISHMENT 163
- TREES 50
determination, origins, solidity

ROPE
- RESTRICTION 169
support

ROSE
- FLOWERS 53
- LOVE 126

ROULETTE
- GAMBLING 139

RUBBISH/GARBAGE
- REFUSE 119

RULER
- CALCULATION 77
- DISCIPLINE 163

RUNNING
- ACTIVITIES 144
- PURSUIT 147
flight

RUST
- EMOTION 130
disability, disuse, stiffness

S

SABOTAGE
- ANGER 123
- WARNING 159
antagonism, damage, resistance

SACK
- CONTAINERS 108

SADISM
- EROTIC DREAMS 96

SADNESS
- EMOTION 130

SAFE
- DECEPTION 152
protection, safety, secrecy

SAGITTARIUS
- THE ZODIAC 69

SAIL
- MOVEMENT 148
- TRAVEL 134
ships

SAINT
- IMAGE 165
- RELIGION 180
goodness, virtue

SALARY
- MONEY 110
- SECURITY 153
regularity, reward

SALE
- CHANGE 168
bargains, rejection

SALESPERSON
- OCCUPATIONS 148
persuasion

SALT
- FOOD AND DRINK 106

SALUTE
- ACHIEVEMENT 167
- AUTHORITY 162
- DISCIPLINE 163
greeting, honor, respect, welcome

SAND
- EARTH 48

SAP
- TREES 50

SATURN
- MYTHOLOGY 64

SAUCE
- FOOD AND DRINK 106

SAUCEPAN
- UTENSILS 109

SAUCER
- UTENSILS 109

SAUSAGE
- FOOD AND DRINK 106

SCAFFOLD
- GUILT 124
- INSECURITY 121
- PUNISHMENT 170
construction

SCALES
- JUSTICE 164
weight

SCANDAL
- GUILT 124
- IMAGE 165
disgrace, immorality, shock

SCARECROW
- IMAGE 165

SCHOOL
- AMBITION 151
- DISCIPLINE 163
- GATHERINGS 174
- YOUTH 89
knowledge, nostalgia

SCISSORS
- UTENSILS 109
rejection, severance

SCORPIO
- THE ZODIAC 69

SCORPION
- SWIMMERS AND CRAWLERS 44
- WARNING 159
threat

SCREAM
- COMMUNICATION 137
- FEAR 120
- WARNING 159

SCREW
- UTENSILS 00
firmness, immovability

SCRUBBING
- CLEANSING 146

SCULPTURE
■ CREATIVITY 73

SEA
■ WATER 46

SEAT
■ GATHERINGS 174
buttocks, furniture, rest

SECRET
■ DECEPTION 152

SECURITY 153

SEDUCTION
■ IMAGE 165
sex

SEED
■ CREATIVITY 73
children (wish-fulfillment), fecundity

SEESAW
■ GAMES 132
indecision

SELLING
■ MONEY 110
betrayal

SEMIPRECIOUS STONE
■ JEWELRY 114

SENTRY
■ SECURITY 153
protection

SERPENT *see* **SNAKE**

SERVANT
■ SERVICE 141
inferiority, loyalty

SERVICE 141

SEVEN
■ NUMBERS 80

SEWER
■ REFUSE 119
waste

SEWING
■ ACTIVITIES 144

SEX
■ EROTIC DREAMS 96

SHADOW, THE 97

SHAME
■ GUILT 124

SHAMPOO
■ CLEANSING 146
■ THE BODY 91

SHAVING
■ THE BODY 91
hair

SHEEP
■ MAMMALS AND
REPTILES 42
blind obedience

SHELTER
■ WEATHER 49

SHIELD
■ SECURITY 153
protection

SHIP
■ VEHICLES 116
■ WATER 46

SHIPWRECK
■ DISASTER 160
■ LOSS 171
■ WATER 46
destruction, hopelessness

SHIRT
■ CLOTHING 84

SHOE
■ CLOTHING 84

SHOP
■ WORKPLACES 116

SHOPLIFTING
■ GUILT 124
betrayal, inappropriate desire, theft

SHOPPING
■ WISH-FULFILLMENT
150

SHOWER
■ CLEANSING 146
■ WATER 46
■ WEATHER 49

SIGNAL
■ COMMUNICATION 137
■ WARNING 159

SIGNATURE
■ IMAGE 165
self

SIGNPOST
■ COMMUNICATION 137
direction

SILK
■ CLOTHING 84
luxury

SILVER
■ JEWELRY 114

SINK
■ CLEANSING 146

SISTER
■ THE FAMILY 90

SIX
■ NUMBERS 80

SKATING
■ ACTIVITIES 144
■ MOVEMENT 148
■ SPORTS 134

SKELETON
■ DEATH 86
■ IMAGE 165
lucidity, minimum

SKILL 72

SKIN
■ THE BODY 91

SKIRT
■ CLOTHING 84

SKITTLES
■ GAMES 132

SKULL
■ DEATH 86

SKY
■ AMBITION 151
■ FLYING 147
freedom, nature

SLAVE
■ SERVICE 141
domination

SLICE
■ CALCULATION 77
care, caution

SLIDING
■ INSECURITY 121
■ MOVEMENT 148
ease

SLIPPING
■ INSECURITY 121
■ MOVEMENT 148
carelessness, mistaking

SLOPE
■ LANDSCAPE 58
effort, lack of effort

SLUG
■ SWIMMERS AND
CRAWLERS 44
laziness, reluctance, slowness

SLUM
■ BUILDINGS 100
condemnation, squalidness

SMILE
■ IMAGE 165
encouragement, welcome

SMOKE
■ AIR 48
obscurity

SMOKING
■ HEALTH 93

SMUGGLING
■ ACTIVITIES 144
■ GUILT 124
secrecy

SNAIL
■ SECURITY 153
■ SWIMMERS AND
CRAWLERS 44
slowness

SNAKE
■ DANGER 158
■ MAMMALS AND
REPTILES 42

SNOOKER
■ GAMES 132
■ SKILL 72

SNOW
■ DIFFICULTY 172
■ DISASTER 160
■ WEATHER 49
beauty, coldness, purity

SOAP
■ CLEANSING 146
fiction, flattery

SOCKS
■ CLOTHING 84

SODOMY
■ EROTIC DREAMS 96
sex

SOIL
■ EARTH 48

SOLDIER
■ OCCUPATIONS 148
■ WAR 140

SOLICITOR
■ GUILT 124
■ JUSTICE 164
business

SOMERSAULT
■ ACTIVITIES 144
■ SKILL 72
change of mind, reversal

SON
■ THE FAMILY 90

SONG
■ ENTERTAINMENT 178
■ MUSIC 70

SOOT
■ REFUSE 119
depression

SORE
■ ILLNESS 95

SORROW
■ EMOTION 130

SOUP
■ FOOD AND DRINK 106

SOW
■ MAMMALS AND
REPTILES 42

SPADE
■ TOOLS 115
disclosure, excavation

SPAGHETTI
■ FOOD AND DRINK 106
tangle

SPARK
■ CREATIVITY 73
excitement, ideas, ignition, interest

SPEAKING
■ COMMUNICATION 137

SPEAR
■ WEAPONS 118

SPECTACLES
■ UTENSILS 109
clarity, observation

SPEECH
■ COMMUNICATION 137

SPELL
■ THE SUPERNATURAL
60
■ WISH-FULFILLMENT
150

SPHINX
■ MYTHOLOGY 64
■ THE SUPERNATURAL
60
knowledge, mythology

SPICE
■ FOOD AND DRINK 106
excitement

SPIDER
■ FEAR 120
■ SWIMMERS AND
CRAWLERS 44
■ WARNING 159
luck

SPIKE
■ WEAPONS 118

SPINE
■ THE BODY 91
courage

SPIRE
■ BUILDINGS 100

SPITTING
■ ACTIVITIES 144

SPLINT
■ THE BODY 91
support

SPOON
■ UTENSILS 109

SPORT 134

SPOT
■ IMAGE 165
■ THE BODY 91

SPOTLIGHT
■ THEATER 81
clarity, conspicuousness, exhibitionism, observation

SPRING
■ WEATHER 49
beginnings, fecundity, nature

SPY
■ ACTIVITIES 144
■ DECEPTION 152

SQUIRREL
■ MAMMALS AND
REPTILES 42
bustle, hoarding, prudence

THE WORLD
OF NATURE

FANTASY &
FABLE

ARTS &
SCIENCES

THE HUMAN
BODY

BUILDINGS &
INTERIORS

EVERYDAY
THINGS

HUMAN
EMOTIONS

HUMAN
ACTIVITIES

HUMAN
CONDITIONS

RITUALS &
RELIGION

THE DREAM
THESAURUS

THE WORLD
OF NATURE

FANTASY &
FABLE

ARTS &
SCIENCES

THE HUMAN
BODY

BUILDINGS &
INTERIORS

EVERYDAY
THINGS

HUMAN
EMOTIONS

HUMAN
ACTIVITIES

HUMAN
CONDITIONS

RITUALS &
RELIGION

THE DREAM
THESAURUS

STAGE
- THEATER 81
display

STAIN
- DIRT 119
- CLEANSING 146
- GUILT 124
disguise, impurity

STAIRCASE
- AMBITION 151
- BUILDINGS 100
calamity, dismay, progress

STAMMER
- COMMUNICATION 137
hesitancy, inability

STAR
- AMBITION 151
*admiration, nature,
prominence, vanity*

STARVATION
- IMAGE 165
- THE BODY 91
deprivation

STATION
- TRAVEL 134
beginnings, endings

STATUE
- IMAGE 165
immobility, inactivity

STEAMER
- WATER 46

STEEPLE
- BUILDINGS 100

STEERING
- VEHICLES 116
control, direction

STILLBIRTH
- BIRTH 86

STING
- SWIMMERS AND
CRAWLERS 44
- THE BODY 91
*activation, persuasion,
reminder*

STITCH, STITCHING
- CLOTHING 84
repair

STOCKTAKING
- WORKPLACES 116

STOKER
- FIRE 45

STOMACH
- THE BODY 91

STORM
- DANGER 158
- DIFFICULTY 173
- INSECURITY 121
- WARNING 159
- WEATHER 49
excitement

STOVE
- ENERGY 73

STRANGER
- THE SHADOW 97
*hospitality, intrusion,
mistrust*

STREAM
- WATER 46

STREET
- LANDSCAPE 58

STREETCAR
- VEHICLES 116

STROKE
- ILLNESS 95

STRONG BOX
- DECEPTION 152

SUBMARINE
- WATER 46
concealment

SUCCUBUS
- THE SUPERNATURAL
60

SUCKING
- FOOD AND DRINK 106

SUFFOCATE
- AIR 48
- RESTRICTION 169
physical discomfort

SUGAR
- FOOD AND DRINK 106
flattery

SUIT
- CLOTHING 84

SUN
- DANGER 158
- WEATHER 49
comfort, optimism, warmth

SUNDIAL
- TIME 80

SUNRISE
- EMOTION 130

SUNSET
- EMOTION 130

SUNTAN
- IMAGE 165

SUPERMAN
- MYTHOLOGY 64

SUPERNATURAL, THE 60

SURGERY
- THE BODY 91
alteration, correction

SURREALIST DREAMS 82

SWAN
- WINGED CREATURES
43

**SWIMMERS AND
CRAWLERS 44**

SWIMMING
- WATER 46

SWIMMING POOL
- WATER 46

SWINGING
- ACTIVITIES 144
indecision

SWORD
- WEAPONS 118

T

TABLE
- ROOMS 103
*discussion, display,
furniture, stability,
sustenance*

TADPOLE
- CHANGE 168
- SWIMMERS AND
CRAWLERS 44
beginnings, fecundity, sperm

TAIL
- THE BODY 91
endings

TAILOR
- IMAGE 165
*compliment, enhancement,
flattery*

TALK
- COMMUNICATION 137

TANTRUM
- CHILDHOOD 88
violence

TAP
- DISCIPLINE 163
- WATER 46
control, restraint

TARGET
- ACHIEVEMENT 167
- AMBITION 151
- SKILL 72

TAROT
- PREDICTION AND
PRECOGNITION 62
- THE SUPERNATURAL
60
- THE ZODIAC 69
the future

TASTE
- FOOD AND DRINK 106
*like/dislike, opinion,
predilection*

TATTOO
- IMAGE 165
decoration, permanence

TAURUS
- THE ZODIAC 69

TAX
- MONEY 110
burden, contribution

TAXI
- VEHICLES 116
availability, hire

TEA
- FOOD AND DRINK 106
home, hospitality

TEACHER
- AUTHORITY 162
- CHILDHOOD 88
- GATHERINGS 174
- YOUTH 89
knowledge

TEAM
- DISCIPLINE 163
colleagues, togetherness

TEARS
- EMOTION 130

TEASPOON
- UTENSILS 109
frugality, measurement

TEETH
- ILLNESS 95
- IMAGE 165
- THE BODY 91

TELEGRAM
- COMMUNICATION 137
importance, speed, urgency

TELEPHONE
- COMMUNICATION 137
- DANGER 158

TELEVISION
- COMMUNICATION 137
- ENTERTAINMENT 178
- PICTURES 76
- THEATER 81

TEMPTATION 169

TENNIS
- AMBITION 151
- GAMES 132
- SKILL 72
approval

TENT
- BUILDINGS 100
*impermanence, protection,
vulnerability*

TERROR
- NIGHTMARES 154

TERRORIST
- HOSTILITY 122
*antagonism, attack, power,
violence*

TESTICLES
- THE BODY 91
*procreation, virility,
vulnerability*

THAWING
- EMOTION 130

THEATER 81

THIEF
- CRIME 140

THEFT
- ACTIVITIES 144
- GUILT 124
- PUNISHMENT 170
envy

THERMOMETER
- CALCULATION 77

THESAURUS
- DIFFICULTY 172

THISTLES
- OTHER PLANTS 52

THORNS
- FLOWERS 53
*affliction, antagonism,
annoyance*

THREAT
- ANGER 123
- HOSTILITY 122
- PUNISHMENT 170
pain

THREE
- NUMBERS 80

THROAT
- THE BODY 91

THRONE
- AUTHORITY 162

THUMB
- THE BODY 91

THUNDER
- ANGER 123
- DANGER 158
- FEAR 120
- WEATHER 49
darkness, depression

TICKET COLLECTOR
- AUTHORITY 162
- SERVICE 141
- TRAVEL 134
label, politics, price

TIDE
- EMOTION 130
- WATER 46

TIE
- CLOTHING 84

TIGER
- MAMMALS AND
REPTILES 42

TIGHTROPE
- ENTERTAINMENT 178

TIME 80

TOE
- THE BODY 91

TOLL
- MONEY 110

price, tax

TOMBSTONE
- COMMUNICATION 137
- DEATH 86

memory, nostalgia

TONGUE
- COMMUNICATION 137
- THE BODY 91

speech

TOOLS 115

TOOTHACHE
- THE BODY 91

TORCH
- UTENSILS 109

hope, light, revelation

TORPEDO
- WEAPONS 118

destruction

TORTURE
- PUNISHMENT 170

confession, pain, secrecy, violence

TOUCH
- COMMUNICATION 137

TOWN
- LANDSCAPE 58

TOY
- CHILDHOOD 88
- EMOTION 130
- ENTERTAINMENT 178

affection, lack of value, trifle

TRACK
- COMMUNICATION 137
- LANDSCAPE 58

TRAFFIC
- ACTIVITIES 144
- VEHICLES 116

illegality

TRAFFIC LIGHTS
- DISCIPLINE 163

approval (if green) /disapproval (if red), permission, restriction

TRAFFIC WARDEN
- AUTHORITY 162
- OCCUPATIONS 148

TRAIN
- COMMUNICATION 137
- INSECURITY 121
- TRAVEL 134
- VEHICLES 116

TRAITOR
- IMAGE 165
- GUILT 124

disloyalty

TRAM-CAR *see* **STREETCAR**

TRANSFUSION
- ILLNESS 95

encouragement, renewal

TRANSPLANT
- CHANGE 168
- EMOTION 130
- IMAGE 165

replacement

TRANSVESTISM
- IMAGE 165

sex

TRAP
- DECEPTION 152
- GUILT 124
- RESTRICTION 169

detection

TRAPEZE
- ENTERTAINMENT 178
- SKILL 72

balance, indecision, uncertainty

TRASH
- REFUSE 119

rejection, worthlessness

TRAVEL 134

TREASURE
- EMOTION 130
- LOVE 126

value

TREES 50

TRIAL
- AUTHORITY 162
- GUILT 124
- JUSTICE 164
- PUNISHMENT 170

TRIBE
- GATHERINGS 174

custom, social behavior

TRICK
- DECEPTION 152

habit, illusion, meanness

TROUSERS
- CLOTHING 84

domination, gender

TRUMPET
- MUSIC 70

TRUNK
- CONTAINERS 108
- TREES 50

TUNNEL
- BUILDINGS 100
- EARTH 48

concealment, hope (light at the end of the tunnel)

TUTOR
- GATHERINGS 174

knowledge

TWO
- NUMBERS 80

double, pairs

U

UMBILICAL CORD
- BIRTH 86
- THE BODY 91

baby, possession

UMBRELLA
- AUTHORITY 162
- DISCIPLINE 163
- WATER 46

reason

UMPIRE
- GAMES 132

UNBUTTON
- CLOTHING 84

UNCLE
- THE FAMILY 90

UNDERCLOTHES
- CLOTHING 84

intimacy, sex

UNDERGROUND
- DECEPTION 152
- EARTH 48

secrecy

UNDERTAKER
- DEATH 86
- OCCUPATIONS 148

UNDERWEAR
- CLOTHING 84

intimacy, sex

UNDRESSING
- CLOTHING 84
- IMAGE 165

informality, revelation

UNEMPLOYMENT
- ACTIVITIES 144

worry

UNICORN
- MYTHOLOGY 64

sensuality, virginity

UNIFORM
- AUTHORITY 162

conformity, obedience

UNIVERSITY
- GATHERINGS 174
- WISH-FULFILLMENT 150
- YOUTH 89

knowledge

UNPOPULARITY
- IMAGE 165
- INSECURITY 121

UNZIP
- CLOTHING 84

URINE
- REFUSE 119

waste

USHER
- AUTHORITY 162
- SERVICE 141

direction

UTENSILS 109

V

VACCINATION
- ILLNESS 95

prevention

VACUUM CLEANER
- CLEANSING 146
- IMAGE 165

VALLEY
- LANDSCAPE 58

depression

VAMPIRE
- NIGHTMARE 154

blood, threat, unscrupulousness

VAN
- CONTAINERS 108
- VEHICLES 116

transport

VASE
- DECEPTION 152
- CONTAINERS 108

decoration, storage

VAULT
- DEATH 86

VEGETABLES 55

VEHICLES 116

VEIL
- CLOTHING 84
- IMAGE 165

bride, chastity, concealment

VENTRILOQUISM
- COMMUNICATION 137
- DECEPTION 152

pretense

VENUS
- AMBITION 151
- MYTHOLOGY 64

VEST
- CLOTHING 84

VICAR
- AUTHORITY 162
- OCCUPATIONS 148
- RELIGION 180

VICTORY
- EMOTION 130

success

VIDEO
- RECORDING 74

VILLAGE
- BUILDINGS 100
- LANDSCAPE 58

community, society

VINE
- AMBITION 151
- OTHER PLANTS 52

social climbing

VIOLENCE
- DANGER 158

VIOLIN, VIOLINIST
- MUSIC 70

VIRGINITY
- IMAGE 165
- LOSS 171

inexperience, innocence, sex

VIRGO
- THE ZODIAC 69

VISITOR
- COMMUNICATION 137

impermanence

VITAMIN
- HEALTH 93

encouragement, preparation

VOICE
- COMMUNICATION 137
- IMAGE 165

expression, opinion

VOLCANO
- LANDSCAPE 58

extroversion, violence

VOMIT
- EMOTION 130

disgust, rejection

VOTE
- ACTIVITIES 144

assertion, choice, judgment, opinion

VOYAGE
- TRAVEL 134
- WATER 46

abroad

W

WAGE
- MONEY 110

recompense, regularity

WAIST
- IMAGE 165
- THE BODY 91

diet

WALKING
- ACTIVITIES 144

WALL
- BUILDINGS 100

protection

THE WORLD OF NATURE

FANTASY & FABLE

ARTS & SCIENCES

THE HUMAN BODY

BUILDINGS & INTERIORS

EVERYDAY THINGS

HUMAN EMOTIONS

HUMAN ACTIVITIES

HUMAN CONDITIONS

RITUALS & RELIGION

THE DREAM THESAURUS

THE WORLD OF NATURE

FANTASY & FABLE

ARTS & SCIENCES

THE HUMAN BODY

BUILDINGS & INTERIORS

EVERYDAY THINGS

HUMAN EMOTIONS

HUMAN ACTIVITIES

HUMAN CONDITIONS

RITUALS & RELIGION

THE DREAM THESAURUS

INDEX

PICTURE CREDITS

t: top   b: bottom   c: center   l: left   r: right

Archiv für Kunst und Geschichte: Zurich, Muraltengut 20bl.
Bridgeman Art Library: 33tr; *Progress,* 1973, Lucien Mathelin © ADAGP, Paris & DACS, London 1995 6bl; British Library, London 14tl, 19tr, 22tl; Galleria dell' Accademia, Venice 16bl; Giraudon 12tl; Louvre, Paris 13b; Lauros-Giraudon 35; Kunstmuseum, Winterthur 21t; Musée Condé, Chantilly 10tl; National Gallery, London 23br; Prado, Madrid 24, 32bl; Index 2c; Private Collection 36br; Tate Gallery, London 38–39; Zentralsparkasse-Bank, Vienna 37tr. **ET Archive:** 8. **Mary Evans:** 7tl, 7br, 10bc, 12bl, 13tc, 33bl.
Ronald Grant Archive: 15b, 18bl, 27br, 29tl, 29tr. **Hulton Deutsch Collection:** 14crb.
Image Bank: John W. Banagan 26bl. **Mansell Collection:** 10bl, 14cr. **Pictor International:** 27tl.
Science Photo Library: Jean Loup Charmet 10tr; Andrzej Dudzinski 17br, 28bl; James Holmes/Janssen Pharmaceutical Ltd. 17tr; Library of Congress 20tr; Hank Morgan 17cl; National Library of Medicine 20tl; Philippe Plailly 18cb, cl, tl & tca.

PICTURE RESEARCH Anna Lord
ILLUSTRATOR Ian Andrew: 56–57; 66–67; 78–79; 98–99; 104–105; 112–113; 128–129; 142–143; 156–157; 182–183.